A Living Book
Autobiographical Reflections 1

Translated from the French
Original title: « AFIN DE DEVENIR UN LIVRE VIVANT »
Éléments d'autobiographie 1

ERRATA

Page 9, title: read Foreword

Photo insert, 2nd page:
read 29 September 1958

Original edition:
© 2009, Éditions Prosveta S.A. (France), ISBN 978-2-85566-975-5
and: Revised and enlarged edition, ISBN 978-2-8184-0000-5, *Forthcoming.*

Prosveta S.A – B.P.12 – 83601 Fréjus CEDEX (France)
ISBN 978-2-85566-989-2

Omraam Mikhaël Aïvanhov

A Living Book
Autobiographical Reflections
1

P R O S V E T A

TABLE OF CONTENTS

Forward

If I speak to you about myself, it is not so that you will think my life is fascinating, unusual, or for any other such reason. It is only so that I can pass on to you what it has taught me so that you will be able to benefit from my experiences. Otherwise, what use is it? We don't really know other people merely through being interested in the events of their lives, but by understanding how they lived and what wisdom they gained from these experiences. This wisdom is like a quintessence of their lives, something which is truly them but also something which is much greater; it is this quintessence that enlightens and nourishes all those who come near.

… My words are food that I give you, they are pieces of my heart, my soul; this is my life, my blood, I cannot do otherwise. When I speak to you, it is my life that you are breathing, that you are touching.

Omraam Mikhaël Aïvanhov

Master Omraam Mikhaël Aïvanhov gave his first public talk on 29 January 1938 in Paris, and he spoke for the last time on 28 September 1985, at the Bonfin in Fréjus. Over this period roughly 4,500 lectures, talks or simple remarks were recorded either in shorthand or on tape recorders or video tapes.

'Speaking from abundance'... This beautiful expression in the French language, which means the spontaneous improvisation of a talk, seems to be one that the Master made particularly his own. He said, 'In order for me to feel driven to speak to you I need to have the topic given to me in a flash of inspiration, a suggestion which comes to me from elsewhere. I link myself to heaven and I become an antenna, receiving hints and suggestions on what I should speak to you about today, not what I should say any other day, but just for today.'

He also said, 'If I wasn't on this platform I would be seen only from the first three or four rows. It is not my desire to be elevated on a dais, but from this position I can see you all while within I am asking, "Show me, my Lord, how I can come closer to my friends." I look for any little pathway that will allow me to come closer to you.' Many and various were the pathways that he used, among them being his way of slipping in personal remarks as illustration of more general topics. Remembrances of certain experiences, of events in his life, would spontaneously emerge, and as he told them to us we not only saw his hopes and dreams but we were also given totally unexpected glimpses of his sensitivity.

These memories often bubbled up in him and took the Master by surprise so that he would make an excuse for them or take refuge in humour, for he was really very reserved and very modest. But at the same time he was also very simple and spontaneous, so when he hinted, in passing, at what he had lived – allusions of no more than three or four minutes – he shared something fraternal with us. And if it happened that he was taken over by beings, suddenly making him inaccessible, unreachable to us like a distant mountain peak veiled in flaming clouds, he was aware of it, and then he would speak to us about himself, because in telling us about himself he was also speaking about us.

We had to give this book some sense of order and coherence. But although we have given all the facts in chronological order, the Master himself recalled them rarely, often with months or even years in between. It was never his intention to leave us an autobiography and the following pages are only a simple attempt at one.

The editors

1

The mysterious pathways of destiny

I was fifteen years old… Like many adolescents I was filled with longings to do or be something lofty and heroic. At this age there are no limits to the imagination, and so there are dreams of saving the world, of setting out to help suffering humanity, of making the discovery that will cure the incurable disease, of becoming the greatest poet or musician or even of waking Sleeping Beauty herself. I was not exactly sure what it was I wanted to do, but I knew that it had to be grand and noble and beautiful. I had no name for this ideal, nor did I have any idea of what it would take to accomplish it. What I did see quite clearly were all the obstacles that rose up before me. Since the death of my father some years earlier, my family and I lived in the most miserable of conditions. Great qualities of character would be required to pull myself up and out of these conditions, and yet I had very little awareness of what these qualities would have to be. On top of this I did not like school at all; I was bored by it, and my behaviour was both worrying and distressing to my mother. There was a huge gap between my actions and the unattainable ideal that I longed for in my heart, and this conflict tore me apart.

At that time, I came across some books on Hindu spirituality which spoke of reincarnation and karma,[1] and I wondered, 'What could I have done in previous lives to deserve such punishment and now have to deal with so many difficulties, suffer so many hardships? Even if I was bored at school, I still wanted to learn so that I would be able to accomplish great things, but at the same time I felt I lacked the abilities that I would have loved to possess, and all paths appeared to close before me. I could not see any way forward, and I was convinced that I alone was responsible. I needed to be enlightened and guided, but I did not know any adult in whom I could confide, not even my mother. She was a truly exceptional woman, very wise, with a wisdom born of her love; she had received little education and could not deal with my anxieties, or answer the questions I asked myself. In fact, what I needed was a spiritual guide, and it was only two years later that I would meet Master Peter Deunov.

But in reading these books about Hindu spirituality, I had learned also that, when we do not have the privilege of meeting a Master on the physical plane, we can be helped if we know how to link to the great beings who live in certain places on the earth. Many of these elevated beings, I read, live in the Himalayas, and by their presence, by their thoughts, they strive to lead people on the path of light. This was a great revelation to me, and from that moment on I began to concentrate on them, to link up with them.

So it was that from the time of my adolescence I accepted the idea that highly evolved beings lived on earth and that, even though I could not meet them physically, I had the means to reach them by thought. I imagined that these wise and luminous beings agreed to give me their wisdom and their light. And perhaps this is actually what happened; when they saw how much I grieved over my imperfections, and how strongly I wished to improve, they must have had pity on me and agreed to help me. Each day I imagined I was with them, among them, and even helping in their work. I have no idea where this desire came from, or what it was in me that advised me to work in this way. I do know that when I actually linked with these beings I no longer felt alone. I was certain too that I belonged to another family, a spiritual family, and that even if I had not met it, I was living with it.

Thirty years later when I had already been living in France for some time, some friends told me of a well-known clairvoyant who lived in Zurich. Because I am aware of the reality of a world that we cannot see but with which we can be in relationship, I have always been interested in studying the phenomena of clairvoyance and mediumship in people who have been born with this particular gift. I have therefore met a few of them, but this clairvoyant from Zurich particularly impressed me.

In 1945 I had been invited to Switzerland, and I decided to take advantage of this stay to go to Zurich for a consultation with her. As she spoke only German, I had to find an interpreter. I asked the owner of the hotel where I was staying if she could help. She told me that her daughter spoke French fluently and would gladly accompany me, and so the two of us set off together to meet her. She was already very old, but the moment I saw her I was struck by the colour and delicate texture of her skin.[2] The skin of her face showed that this woman was a saint and that immediately gave me confidence. She began by taking my hand, although she then confided that it was just a normal gesture for her: she did not see anything in the hand, but saw directly into the subtle realms. Then she said to the young lady who had come with me, 'Tell the gentleman that he comes from a royal family.' I protested, 'But that's not possible! I know my father, I know my mother, there is nothing royal in our family.' She smiled and repeated, 'Tell the gentleman that he comes from a royal family and that he will understand me later.'[3] And, in fact, I understood later that the royal family I belonged to was not on the physical plane, but the spiritual plane.

She continued, 'You come from a Balkan country, your father died when you were eight years old and, after his death, you lived a life of extreme poverty. You had a younger brother, and in order to bring you both up, your mother got remarried to a man who already had a child, and together they had three more children. Despite all these material difficulties, you studied a great deal. You have been in France for eight years. You belong to a spiritual teaching established by a Master whom I can see there, behind you. He has white hair and a white beard and he is no longer on earth.' So, it was true, the Master had left the earth! At this time, just at the end of the war, I was not able to receive any news from Bulgaria, but I had had certain feelings, I had had dreams warning me. Now this clairvoyant gave me confirmation of it: the Master had departed.

She continued, 'When he saw that the one he had sent to France was carrying on his work and that he could count on him, he was able to depart. You are his heir, he chose you as his heir… And now, listen to me carefully. In the next few years, you will have to undergo some difficult ordeals, you will be threatened by mortal dangers, accidents will befall you, but you will come through them all. Then, you will go to India where you will have some very important meetings, and you will live through extraordinary events. The secret of the Queen of Sheba will be revealed to you.' I was totally taken aback: how was it that this simple, uneducated woman could speak of the Queen of Sheba's secret? She told me many other things, which I may tell you about some other time. Everything that she had seen of my past was absolutely true, and what she foresaw has either come true or is on its way to coming true.

But let's go back to that first phrase of hers: that I belonged to a royal family. If I had wanted to be someone who gave orders, to control and rule others, then clearly the conditions I had been born and raised in were not the best. But even if I was not immediately aware of it, as my true ambition was to become king of my own kingdom, that is master of myself, these conditions were the best.

No one arrives on this earth with a clear knowledge of who they are, what they have come to do, and for what reason. For a long time, for me too, nothing was clear. To incarnate is to take a dive into matter, and matter has such a powerful grip on the soul that it drives out memory. We know that the ancient Greeks described the beyond as a land threaded through by different rivers, of which one was the river Lethe, whose name means 'forgetfulness'. They believed that souls drank the water of this river after death in order to forget the events of their earthly lives. And it was also these waters that they drank at the moment of rebirth. You can find an echo of this belief in one of Plato's books, *The Republic,* where he explains that a soul's destiny is based on the life it lived in previous incarnations. Before descending into matter once again, it knows what awaits it, either because this has been imposed on it, or because it has had the chance to choose, but the moment it descends, this knowledge is taken away from it, for again it must drink the waters of Lethe, and it forgets everything.

Obviously this is only a picturesque way of presenting things but that is the reality; the incarnating soul starts out knowing nothing of its future destiny. Even for the most evolved souls, this remains hidden, but gradually they remember, and that is what differentiates them from others who are condemned to remain in ignorance of why they are here on earth and what they are here to do. Yes, contrary to what some people assert, no one is born with a clear knowledge of their predestination. Of course, at a very young age we can feel drawn in this or that direction, but even so, it still remains quite vague. It takes years and years of research, study, and even suffering, before we discover our true vocation.[4]

So it was after many years and many ordeals that I began to understand how the meaning of a destiny is revealed, and I want what I have discovered to be of use to you so that you, too, will be better able to solve the problems you encounter each day. How many hindrances and difficulties that we meet exist just to force us to take the one path where we could accomplish our predestination as sons and daughters of God! A sublime wisdom rules over all destinies, and we must accept this truth if we do not wish to increase our sufferings. Cosmic Intelligence has no intention of crushing us, but with what it gives us, and with what it withholds too, it puts us in situations where we have to express and produce the best in us.

Since I could see no way out on the outside, I had to look within myself and work tirelessly with thought, imagination and willpower. Everything I succeeded in obtaining later on, what I became, I know now I owe to these limitations, to these hardships imposed on me. For each person, destiny has a special language that he or she must strive to interpret. Each hindrance, each obstacle that I came up against forced me to look for what I needed in the realm of the soul and spirit. And now I want to give you too all that I have discovered.

After many years, I understood that outer conditions are not the determining factor. Or more exactly, they are the determining factor in the sense that they make us work on ourselves. When we cannot move forward and we do not want to go backwards, we can only go deep within ourselves, like the pearl fisher who dives into the depths of the ocean. Or else, we can soar further and higher until we reach the stars. Now, I can tell you; thanks to all the obstacles I met, I have fished many pearls and I have soared to the stars. We must never become resigned to poverty, we must never become resigned to lack, we must never become paralyzed by difficulties, but experience them only as stimuli to go in search of true riches.

The pathways of destiny are always mysterious. Contrary to appearances, destiny had placed me in the best conditions. But what does a fifteen-year-old know about the paths of destiny? And especially, how could I know at that age that before I came down to earth I myself had accepted these conditions? Yes, for now I know – I had accepted them.

Notes

1. See *Man, Master of his Destiny,* Izvor Coll. n° 202, chap. 8: 'Reincarnation'.
2. See *'In Spirit and in Truth',* Izvor Coll. n° 235, chap. 9: 'The skin'.
3. See *On the Art of Teaching – from the Initiatic Point of View,* Complete Works, v. 29, chap. 5: 'On perfection', part 4.
4. See *The Wellsprings of Eternal Joy,* Izvor Coll. n° 242, chap. 7: 'Like a fish in water'.

2

A childhood
in the mountains of Macedonia

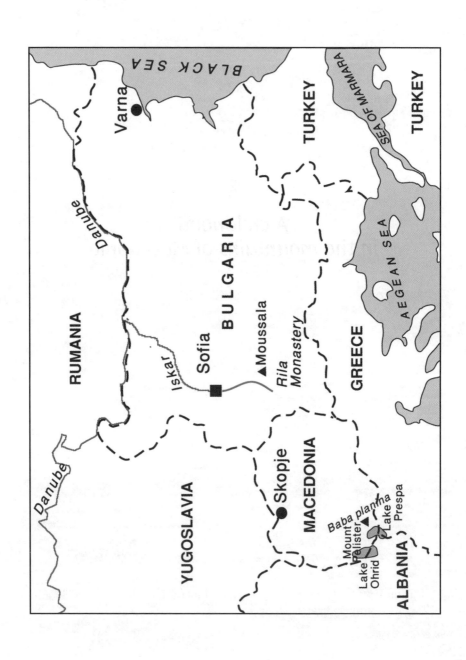

I was born in Macedonia,* in the small village of Baba Planina, 'Grandmother's Mountain', near the base of Mount Pelister, not far from the Greek border. I was born prematurely, at eight months, on a freezing winter's night,** in a house that was almost impossible to heat, and no one thought I would survive. It appears however that not only did I not cry, but I smiled, to everybody's amazement. At that time, and particularly in such a forgotten spot in the mountains, there were none of the clinics we have nowadays to look after premature infants. To this day I am hypersensitive to the cold, but I survived, and many times my mother told me how joyfully the whole family had welcomed me. 'When you were baptized I will never forget how heartily we sang the hymns. After the ceremony, your father served wine to all those present and the orthodox priest got drunk! He assured us that this had never happened to him before, and he came to the conclusion that you would be a child like no other.' Apparently, he also made various prophecies about me.

My mother told me that when I was conceived, and throughout the whole pregnancy, her one thought and

* This means the present republic of Macedonia, which, between 1878 and 1912, was part of Bulgaria.
** 31 January 1900.

desire was to consecrate me to God. By dedicating a child to the Lord, a mother, and a father too, of course, do not necessarily make an exceptional being of the child, but they imprint a mark on it; they engrave certain furrows into its psychic material which make it easier to attract to it currents of good forces whilst at the same time deterring undesirable forces. I have always told you that the true education of a child begins before birth.[1] That is why, well before the birth of her child, while carrying it, the mother must be conscious of the influence she has on it. It is not enough that she already loves her child, she must learn to use the power of this love. When thinking of her child, she can project her love to the sublime realms in order to gather all the necessary elements for its physical and soul growth, and then to imbue the child with them.

The moment a child takes its first steps is always an important one for the family. What happened with me was a little odd. Once again, it was my mother who told me the story. I was about eight months old. At that age, children do not walk yet. Now, one day, I got up and I started walking. Not only my family but the neighbours too, who were often with us, watched me in amazement. They exclaimed, 'How extraordinary, he's walking!… He's walking!' And then two village women came in, women whom everyone feared because it was believed they had the evil eye. Were they in fact the cause that, next day, I became deathly ill? That's what was said. My grandmother's care managed to save my life, but after that I had great difficulty in walking normally. And so it was that, after having been so precocious, I walked later than all the other children.

How should this be interpreted? Thinking about it again, years later, I understood that this apparently inexplicable episode in my childhood indicated that one day I would have to go through a terrible ordeal which would paralyze my activities for a while, but then I would be able to continue my path. And that is what happened. Often, certain events in a child's life will warn of what it will have to face later in its adult life. In a way, these are prophecies to which we do not always pay sufficient attention.

We lived a harsh existence in my childhood village. My parents may have been poor and fairly uneducated but they were very courageous and had strong morals. I rarely saw my father, for in order to support the family he had to go and find work elsewhere.* Of course, he came back from time to time, but only for very short visits, because he could not

* Although the Master never made an explicit parallel, it was probably the absence of his father, who had to leave his family to provide for their basic necessities, which later inspired him with this analogy:'In certain poor countries, men go to look for work abroad, because if they stayed at home they would never earn sufficient money to feed their families. They love their families yet they leave them, and it is just because they love them that they leave them: if they were not to go, their families would die of hunger.

So why don't you, too, go to a foreign country to earn enough money to feed your family? You will say,"Why should we go abroad? We don't need to do that!" I know that, but the foreign country I am speaking about is the divine world: you need to go every day to the divine world in your prayers and meditation to bring back pure gold for all those you love. This gold is purity, harmony, light and joy... As for me, I leave you every day for a few minutes or a few hours, so that I can travel to a distant country and collect the gold I will then distribute to each of you. Why don't you decide to leave your family and friends for a moment? Because you love them, so you say! No, you do not love them, or you love them badly. You leave them to die of hunger, because you aren't capable of feeding their hearts and souls, and so it is not love.' Editor's note take a long absence from the charcoal business he had in a forest near Varna, on the Black Sea. And Varna, especially at that time, was a long way from our village.

My father was a charcoal burner, which is not a highly esteemed job, but it is one full of meaning, as it is linked with fire, the fire of sacrifice. To sacrifice oneself is to be like a piece of dead wood that is put on the fire. Before burning, the wood is dull and of no use. But the moment it is put on the fire to feed it, the wood itself becomes fire, light, heat, life and beauty.[2]

As my father was so often away, I was educated mainly by my mother. But she was always very busy, always ready to run and help a relative or a neighbour who requested her aid. I helped a little bit around the house and in the fields, but she never asked me to do very much.

One day, of course, I had to start going to school. If only you could have seen this school. It was so wretched! It was a wood and mud hovel with windows in which the glass was often broken, which they took their time to replace, and wind blew under the door. From the beginning of the cold season, which arrived early in that part of the world, every day each child had to bring at least one log for the stove. I won't tell you how this stove worked, but it belched a large amount of smoke. At the end of the day two or three children took turns to stay behind after classes to tidy up, sweep and wash everything.

This was a one-class school, and obviously there was just one teacher who had to work with pupils of all different age groups. I well remember the long cane that the teacher used to hit inattentive or unruly students on the head or hands. His methods were not really the best... In order to punish a child, he would make them kneel for a very long time on sand or gravel with their arms held high in the air. At other times, he would shut them in with the pigs in the pigsty next to the school.

At that time, some parents found it difficult to accept that their children had to go to school. They would have preferred them to work at home or in the fields and look after the animals. So, as soon as they returned, in the evening and during the holidays, the children had to do all sorts of tasks. The necessity of participating in the collective life was advantageous for them because they became conscious very early on of being part of a community. Nothing, or almost nothing, protected the villagers from the whims of nature, and therefore no one could think of their own wellbeing and security without being aware of the wellbeing of others; everyone was obliged to help each other. If, later, I held work and physical efforts in high esteem, I owe it also to those past years spent in our village, and to the role models I had around me. How courageous these people were! I remember a neighbour whose husband had also gone to look for work abroad, and he came home much less frequently than my father did. She never complained and when people asked how she was doing she would always reply, 'Don't worry about me. I have everything I need, thank you.'

I lived surrounded by affection in a warm and loving community, but I always felt the cold, and I often felt an indescribable sadness, which came, I'm sure, from the position of the Moon and Saturn in my birth chart and also from the actual circumstances of my birth. During her pregnancy, my mother was greatly influenced by a tragic event and her grief penetrated into me. I remember that I did not play with the other children, I watched from afar, I did not join in their dances, I did not sing with them and, for no apparent reason, I would suddenly be overwhelmed with a despair I could not overcome. Later, I learned how to neutralize these states, but it has been very difficult. I had such a struggle that I do not know even now whether it is cheerfulness or sorrow that predominates in me. No doubt neither of them. Let's say that sorrow and seriousness are for me, and that joy and cheerfulness are for others. If you could see me when I am alone at home, you might not recognize me as the same person who was with you a few hours before.

But even if I was a shy, sad and lonely child at this time, I was like other children in the stupid things I did; I disobeyed my mother, I squabbled with the village boys, I stole fruit from the neighbours' gardens and, above all, as I was unaware of the danger I was causing, I loved to light fires wherever I could find something to burn. Then, obviously, my mother had to do something about punishing me, but she was never angry and she never beat me. She would say, 'This is what happens when you act in this way, and this is what happens when you act in that way… and now it is up to you to choose.' And she would often finish with this sentence: *Krivdina do pladnina, pravdina do veknina,* which means: everything underhand and deceitful lasts just until midday, but whatever is upright and honest lasts for eternity. This proverb did not mean a lot to me as a child: what does a six-year-old understand about good, evil and eternity? And yet look at the effect of those words on me, since I am still quoting them to you eighty years later! They made a much deeper impression on me than if I had been given the smacks that I sometimes deserved. Yet, if I didn't understand what good, evil and eternity were, the love with which my mother spoke those words touched me so deeply that I was often close to tears. But I was much too proud to let her see how moved I was.

My mother also said, 'When you have to do something new, take all the time you need to get it right the first time. Don't rush at it. By going too quickly you may save yourself a few minutes, but just wait and see how much time it will take you to correct your mistakes.' Unfortunately, I was not a patient person by nature and quite often, afterwards, I had the opportunity to note how right she was.

I have many good memories of my grandmother. When neighbours found me picking the fruit from their trees and I was being chased from one garden to another, I used to run and seek refuge in her house. Of course, she didn't encourage me in my petty pilfering, but she protected and comforted me. I would arrive out of breath and anxious, and I never understood how she guessed what had happened. When she saw me she would say, 'So, you have been up to your old mischief again...' 'How do you know that, grandma?' 'I can see it in your eyes. You will be punished, and your mother is right. But until then, come and hide here.'

My grandmother was so gentle! She never scolded me. My mother was much stricter with me. When I had done something stupid, she always knew where to find me, and I had no idea how she was able to guess exactly where I was. She would take me back to the house, and then, when I had been scolded and punished, I would go back again to grandma to be cheered up. That's why, for me, grandmothers are always those who cheer up their grandchildren after they have been punished by their parents. 'Come and eat this apple, sweetheart.' There are always apples at grandma's house to cheer up children. Grandma hugs and comforts the weeping child. I will never forget my grandmother and I want my actions to be like hers. When I see that your 'parents', the beings in the invisible world, have shaken and corrected you, I let you take refuge with your 'grandmother', that is with me. I too always have apples, figs, plums or nuts tucked away to give to you…

Life is not cruel, but it is just, and for each mistake we make it inflicts a sanction. Even if you are unaware of what error you have committed, life will offer no explanations. You may then suffer for years on end without understanding why. As for me, I spend my time explaining to you what you should do and what you should not do if you want to avoid getting the hard knocks. Are you always aware of this? That's another question. So, I am like a grandmother who tries to soften your ordeals. But once again, do you understand it?

Often, I went to my grandmother's so that she would tell me stories. What were these stories about? Battles between the forces of light and the forces of darkness; good and noble kings attacked by cruel, wicked kings; white magicians who had to foil the spells of black magicians and release their victims. What battles! All the forces of nature took part in these battles and, in the end, good always triumphed over evil, light triumphed over darkness. I so loved these stories! They made a really deep impression on me. I am sure that if I had to forget all that I have learned from books since then, these stories that my grandmother told me about the struggle between good and evil and the victory of good would remain with me forever. Among those stories my grandmother told me, there was one which, despite my young age, touched me deeply.

Once upon a time, in a little village, there lived two brothers who were very fond of each other. One of them was married with children, and the other was a bachelor. Their life was a hard one; they raised cattle, tilled the soil and never had time to rest. When their father died, their inheritance was divided equally between the two of them.

Some time later, the married brother said to himself, 'It's not fair. I have a wife and children. God is good, and if I should fall ill, my wife is here at my side. My children will go on growing, and when I become old they will look after me. And there is my poor brother on his own, and I cannot imagine how he is going to cope. Oh, I really should do something for him.' That night, he went surreptitiously to his brother's barn, left a few sacks of wheat there, went back to bed and slept peacefully. Meanwhile the other brother had been thinking things over, too: 'I am single, I am peaceful, whereas my brother has to worry about his whole family. All those children to feed and educate… something is not quite right here. I must do something to help the poor chap.' He went to his barn, filled up a few sacks with wheat, and making sure that he wasn't observed, he emptied them in his brother's barn.

Next morning, imagine the surprise of both brothers when they found that each of their stores of wheat had not diminished at all! They both said to themselves, 'Did I dream, did I actually carry that wheat to his barn or not?' The following night they did the same thing, but the next day the result was still the same: the level of wheat was exactly the same as it had been the evening before. They kept on questioning themselves, 'What is going on here? Have I been dreaming? I must try again tomorrow night…' This went on for several days until, one night, despite all their precautions, they bumped into each other: 'Is that you?' 'So, it was you who…' They hugged each other, wept with emotion, and then the married brother said to the bachelor, 'Look, there is plenty of room for you in our house. Move in, and let us live together.' And that was what they did, and they lived happily ever after. I often asked my grandmother to tell me this story.

Other members of my family, very old men and women who were both very wise and very deep, also had a great influence on me as a child. Some of them were not able to read or write as they had never been to school, but they were able to give wise counsel and they always weighed all their words and gestures so carefully! Their manner made a great impression on me; I observed them, and when they came to visit us, with what joy I welcomed them! Like my grandmother, they knew stories in which the forces of good and evil struggled with each other. And it was always good, the light, which was victorious. I never tired of hearing these stories; each time these relatives came, I asked them to tell me a story, and they did it so patiently! I remember one in particular: his name was Mikhaël.

When I think back on these relatives, I have the impression that they were placed there in order to imprint on me, at such a very young age, something good, beautiful and, above all, true. Even now, I live in these stories that they told me as often as I asked them to; I live this battle of light and dark, of the forces of good and the forces of evil, and I know that one day good will triumph: *Pravdina do veknina,* as my mother told me. It was with these wise words that I was fed.

Even if a child is not old enough to understand, what is more important for it to hear than that light always triumphs over darkness? This is recorded in the child, just as everything is recorded. That's why I always tell parents to be vigilant, to protect their young children by seeing that no adult, through their words or behaviour, leaves any trace of darkness in their souls.

A few years later, I went to a play in Varna in which good and evil, personified by angels and demons, confronted each other. At various moments in the production, a great angel would step forward alone to the front of the stage and each time would say this single sentence: *Vetchna istina, vetchna édinstina; vetchno é samo dobroto i krassotata*, 'Eternal truth, eternal unity; only goodness and beauty are eternal.' The actor who played this part wore a magnificent costume with large wings, but what was most striking about him was the way that he delivered this line. He did not shout, but his voice vibrated with such tremendous intensity that we were transfixed. This phrase resonated in my head like an echo of all that I had heard and learned as a young child: *Vetchna istina, vetchna édinstina…*, and now I still shiver whenever I say these words. All that I have told you in my lectures over the years is based on this certainty, that only goodness and beauty are eternal. Never forget that, and you, too, can repeat these words.

I have many other memories of my grandmother. At a time and in a country where medicines as we now know them hardly existed, we relied particularly on plants. My grandmother was capable of healing all sorts of illnesses. She was constantly busy making various remedies. She would go out nearly every day to gather plants whose qualities she knew. Sometimes, she would boil them before sunrise while whispering certain formulas over them. She would then pour this brew into a tub filled with water at a specific temperature and tell the sick person to get in the water, and the patient would get out completely healed.

She also made up a mixture of vinegar and garlic, which she put outside for the night. Occasionally, I saw her go out to a nut tree with a bottle of wine and put some living rootlets of the tree into the neck of the bottle. Then, she would carefully re-cork the bottle and bury it. Some weeks later she would dig it up again. The wine had been absorbed completely by the sprouts, and the bottle was filled with a blackish liquid which she gave to certain patients to drink. If people had jaundice, she told them to drink their own urine, making sure, of course, that they took certain precautions.

She also strongly believed in the power of the stars. When the night sky was clear, she would lay a patient out under the starry sky, and she would sit praying beside him or her. On other nights, she would care for her patients beside a stream. The clear, pure water flowed over little white pebbles, and my grandmother would use these little pebbles while she murmured certain ritual formulas.

My mother inherited from her mother this knowledge of plants, which she used to make herb teas and herbal baths, and she, too, had the true gift of healing. She would place her hand on a patient's solar plexus for a long time, because, by harmonizing all the currents passing through their body, she could restore many things in the organism. Sometimes, she just concentrated on the navel. And with what love she approached a sick person to touch them and ease their pain! One day, when I was still very young, I asked her, 'Mama, what do you do to heal people? What do you do to the sick person?' She replied, 'When I am with someone, I forget everything else. I begin by calling on God, on his power, on his love, and then I use all the powers of my soul for healing.' She told me that she herself was weak, that only love was all-powerful, and that it was love which worked through her. She was like a child holding a wire in its hand through which pulsed a mighty current. That was my mother when she was caring for someone; all she needed to do was to hold the wire. During my childhood and adolescence, I should have died twenty times, and it was always she who pulled me back from death.

Now, if I told you about all the 'medicines' that I saw used in this little Macedonian village, you would be amazed.

If someone had a boil or an abscess, they took, for example, a perfectly ripe fig and put it on the sore spot, saying to the entity which had caused this problem, 'Come, eat, it's for you.' After a moment or two, the pain would leave the person, and then all that had to be done was to throw away the fig.

The remedy for bronchitis or pneumonia was to curdle two or three litres of milk with lemon juice. Then, the whey was drained off, and after the curd was warmed it was put on the patient's chest. As with the fig, the curd was used as food for the beings responsible for the illness, and when they had eaten their fill they left.

If someone had mental problems, it was believed that they were victims of dark forces. So, a small bread roll was prepared on which was spread a large amount of honey. Then musicians were invited to come and play, and at the same time the harmful spirits were invited to eat the bread. Finally, they took the bread and, while singing and reciting formulas of exorcism, they left the village in procession and threw the bread as far away as possible. The evil spirits rushed forward to eat the bread and liberated the patient; this was how they got rid of undesirable entities by sending them elsewhere. Such practices probably seem very odd to you. But read the Gospels where it is reported that Jesus commanded demons to leave the body of one who was possessed and ordered them to go into a herd of swine; the swine then jumped into the sea.

These practices, which date from a distant past, can still be found in places where people use traditional medicine. They are based on very sound knowledge. But, of course, their true efficacy depends on the moral standing and experience of the one applying them, for without these moral qualities and this experience, the 'healer' runs the risk of being attacked.

Some problems seemed to have been caused by black magic, by an evil spell cast on someone. In such cases, I have seen women use tongs to take a piece of burning charcoal and thrust it into a pot of clear water, saying, 'As this charcoal is extinguished, so may all the evil thoughts and feelings directed at so-and-so be extinguished.' This action and formula would be repeated three times, and then the water would either be used to wash the eyes or a mouthful would be given to the patient to swallow. And sometimes they used these methods themselves for their own protection.

When someone died, the tradition was to place a sprig of basil on the body, which, it was said, would stop evil spirits entering the body. You should know that at this time in the Balkans, belief in vampires was very widespread. I remember hearing that such-and-such a person, who had been dead some time, had become a vampire and that people had gone secretly at night to dig up the corpse and had driven a stake through its heart. They even talked about *varkolak:*

the werewolf. What it was exactly, I don't know; I was much too young to understand anything of these stories, and I asked no questions. But I was used to listening and watching everything that happened around me, and even if I did not understand very much, all that I saw and heard has remained stamped in my memory.

It is difficult to make a definitive statement on the future development of some children who seem to be mentally slow for their age. The spirit enters the abode of the physical body at different times for different beings. Some parents worry when they see their children being slow to understand, dreaming, absent, especially when they do not get good results in class. But we cannot make statements with any certainty about children's development until they have passed through adolescence, because sometimes something is suddenly released and they make up for lost time.

I was one of those apparently retarded children. Until I was eight years old, I lived in the clouds, floating along as if I was out of my body. It looked as if I was asleep, with nothing going on, but so much was happening inside me: the invisible world was opened to me and I saw all the beings there, not just angelic beings but also nature spirits. Later in life my mother told me that I would speak of events which were going to happen and everyone was astonished, but I have no memory at all of this. I don't know the effect that I had on the people in my village, but despite all the foolish things that I did sometimes, I felt they regarded me in a special way and they loved me greatly.

In those days, there was an enchanting custom: the morning of New Year's Day, all the children were sent out on the streets to go from house to house wishing everyone a

Happy New Year, because children, in their innocence and their purity, bring only good to everyone. On that morning, each child would carry a branch of dogwood, which was sometimes decorated with ribbons. They would go into the houses and, with this branch, would touch each person in the family wishing them health, success, good crops and livestock. They were thanked with gifts of fruit, sweetmeats and cakes, and that is why on this particular morning each child carried a sack which was nearly as big as they were in which to put all their gifts.

When I was very small, I too took part in wishing everyone in the neighbourhood a Happy New Year. I don't know how people discovered that I was able to bring them blessings, but there were many families who asked my mother to send me to them very early in the morning, before the other children. So, she would wake me, dress me, which was very hard for me, because I was sleepy, and I would have to go out into the cold and snow – you know, the winters in the Macedonian mountains are not at all the same as winters on the Côte d'Azur! But I did it. Half asleep, I went into the houses to touch everyone there with my little branch, and I would whisper the words that my mother had made me learn by heart, words that I didn't really understand. It was a lovely custom.

Yes, I believe that I spent a part of my childhood partially out of my body in a sort of waking dream. I didn't pay much attention at school, but one day something strange happened. The teacher read us the story from *Genesis* about the creation of the world: *'In the beginning, God created heaven and earth…'* and suddenly, it was like a revelation. I must have been six years old, certainly no older, and I could hardly understand what was said, but each word at that moment so strongly impressed me that almost immediately I knew the text by heart. The teacher and my parents were all amazed. And with what pride I would say to them what God did on the first day, the second and third days. What had happened in order for me to grasp this text so easily? Then what really impressed me was the story of the Flood: the disappearance of the earth under the waters, Noah taking refuge in the ark with his family and two of each animal species. But all the same the recitation about the creation of the world made the strongest impression on me. Now, I no longer know it by heart; all that faded a long time ago, but I have continued to think about it, I have studied it and meditated on it for a long time, and I have also sometimes commented on it for you.[3]

It could be said that in childhood there are a few brief moments of illumination, and what was lived then comes back much later in a different form. In the same way, we must seek the destiny of beings in the tastes and tendencies they expressed when they were very young.

My first clear memory goes back to when I was about four years old: I see myself again picking up pieces of thread. Whenever I saw a piece of yarn or string, I picked it up. What did I do with it? Nothing, I was happy just to pick it up and put it somewhere. It appeared to be quite a harmless passion, until the day when I wrought the most terrible havoc. Sometimes, I would watch one of my relatives weaving at a big loom. One day, I found myself alone in the room with this big loom and its coloured threads all lined up. I don't know what came over me, but those threads fascinated me so much that I wanted to have them too, so I cut them with scissors... When I was discovered in the middle of this pile of threads, there was uproar. I can still see everyone running here and there, and I didn't understand why they were all in such a state.

Where did my need to collect threads come from? What was it that I saw in these threads? Did I, even at that young age, have the intuition that, from plants to our physical bodies, threads form every living thing? Trees with their roots, trunks and branches are just a collection of threads. In the same way, our bodies are made up of threads, strands, filaments; our muscles, nerves, blood vessels are threads. Even chromosomes, which carry the determining hereditary factors, are also threads...

It's worth spending a little time reflecting on this question of threads. The flesh we are all made of is a cloth woven out of different kinds of thread. If the physical body becomes ill, it is because 'the weaver' didn't use a sufficiently strong thread, so it often breaks. The weaver knots the two ends together, but the thread breaks again. So there are knots everywhere. On what does the strength of the thread depend? On the quality of the thoughts and feelings nurtured by the weaver. Because thoughts and feelings weave threads too. Thoughts go from right to left and feelings from left to right, and together they weave actions. Actions are the cloth, and the physical body is just the materialization of these acts. Yes, the physical body is just materialized cloth, and according to whether it is coarse or fine, soft or hard, we can know the mental and emotional qualities of the weaver.

Nature works with threads, and the whole world also works with threads. From our clothes to our telephone, to radios, computers, and so on, how many threads there are tangled together! And what are human relationships? Threads that we offer to others and that we sometimes also cut, which is something we must do with discernment.[4] For, if some connections are good to make, there are others which are better cut. What is freedom? The ability each person has to know to whom and what they should be linked, and also from whom and what a link should be severed. The connective force is love, and that which disconnects is wisdom.

There is still so much more to say about threads! What is a magic wand?[5] A thread which binds the world below and the world above. What are the sun's rays? Threads that it sends down to us so that we can lift ourselves up to it.

When I started thinking about this apparently inexplicable taste for threads which I had had from childhood, I wondered why I was interested only in threads and not needles, and yet needle and thread go together. But no, needles didn't interest me. I found the answer by transposing this behaviour to the psychic and spiritual realms and interpreting it there. I was not looking for needles, because needles represent the masculine principle. I already possessed this masculine principle, a principle which is active and determined. So I needed the feminine principle, matter, threads, so that I could weave, create patterns, pictures. And now, after many years of work, I have the threads too; the Lord allowed me to find them.

In this Macedonian village where I spent my early years, springs bubbled out of the ground in several places. There was one just near our house. Once I had discovered it, I felt myself irresistibly drawn to it. I must have been about four or five years old… With its purity and the transparency of its water, this spring surely talked to me, and I would listen to it for hours on end. I would gaze at it with love. I was captivated, enchanted by these crystalline drops of water which I saw springing from the ground. I could not tear myself away from them. I would almost have forgotten to go home, and when my mother called or came looking for me, I was not happy.

Those images of the water and the sensations I felt have since remained engraved on my soul. Whenever I see pure, clear water, I am overcome by an indescribable feeling. That is when I wish I were a poet so I could speak about water, the limpidity of springs, the song of streams and waterfalls, of rain drops or dewdrops on leaves and flowers, especially when a ray of sunshine strikes them and, one after the other, colours appear as pure as those of a prism. And then I'm told that there is no proof God exists! If water were the only thing that existed, is that not itself irrefutable proof? And when I see crystalline water in a crystal glass, I think I hear music...[6] Then, in my thoughts, I take this water, I raise it very high, higher than the highest mountain tops, and I expose it to the sun, to the air, and I drink it.

Water is a daughter of God, which is why I talk to it; I bless it and it's happy. I know that it will pass on the messages I entrust to it. Yes, for its nature is to be receptive, every-thing is imprinted in it. It is a marvellous messenger. Often, when I pause by a lake, a river or a fountain, or when I look at a crystal, which is a kind of frozen water, I feel the water as a presence in me which comes from much further back than those experiences of my childhood. It is as though, in previous lives, I had studied for a long time the virtues of water, its power, its meaning, and everything it represents in the universe.

Even now, that little spring of my childhood is with me, in me, and I can see it, as I saw it then, with the same wonder. I have no doubt that it impregnated my being. All my life since, I have lived with the memory of this spring; the image of it has accompanied me and sustained me throughout all my ordeals.

When, years later, I gave my first lecture* in Paris, I began with the image of the spring.[7] Perhaps that again was a recollection of the little spring of my childhood. That is why that lecture brought many others. It, too, was a spring. Whenever water flows, life appears: grass, trees, animals and people.[8]

Don't be surprised if I am preoccupied with water, speaking to you often about water. Water, and fire, too. As much as I loved water, I loved looking at fire too, and whenever I could I lit one. The dancing flames fascinated me, and I carried out all sorts of experiments; I observed how it consumed paper, wood, rags... It was better not to leave matches within my reach. How many times my mother had to put out fires that I had imprudently lit! I even scared my neighbours, because as soon as I saw wood lying about, I wanted to burn it, simply to watch the fire. To me, it was a magnificent spectacle; I loved to watch it, and I never could understand why everyone was scurrying around with buckets of water to put out the fire, or why my mother punished me.

One day I even set fire to my parents' hayloft. I thought to myself, 'There is nothing but old stuff in there.' I was six years old, and yet I knew already that old things must be burned! When I finally began to see the danger I was in, I took to my heels and as usual ran straight to

*29 January 1938.

my grandmother. When she saw the smoke and my panic she understood everything. Of course, once again I was punished.

Since then, life has taught me that fire needs to be handled with the utmost care. In some situations, it can take hold and spread with such speed that there is no time to stand and stare at it. Some years ago, I went to Florence. I was with a couple of friends, and I was looking forward to seeing all the magnificent monuments and visiting the museums. We were driving along a deserted little road in the hills above the city when we saw a fire that had taken hold a few metres away in the undergrowth. A driver perhaps had tossed a cigarette butt out of the car window. The fire brigade would have taken a long time to reach this place, which was quite difficult to get to, and something had to be done quickly. No other cars were passing by and we couldn't warn anyone. So, I said to my friends, 'It is imperative we put out this fire, otherwise it could spread down to the town.' After a lot of time and effort we managed to put it out. I don't know if we actually saved Florence that day, but I was happy about it and said to myself, 'Well, at least I have been able to make up for one of the transgressions of my childhood!'

But in fact I have never lost the desire to light fires, because each of us is born with certain tendencies we can never shake off. They just have to be transposed to a higher plane, by giving them a more spiritual expression. So, if you like, let's say that I was born an arsonist, but I learned not to go on lighting fires in log piles or haylofts. Now I strive to light other fires: in hearts and souls. Yes, I want to ignite in you an inextinguishable fire, the fire of divine love, so that it enlightens you, warms you and gives you life.

So I began my first lecture using the image of the little spring, but in that same lecture I also commented on the passage in *St John's gospel* where Jesus said to Nicodemus, *'No one can enter the kingdom of God without being born of water and Spirit.'* To be born of water and spirit is to be born of fire and water, of wisdom and love. You look at water, you look at fire, and because you see them you think you know them. No, when you understand them as symbols of the two principles – the masculine and the feminine – which are the two principles of creation, when you have deeply understood their relationship with each other, when you give them their true dimension – their psychic, spiritual, magic and cosmic dimension – only then will you know them, not before.[9]

When I recall my childhood, I also see the pine forests and the mighty poplars next to our house. How I loved climbing those poplars! I climbed as high as I could, then I would stay there for hours on end. I felt like a bird and I was so happy to be able to see the countryside as far as the horizon. I wouldn't go so far as to say that it gave me a feeling of superiority, but I did love the fact that when I was up there I could see things that others down below could not see. When my mother needed me she would call, and then, 'zip', I would slide all the way down the tree trunk. As, on hot days, I would often not be wearing a shirt, my stomach ended up as rough as an elephant's hide.

Still now, I find myself feeling like that child who climbed trees to see far off things from on high. I don't have any of the abilities that would allow me to be recognized as a man of science, and there was a time when I regretted that. I would have liked to be an astronomer, a botanist, a chemist, a physicist... but I am just a child who climbs trees. But from up there, I have the best vantage point; I see things which those down below may not see for goodness knows how long. I am interested only in the vantage point, the view from the top. From where I am, I can see the reality of things. Others are much more intelligent and able than me, but they have stayed in places where they cannot have this vision from on high.

If I am here before you speaking to you, it is not because I am so much more intelligent or better educated than you. No, it is because of the vantage point to which I have successfully raised myself, the view from the top, and I am striving to take you along with me. I place you near me on a branch, but look, you have brought a saw with you, and you begin to saw the branch on which you are seated and you fall. On the ground, you begin to concoct a logical explanation for your fall, and you blame your family, your surroundings, society, the government and so on. As for me, once again I must spend time and energy to lift you once more onto another branch. Why do you persist in working against your best interests?

In 1964 I went back to the village where I was born.* Fifty-seven years after having left it, I was still able to find some of my family: lots of cousins and the children and grandchildren of those I had known. They all threw themselves on me to hug me. And because they did not know what presents to give me, they gave me their most prized possessions: bottles of rakia. I don't know if you have ever drunk this, but it is an extremely strong brandy. And

*Macedonia was then part of the Federal Republic of Yugoslavia.

I who never drink alcohol!... I took a little sip to show my appreciation, but when you are not accustomed to drinking it, it burns the throat fiercely. When they saw me pull a face, they laughed to see this cousin who couldn't manage the drink they thought was so delicious. Then they asked me to take part in a wedding. What a party that was! It was a type of celebration they still had in these countries, with bright traditional costumes, and songs, and popular dances. I filmed it all. And then, what a feast! I had to continually make sure that they didn't keep filling my plate... or my glass!

These reunions were, of course, filled with great emotion, because it was there that I met my mother again, whom I hadn't seen since I left Bulgaria in 1937. I was told many things about my family which I didn't know. I was happy to learn that I had a grandfather who used to build roads throughout the country. What a magnificent job it is to build roads! I also found the cousin whose weaving I had destroyed by cutting the threads. Her husband was with her and they were both very old. I gave them presents so that they would forgive the wrong I had done them in the past.

All these years later, I wanted to climb Mount Pelister, which, as a child, I only ever saw from a distance. I particularly longed to walk in the pine forests, which, I had been told, were the most beautiful in the world. I wanted to believe it, but I was not sure. Knowing Bulgarians, their pride makes them exaggerate the beauty and importance of their country. I remember once seeing some country folk in Sofia dancing in a circle singing 'A city bigger than Sofia*... does not exist... A river deeper than the Isker**...

* The capital of Bulgaria since 1879. Around 1930, its population was about 350,000.
** Tributary of the Danube, which flows 8 km from Sofia.

does not exist. A mountain higher than Vitosha*... does not exist...'

So, with various relatives and friends, who knew the paths very well, I climbed Mount Pelister. In all the countries I have visited (India, Sri Lanka, the United States, Sweden and Norway) I have seen many pine forests. Some of them may have been bigger with taller trees, but they were certainly not more beautiful. Their colour, the thrust of their trunks, the placement of their branches, the shape of their needles, the scent which filled the air and all that emanated from them, what a marvel! Even the pebbles and the moss at their feet. It was something indescribable. You have to be there to have any idea of it. How I would love to go back now to Mount Pelister to spend a few days in these forests! Pines are the trees among which I feel the best.

Threads, water, fire, trees – that is what attracted me most in my childhood, and when I thought about it later, I realized that fundamentally I had not changed. The inclinations that I had then I have just deepened; they have become conscious in me, and threads, water, fire and trees have occupied an essential place in my philosophy.

There are still many things I saw or experienced between the ages of four and seven or eight years old which have remained as alive in me now as when they happened. I remember in particular some sensations which, when I analyzed them later, seemed to me to be intuitions of what my life would be, where I wanted to go, the choices I would make. And you, too, if you look back on your life, will discover that what you have become, the choices you have

* Mountain range overlooking Sofia which is 2230 m at its highest point.

made and the tastes and concerns you have now all have their origins in your early childhood.

Notes

1. See *Education Begins Before Birth*, Izvor Coll. n° 203.
2. See *'Know Thyself': Jnana Yoga*, Complete Works, v. 17, chap. 5: 'Sacrifice'.
3. See *'Cherchez le Royaume de Dieu et sa Justice'*, Synopsis Coll., Part II, chap. 1: 'Au commencement Dieu créa le ciel et la terre'.
4. See *Love and Sexuality*, Complete Works, v. 14, chap. 26: 'The bonds of love'.
5. See *The Book of Divine Magic*, Izvor Coll. n° 226, chap. 3: 'The Magic Wand'.
6. See *The Fruits of the Tree of Life – The Cabbalistic Tradition*, Complete Works, v. 32, chap. 10: 'A bowl of water'.
7. See *The Second Birth – Love, Wisdom, Truth*, Complete Works, v. 1, chap. 1: 'The second birth'.
8. See *The Mysteries of Fire and Water*, Izvor Coll. n° 232, chap. 4: 'Civilization, a product of water'.
9. See above, chap. 1: 'The two principles of creation, water and fire'.

3

Life in Varna, beside the Black Sea

In this little corner of Macedonia where I passed my earliest years, I instinctively learned to respond to the beauties of nature. The pure atmosphere of the surrounding mountains, the large trees, the river, the little spring where I spent hours in contemplation left indelible traces on my soul. But, one day, suddenly, we had to flee and it was heartbreaking.

At that time, the frontier between Macedonia and Greece was not secure, and the attacks from one direction or another were increasing. One evening, we saw a troop of Greek soldiers coming towards our village; some of the villagers fled and hid as best they could. My mother and I, as well as several other relatives and neighbours, spent the night in the river, hidden in the undergrowth, and from there we were able to see our village go up in flames. I was just seven years old at the time and I have never forgotten that night. The next day we found nothing but ruins and the bodies of men who had tried to defend the village. Nothing remained of our house. My mother decided then that we should go to join my father in Varna.

Varna was not a very large town, especially at that time, but how different it was from the little village I had just left. Everything was new for me. We lived in the Turkish quarter on the outskirts of the town. It was a wretched area with filthy little alleys that threaded their way up and down; whenever it rained these alleys became rivers of mud. In the winter, when it snowed, the ground froze, and walking up these slopes became quite an effort. I had to leave home very early in the morning if I was not to be late for school.

My father had chosen to live in this area because it was convenient for his charcoal business: all transactions, the buying and selling of charcoal, took place there. And, meanwhile, he had not been able to find anywhere better and more comfortable for us to live. A notable feature of these houses was that inside each one was a small door, allowing people to go into their neighbour's home, from there into another neighbour's home, and so on. It was impossible to know how far this went, and that is why people sought by the police could escape through these myriad connections. So, this is where we lived, among Turkish families and as we met them every day I was able to pick up a little of the language. Now, Varna has become a very modern city that attracts tourists from all over the world because of its beaches, and of course this quarter has been completely modernized.

I suffered at having to leave my little village, my grandmother and all the old relatives I loved so much, but I was so happy to be reunited with my father. He, too, was delighted, and that was why he was very indulgent towards me. For example, he would often leave a few small coins on a table knowing that I would take them to buy ice cream or candy. My mother did not approve of this at all and would reproach him, saying that it was not a good way to teach me…

Slowly, I began to get to know the children of the neighbourhood; they were not like the children I had known in our village. They were much more aggressive and cunning. When we are young, we don't choose our friends but just play with the children in the neighbourhood, and even parents often cannot do much about it. You have no idea what the boys who I grew up with were like. I often got involved in brawls which could have turned out very badly; Bulgarian boys against Turkish boys, as obviously we reproduced at our level the hostilities of our elders. Because I was a little naïve, a bit of a dreamer, my comrades took advantage of me. They would say we were going on an 'expedition', and then we would wreak havoc. As soon as the adults turned up, furious, the others would take off to save themselves, but I stayed there, nailed to the spot. I had nothing to say to the questions they asked me, and so I often got quite a beating. I don't know why, I never made any excuses. And, then, when my mother learned what had happened, she would punish me too.

So, one day, feeling that I had been the victim of too much injustice, I decided to leave home. I had no idea where I was going. So I left and made for the train station. There, I observed the comings and goings of the travellers. It was new and quite fascinating for me. But, after a few hours, I began to realize what it was to be alone, far from home and family. Firstly, I decided that I would not eat. But night came: where would I sleep? I found a small shack close to the station; it was empty and I could stretch out in it. But the sun had been heating it up all day, the air was stifling, and I left to find another shelter. I could not find anything, and I ended up stretching out on a bale of straw left lying on the street. I felt free and I was happy. I thought, 'There, my parents won't be able to find me. They don't understand me at all… I will have my revenge and they will be punished.' I knew that my mother would be distraught at my disappearance but, for the first time, I felt pleased at the thought of making her suffer. Then, hungry and exhausted after having walked for hours, I fell asleep.

The next morning I was woken by a few gentle kicks. It was a station employee. Shocked to find a child fast asleep on a pile of straw, he demanded, 'What are you doing here? Why are you sleeping here? Haven't you got a home to go to?' 'I have left home.' 'What? You have run away from your parents? Now, hurry up, and go back home or I will take you to the police station.' I got up and left, my head low. Once I got home, I was greeted by an outcry, 'There you are at last! Where on earth have you been? We've been looking for you everywhere…' and I could see by the look on my mother's face what anguish she had been through. Oh, I was not at all proud. My running away had no dire consequences, but it certainly made me think; I realized that I would never be as well off as when I was at home with my parents and I never ran away again.

However, I still followed my friends. They were always coming up with new ideas, new adventures. One day they decided that we were going to take down the flag that fluttered from the pediment of the Turkish legation in Varna. We didn't know much about the centuries' long domination of Bulgaria by the Ottoman Empire, but we were well aware that Bulgarians did not regard the Turks as friends. So, off went our little gang to haul down the flag. And we succeeded in doing it! Not surprisingly we were quickly discovered and the police were called. As usual, my companions took to their heels and I was left alone with the flag.

Taking down the flag of a foreign legation and, in particular, one from the Turkish legation was, of course, a serious offence, and I was taken to the police station. In those days, the police travelled by horse. So we set off, me on foot, carrying the flag, flanked by two officers on horseback. We crossed the town in this way and all the passers-by stopped to look at us. When we arrived at the police station, I was obviously a little nervous, wondering what they were going to do to me; once again, I would be the one to be punished, maybe even treated roughly. But I watched the officers whispering together, some of them even smiling a little. I waited… and then, after speaking very severely to me, and making me promise never to do it again, they told me that I could go home. Perhaps, after all, they were rather proud of what my friends and I had dared to do at such a young age.

One day, I began to understand that I really needed to distance myself from these lads, and even if I sometimes let myself be drawn into their escapades, they never managed to get me to take part in any of their criminal activities like thieving or fighting. They kept badgering me to join them, but fortunately something in me held steady and I felt that I should no longer follow them. I tell you from time to time about other foolish things I did, but they were nothing compared to what I could have done if I had stayed with the gang. All these boys ended up badly one way or another, either in prison, murdered or shot.

Of course, we cannot ignore the power of influences, but we should not think that outside influences are the determining factors. If people allow themselves to be drawn into behaving badly, it is because they already possess elements within them which will attract them almost magnetically into such actions. That is why, as I have often told you, it is so important what a mother puts into her child during pregnancy through her thoughts and feelings. Then, the example set by parents is also important, and that given by my parents was the best. From this point of view, I was very privileged.

At that time we lacked nothing, but we always lived in a very modest way. From my honest and upright parents, I learned that we must work, endure, toil, struggle. Also, I was always ready to make an effort, and I was amazed to see that some of my friends were brought up differently. It was thanks to the upbringing I received that I was able to come through some tough ordeals later in life; in some way, I was prepared then and I would not break down, to the point where, when the situation improved, I could not believe it. As soon as things lightened, improved, I asked myself questions: I did not find it quite normal.

When I think back on the upbringing I received, I bless heaven that I was born into a family which inculcated me with such a conception of life: I knew already that difficulties and ordeals are inevitable, and everything which was a little lighter, a little clearer, became a true blessing. What a surprise to see that other people not only failed to rejoice, but still complained about situations, when I was so joyful and so grateful! My father was concerned for my future; he had great plans for me, but even though he worked so hard himself, he never told me that the path to success was to make money, and neither did my mother. There, at least, I was not subjected to the pressures that so many children are under, from their earliest days, from their parents telling them over and over that they must prepare themselves for the purpose of obtaining lucrative and prestigious professions. If these children showed the least idealistic tendency, their parents reminded them of reality. My parents, however, left me free to blossom freely.

It was not quite two years since I had left Macedonia, and I hadn't changed inwardly in that time. I was still a little sleepy, a bit of a dreamer, and I felt so protected by both my parents. When my little brother was born, we were very happy. However, my father suddenly fell gravely ill and died. What a violent shock that was and it hurled me into reality. It was a terrible realization. My mother, grief-stricken, became ill, and her sorrow was increased by the anguish of having to support her two children.

In those days, most women did not really have any profession; my mother, who knew nothing of business affairs, was absolutely incapable of running my father's business, which just collapsed. Many of those who owed money managed to wriggle out of paying their debts, while others who were owed nothing started to lodge complaints. We lost just about everything, and we had to leave our home for a much smaller and less comfortable one in the neighbourhood. Some years later, we were able to obtain a small plot of land near the park overlooking the beach; the view was magnificent, and there we built a little house with the materials from our old home, which we had demolished. But for the time being we lived in an unhealthy house, my mother was ill, and we had hardly anything to eat. I was well aware of the seriousness of the situation, but I was eight years old; what could I do? With the help of a neighbour, I looked after my mother and took care of my little brother.

A short while later, in order to raise my little brother and me, my mother agreed to remarry. It was a very unhappy marriage, and our situation only became worse. I remember shoes with holes in and secondhand clothes that didn't always fit me. Sometimes, at night, I would dream that I found a few coins or that someone gave me a wonderful penknife with several blades. What disappointment the next morning when I found neither money nor penknife!

Of course, I went to school, but often I went without breakfast as we were too poor. That is why, during classes, I was almost always sleepy. I only had a notebook as my mother could not afford any textbooks. So, at breaktime, my willing friends would lend me their books, and I would read the lessons once or twice, as quickly as possible. When I was questioned, I spent a long time remembering what it was that I had read so quickly. I would begin by being silent, and my classmates would laugh, while the teacher walked up and down the classroom waiting for when I would finally say a few words. After a while, seeing that I was still silent, he sent me back to my seat, and that was the moment when I finally opened my mouth… The teachers did not know that if I took so long to answer, it was because of the bizarre way that I had had to study the lessons. So they concluded that I was very slow and they became used to waiting for me.

Learning under such conditions could not be anything but harmful for my nervous system, which I was mistreating. How could I be interested in topics that I was learning so badly? That is why I never liked school, and when I think about those years at school, I have very few memories of what I learned there. I remember more some of the teachers and some events that I lived through with my friends.

During the First World War of 1914-1918, most of our teachers had to leave for the front, and so we had substitutes who came for a short while to teach us. One year, we had two mathematics teachers in succession. When the first one came into the classroom the place erupted in a deafening hubbub: the students were all laughing and joking... He tried to do everything to re-establish silence. He shouted, gesticulated and threatened, but all to no avail. He even went off to fetch the head teacher, but as soon as he was gone the racket and laughter began once again. He was a nice man and I felt sorry for him; I didn't understand why my classmates were being so cruel. One day, I was so shocked that in his absence I took the opportunity to speak up and reproach them for their behaviour. They agreed that they would change their attitude, and for a day or two it was better. Then, once again, the rioting started up. Really, you could say that, just by being who he was, the teacher himself was responsible for provoking such reactions in the pupils; there was something in him that just released that hilarious hubbub.

One day, he left, and he was replaced by a small gentleman who came quietly into the classroom, without even looking at us. But, as soon as he came in, the pupils went to their desks in silence and did not move; he placed the register on his desk and began the lesson in a calm, peaceful voice. He never got angry, he never threatened us, and he never punished any of us. He knew his material perfectly, he never hesitated, and the students couldn't do anything but pay close attention. I was much struck by this, and so this insignificant man, who had apparently nothing remarkable about his appearance, has remained in my memory. It was not only his knowledge, but also his presence, what emanated from him, which commanded respect both from the students and other teachers. I couldn't explain it, I didn't understand it, but I noticed it, and it made me think.

I am aware that I was not always a model pupil; I didn't always try to understand my teachers. I acknowledge that sometimes I, too, made fun of them. As long as there are teachers and students, students will make fun of their teachers; very rarely in front of them, of course, but when they are together at break time, they imitate their gestures, the way they talk, the way they walk, their nervous twitches.

We had, in particular, a religious instruction teacher who was the butt of all our mockery. My God, how strange he was! He always wore the same worn out, darned old clothes, which he never changed, and the same hat, the same umbrella which had completely faded. And his shoes!... When he questioned a student, he made him come up close to him, and he would ask, for example, a question about some biblical patriarch: Abraham, Isaac or Jacob. If the boy did not know the answer, he began by speaking to him at length, quite quietly, in measured tones, as if he wanted to help him find the answer… or else he would start talking about something completely different; and then, when the student was least expecting it, he would hit his hand hard with a ruler. As we were well aware of his methods, the student being questioned was very distrustful, knowing what would happen if he didn't give the right answer. He was quite right to be suspicious, because at any moment he would be taken by surprise and 'whack!' he would feel the smack of the ruler. How often we mocked this teacher! How often we imitated him!

One day, a snake charmer was invited to the high school to demonstrate his skills. He was dressed entirely in yellow and carried sacks of snakes, all of which were poisonous; to prove this point, he gave a small animal to the snakes, which was bitten and died almost instantaneously. Then he let several snakes out of a bag and let them slither around the stage. He controlled them with his eyes and this look of his was truly powerful. He would bring his face very close to the snakes and stare so intensely at them that the snakes would recoil. We were both fascinated and terrified at the same time. Some short while later, we learned this man was dead, bitten by one of his snakes. I have often thought about him: what did he do wrong? He had so impressed me with that look of his and his mastery! Was there a moment when his attention slipped?

In 1909, Blériot, the French pioneer of aviation, made the first crossing of the Channel. Of course, the news of this extraordinary feat reached us in Bulgaria... So, imagine the excitement in our high school when we heard some time later that Blériot was coming to Varna for an air show! Our teachers led us out to the land where it was going to take place – the same land where, much later, my family got permission to build a new house. I will never forget how excited and how moved we all were to see the aircraft take off from the ground and rise into the air...

I loved walking by the sea. It was a new experience for me. I do not know what it is like now, but in those days these seashores were magnificent. The cemetery too where my father was buried was there. I accompanied my mother when she went to pray at his grave; she would bring some oil and light a small nightlight. A feature of this cemetery was that it was planted with fruit trees, and my enduring memory is that I have never eaten tastier fruits than those

I picked from those trees. Sometimes I would go there by myself; at least, there, no one accused me of stealing fruit.

Perhaps some of you are thinking, 'Eating fruits from a cemetery – how disgusting!' Where do you think the fruits that you eat come from? How many generations of people have lived and died over thousands of years? Where do you think their bodies are? The whole earth is nothing but a cemetery. Wherever we go, we are walking on corpses and our daily food grows out of them. The miracle is that plants are the greatest alchemists and they transform everything. Whether they are given chemical fertilizer, waste, or even corpses, they will grow flowers and fruit for you. If I so enjoy looking at peach trees, plum trees, apricot trees and others at the time when they are bearing ripe fruit, it is because I think of the work of transformation they are capable of doing. I too want to realize this work in myself, in order to give beautiful, fragrant and delicious fruit. So, I go up to them, I speak to them and I ask them to help me become like them. Think of doing it yourself from time to time.

My mother let me come and go freely in Varna, and this is when I had some interesting encounters. There were many gypsies in Bulgaria, and the women would tell fortunes. One day, I was passing by one of these women in the street when she stopped me. She told me that I had many enemies. Imagine that, at nine years old! Astonished, I asked her, 'But why? What have I done?' She added that I also had many friends. Then she took my hand and looking at my palm said that she could see a pretty girl, but big and fat, who loved me. Once again, astonished, I asked her, 'Is she really as big as that?' Then, she told me that, the same morning, she had fallen off her donkey and that had stopped her from seeing clearly. After that she put out her hand asking me to give her a few pennies! Bulgarians prefer to read the future in coffee grounds, and I remember a woman in Varna who was invited by all her neighbours to have a cup of coffee with them so that she read the grounds at the bottom of their cups.

In the centre of Varna, there was a tall tower and on top of that was a clock. When it struck the hours, you could hear it all over town. At that time a poor man lived there whom everybody knew. In the past, he had been quite a well known orchestral conductor, but because he had been through some terrible, testing times, he had lost his mind. He lived in utter destitution and all he did was sing to himself or smile blissfully. He could be heard repeating over and over again, 'He gives, he gives, he gives…' He was a gentle, harmless soul, and he never lost his temper with the children who danced behind him on the street and mocked him. Adults were more likely to take pity on him and so would bring him food and clothing, but he gave them away to others whom he thought were more unfortunate than he was. He kept almost nothing, so that most people had given up trying to help him.

I sometimes went to visit this man. Occasionally, I would find him sitting on the weight of the clock singing. I remember in particular how he sang *La Paloma*, and this song had an almost magical effect on me; I was flooded with romantic, even mystical, feelings. I know very well that some kinds of music can make people feel overly sentimental. Still now, when I hear someone play or sing *La Paloma*, I see again this poor eccentric and those days of my childhood come back to me. He was so good, so generous! As he had been a conductor he also knew many operas. So, I asked him to sing me some arias from *Il Trovatore* and *Aida* amongst others, and it was thanks to him that I learned many things about music. He would close his eyes, searching for inspiration; his face would become radiant and then he would sing. Hardly eating, living in wretched conditions, with no mattress or blanket in winter, he would be chilled to the bone. I would see him shivering, teeth chattering because of the cold, and I was unable to help him because I was too small and we, too, were so poor! And yes, it was true, he gave away almost everything to other people. But he sang, so I went to be with him and I communicated with his soul.

There was also an old beggar who could usually be found at the door of Holy Trinity church. With a friend, I went to talk to him from time to time. He told us many wonderful things, and that is why, despite his dirtiness, his unruly hair, beard and moustache, we enjoyed listening to him. One day we said to ourselves that we could not leave this likeable man in such a wretched situation; we had to do something for him.

I knew a woman who, because of her position, would be able to intervene with the local government. She had translated, amongst others, the books of the French astronomer Camille Flammarion into Bulgarian. So, I went to see her with my friend to tell her about this situation, and she promised to do something. So, soon, the beggar was found lodging, he was clean and properly dressed in a municipal care home where he lacked nothing, and we were very pleased with our good deed. Imagine our surprise to learn one day that he had escaped from the home and that he was back once again begging at the church door! That was quite a lesson for us, who had believed that he would be delighted at not having to beg for a living!

It is important that children should open up to the world from a young age, that they should store up as many impressions as possible, because having these experiences while very young will enrich their understanding of other people and of life in general. Their parents must also encourage them, while watching that they are not exposed to danger, of course, to become aware of all that is going on around them. Children go to school where they acquire a store of knowledge. This is necessary, but it is not enough. It is also important that they feed their intelligence and their sensitivity by meeting the greatest possible number of people.

Obviously, I did not spend all my time coming to the aid of the unfortunate. I had drawn away from the scoundrels in my neighbourhood, because I felt being around them could be dangerous, but I did not need them to cause a ruckus and disturb the neighbours' peace, as I had plenty of my own ideas, and if I was going to get up to some tomfoolery, I preferred to do it on my own. France had a notable chemist, Berthollet, who made a formula for explosives starting from a chlorine base, called 'Berthollet's salts'. I managed to get hold of some, and with what pleasure I caused explosions! I never caused any damage, but these explosions made a terrible noise, and the neighbours, scared out of their wits, would come running out of their houses. I did not wait for them but quickly ran away to hide. That was not very brave of me, but if I had not fled, not a scrap of me would have remained!

When I returned home, my mother, of course, would already have received visits from the neighbours. I cannot tell you how many times they came to complain to her!

They would say, 'Your son is a crook and a scoundrel', and she would reply, 'No, no, he's not a bad lad. You don't know him. One day you will see that he will change, and he will do very good things.' Of course, she would punish me sometimes, but I would begin again. Why did I feel the need to create explosions to shake people up? I've been told that years later people still remembered them.

I never did any irreparable damage, but I know what it is to be a child whose energies are not channelled. That's why, when parents come to talk to me about the difficulties with their children, which often happens, I tell them that they don't necessarily need to worry. They must find activities that will allow their children to direct their energies in a better way. Even though it may be more peaceful, parents shouldn't wish to have good and obedient children who agree with them all the time, for this apparent wisdom and obedience is often no more than passivity, and though these children may do nothing bad later on, they may also do nothing good. There are even cases where children and adolescents who have been totally passive wake up later on to become dangerous criminals.

Children should not be bullied; they should be watched over, corrected if necessary, but most of all they should be shown that they could always do better, that they are thought capable of doing better. That was the way my mother behaved. She had such faith in me, it undoubtedly had an effect, and I remain ever grateful to her for that. If children are to improve, they need at least one person who can show them such trust.

Of course, I lacked a father; I needed an authority figure. My mother was strong, but her strength came not from her will but from her love and her sense of sacrifice. She educated me by her love, not by her will, and it was her love that controlled me. I was always deeply moved by her attitude which made me feel ashamed. I realized how much anxiety I had caused her, and I wanted to throw myself at her feet to ask her forgiveness. I did not do so because I was much too proud, but when I had left her I would cry for a long time. I made good resolutions; I would be good, but it was so very difficult!

One day, I was walking down the street on my way to the park in Varna when I saw a travelling salesman who was selling pamphlets and bargain books. I stopped to look and found a pamphlet about the life of St. Athanasius. I leafed through it and was amazed. Of course, I understood nothing of the theological disputes he was involved in, but I was completely taken by this extraordinary man who had been able to triumph over a multitude of hardships. I really wanted to buy this pamphlet but it cost a lev. A lev is nothing, but for me, who had little money, it was a vast sum. So I prayed, 'Oh dear Lord, please help me find a lev so that I will be able to buy this pamphlet!' I continued walking down the street and, suddenly, I saw a lev on the ground. I picked it up quickly, and with what joy I ran back to buy the book! I read it, I reread it and I loved it so much that I decided I too was going to become a saint. I began by repenting of all my sins, which I thought were huge! For a few days I behaved myself, but of course this period of saintliness did not last long.

Another time, I borrowed the *Proverbs* of Solomon from the school library. I have no idea how or why this title attracted me. I opened it and read it: *'Hear, my child, your father's instruction, and do not reject your mother's teaching.'* I was bowled over. What is written in this book is difficult for a child to understand, but those words stirred something in me beyond understanding and awoke memories of the past.

For the first time, I had made contact with wisdom. I read and reread that book so much that I did not want to return it to the library. I found it so precious that I did not think anyone else would be worthy of having it. I did return it in the end, but meanwhile I kept it. I always read it with the same emotion, I bitterly regretted my faults, I wept while begging God's forgiveness, and I promised that I would become wiser. Obviously, once again, these good intentions did not last long, and I did not understand why it was so difficult to improve. Even so, I had a new awareness. The book of *Proverbs* stayed with me; I would often refer to it, and at least for a while I managed to behave well.

It may seem odd that this book played such a big part in a child's education, but that was how it was. Many years later I came across the *Amphitheatrum Sapientiae Aeternae,* 'The Amphitheatre of Eternal Wisdom' by Kunrath, which used *Proverbs* for an inspired cabbalistic commentary, seeing in it analogies for the preparation of the philosopher's stone. This sent me back again to the book, and I made many very interesting discoveries in it, but these new discoveries never erased all those feelings that stirred within me on my first readings.

Later still, during the school holidays, some of the workers who knew my father well and who had stayed in touch with the family took me with them up to the forest where they made charcoal. I was twelve years old. I spent a month up there. I watched how they prepared charcoal and some-times I helped them. They had built me a little hut and even made a ladder so that I could climb the tree beside the hut.

One day, one of them gave me the Gospels to read. This was the first time that I had read them and I did it with the utmost attention. There was such a great silence, such deep peace around me there!

I will never forget that mighty forest and its magnificent trees. There, I was tranquil as I read the Gospels, undisturbed by calls from my school friends to come and brawl with the Turkish children in the neighbourhood, and I no longer thought about creating explosions. Given my age at the time, what impressed me most in the Gospels were the miracles that Jesus did – how he healed the sick and drove out evil demons. I was particularly taken with the story of the possessed man whom no one could control; they had chained him, but he would break the chains, run naked everywhere and sleep amongst the graves. And then Jesus arrived. He asked him, *'What is your name?'* The man replied, *'Legion'*, for, according to the Gospel, several devils had entered into him. Then Jesus ordered the devils to leave, and suddenly the man came to his right senses, freed; he agreed to put on some clothes and sat at Jesus' feet, calmed.

How amazed I was by this image! A man who, just a short while before, had been behaving like a madman and who suddenly regained his senses. I pictured it so clearly: there he is, sitting down, his face at peace, a new light in his eyes and looking at Jesus with love. Why was I so struck by this? Because, to some degree, I identified with him. Try and understand what goes on in a child's soul!

Ever since I became aware of my faults, I considered myself the greatest criminal. That's why I was so overwhelmed by the story of this man saved in such a miraculous way by Jesus. I would have so wished him to do the same thing for me! So, I wept, I wept and pleaded that I, too, could be freed of my 'demons'. At times, I felt that I was that man, no longer possessed, but calm, at peace and sitting at Jesus' feet... This feeling lasted for a short while and even though it must have left deep traces within me, it faded somewhat; I was not transformed as quickly as I wished.

Of course, I went to church with my mother. But religious services are not particularly made for children, especially if no one explains anything to them. Then, they are bored, and later, they remember only the boredom and a few picturesque scenes. I used to love the Christmas festival because of the hymns and the lights, but I was more interested in the way that New Year's Day was celebrated.

In the morning of the first of January, a large crowd would assemble on the beach. All the Orthodox priests, led by the bishop, were there also for a religious service. However, the aim of this gathering was not entirely religious. The priests and the bishop would board a boat, and men were seated in other boats alongside. They were muffled up in thick coats, but underneath they would only be wearing a pair of underpants. The priests prayed and sang... This ceremony, as always in the Orthodox Church, would last a long time. Finally, the bishop would throw a crucifix into the water, and the men, casting off their coats, dived into the water to retrieve it. The first person to find it was entitled to a reward; he would then run through the town carrying a container which we call a *kotelché,* meaning a little cooking pot (*kotel* means cooking pot). The victor would carry this pot, usually made of copper, through the town and every one gave him a coin.

If it did not take place on the sea, the same ceremony would take place on lakes or rivers. This tradition most assuredly originated from a ritual of purification. I do not know if it is still carried out, but what good memories I have of it!

I also loved the Easter festivals, which in the Orthodox religion lasts for three days. They were preceded by another tradition; on the arrival of spring, everyone pinned two little pompoms, one red, the other white, on their clothes. I explained to you once the symbolic meaning of this custom whose origin is unknown.[1]

On Easter morning, the church would be full; the priest would light a candle and then pass the flame to the one officiating beside him, who in turn lit the candle of his neighbour, and so on… Watching the candles lighting one another, you would have said that fire was on the march, until the moment when the whole church was filled with a multitude of little flames. It was so beautiful! Then, of course, the service followed, and it was so long! There were hymns, of course, but the priest would read interminable passages from the Old and New Testaments, along with some prayers, all done in a very monotonous voice, and it was boring! Was he aware of what he was reading?…

So, I was there, obviously with children of my age. We waited impatiently for it all to end, because the only thing that interested us children were the eggs we had in our pockets. Our mothers had given us these hard-boiled eggs, which we had painted in bright colours, and we had to be very careful not to crack the shells, because when we left the church we were going to play a game we loved. We would take an egg in our hand and go and bang it against another child's egg. What a hubbub! Each one of us would take the egg out of our pocket and hit it against another child's egg! The winner, of course, was the one who could keep their egg intact the longest.

Ah yes, it was Easter, and we were children, and children like to play with coloured eggs. If only someone had explained what these eggs represented, they could at least have begun to be aware of the living book of nature, and then the celebration of the resurrection would have become something else for them and not just ceremonies which they couldn't wait to end.[2]

I must say that at that time it was not religion which contributed the most to my upbringing, but rather it was my mother, thanks to her behaviour and the example she set. Her life was so difficult! But she never complained, and when sometimes she did cry, she always did it out of sight. I often saw her crying, but she did not know that I had seen her. If, at that moment, a neighbour came to talk about her own difficulties, she would quickly dry her eyes, erasing all traces of her own sorrow, and would listen patiently to the account of some situation which was often much less serious than her own and succeed with her wise words in renewing her neighbour's confidence and courage. My mother was the first to teach me what love is. There are times when I feel crushed under mountains of difficulties, but with love, even if I were dying, I would hide my pain. It is this love that allows me to rise above everything. Love always has the last word and it resuscitates me. Love is true strength. My mother was wise, but above all she was full of love.

One day when I had to go out she said to me, 'Eat this bread that I've made for you before you go.' She opened the oven, and taking out a little roll she gave it to me. It tasted so good, but more than that, after I had eaten it I wasn't hungry for the whole day, and I was full of energy. When I came home I asked what she had put in the bread.

She replied, 'I put all my love into it. When I was making it I prayed that it would satisfy you and give you strength.' This is why I advise mothers to cook their young children's food themselves as often as possible, putting all their love into it.

It was my mother's love which enabled her to work tirelessly. She was always ready to help; she never stopped. If I said, 'Mother, just sit down; be calm, and rest a little', she would reply, 'I can't do that. If I rest, I will become ill.' And when she was ill, in order to get better she would get out of bed. Since my childhood I had seen her behave like this; it was her philosophy. When we met again in Yugoslavia in 1964, she had not changed. She was surrounded by many much younger relatives, but she was the one who got up, who went to find what was needed to serve others… I told her that such behaviour was making every one around her lazy and that was not a good education for them, but she replied, 'I cannot do anything else.' Believe me, if I have always treated women with the greatest respect, I owe it all to my mother.

So, after the fire in the village of my birth, I had left with my mother to rejoin my father in Varna, but he had died two years later, and after that we lived in poverty. Of course I was miserable, of course I suffered, but I had learned from my mother not to rebel, and I was never envious of other more fortunate children, who would come to school eating croissants when I had had no breakfast. It was as if there was something deep inside me which went far beyond my childish understanding, which knew, even at that tender age, that things were as they had to be. When I reflect on it now, I think that the harsh conditions forced upon me were the very best for the formation of my character. I could not draw the slightest superiority from my family's social standing. It was up to me to make every effort to prove what I was capable of. Now, I can see quite clearly why I had this childhood.

When one has been raised in poverty and destitution one remembers it all one's life and then understands how much suffering there is for the hungry. In Bulgarian we say, *'Sityatt né viarva na gladnyatt,'* which means that people who are satisfied do not believe the starving. And if, one day, those people benefit from better conditions, they always feel they owe something to the less fortunate. Fortune and social standing do not impress me; on the contrary, I am sometimes very severe with those who think that these external advantages merit sympathy and consideration, while I look for hidden virtues behind a person's insignificant appearance. When one is destined one day to enlighten and nourish souls, it is better to have learned very early on to recognize their worth and forget the criteria current in society – family origin, fortune, rank and professional prestige. Compared with the true values of the soul and spirit, this counts so little!

Notes
1. See *The Living Book of Nature*, Izvor Coll. n° 216, chap. 9: 'Red and white'.
2. See *Sons and Daughters of God*, Izvor Coll. n° 240, chap. 8: 'Christmas and Easter: two pages in the Book of Nature', and *The Philosopher's Stone – in the Gospels and in Alchemy*, Izvor Coll. n° 241, chap. 11: 'The regeneration of matter: the cross and the crucible'.

4

Apprenticeships

Some children do not enjoy school because they are bored, but they just love reading; they find that other books are far more interesting than the classroom textbooks. I was one of those children. Between the ages of twelve and fifteen I read voraciously and I particularly enjoyed novels. My greatest delight was reading, and at that point in time I had no other ambitions; I just wanted to read and saw myself doing just that all my life.

In Bulgaria we may not have had many great writers, but you could find translations of all the great writers in the world. I do not know how it is now, but at that time Bulgarians translated a great deal, and that is why I was able to read so many books by English, American, German and Russian authors, etc., and I began to get to know French literature: Victor Hugo, Balzac, Alexandre Dumas, Jules Verne, Eugène Sue... I read not just one or two novels, but almost all their work. I found these books in the school or town libraries, or else I was loaned them.

At high school, I continued my practice of borrowing textbooks from my friends to glance at the lesson before class. Now that I was used to it, I found that was all it needed. I even looked with a little scorn and some pity at those students who took so much time learning their work by heart. They got the better grades even though they were not always the most intelligent of pupils, and I had no desire at all to be like them. Was it really worthwhile putting so much effort into getting good grades? I could see quite clearly that they were learning not because they were really interested in the subject, but to be top of the class.

Often, while teachers were giving their lessons, I would read other books, not just novels but biographies, history books, books on the theatre or on poetry. When I got home, I continued to read. That is why, when I was asked questions in class, I brought up facts or gave explanations that were not in the books I should have studied. But as they were always relevant to the topic, the teachers, while wondering where I had found the information, usually gave me a grade 3, which, in Bulgarian schools at that time, was average. The best grade was 6.

I really wanted to learn, but in my own way. When adolescents make decisions on their own as to what they are going to learn, it can lead to strange results. One day, I came across a chemistry book, and I decided that I was going to do some experiments. Our house at the time had an old stable. I loved this spot because a jujube tree had taken root there, and over the years its branches had grown right out of the window. With my mother's permission, I set up my 'laboratory' there. I begged so hard that she ended up buying me a few test tubes. Once, I made a sort of chloroform, because I liked the idea of making people fall asleep; I had great fantasies about all the things I could do while they were asleep! However, it was difficult to put this project into action, and so I quickly abandoned it.

The truth, too, was that I was not really able to understand the instructions in the book I had found. Then, one day, I made a mistake when measuring amounts, or perhaps I just mixed together substances that should not be mixed… and everything exploded! It caused a lot of damage and my face was quite badly burned. Imagine what a state my mother was in… But how gently she nursed me! Thanks to her care, my new skin grew quite quickly.

At that time, I had a friend the same age who was mad about mechanics: he built engines by finding bits and pieces here and there in garages around town, and these engines worked. I really enjoyed watching him do it. But I was not interested in making engines; I, myself, was a chemist… an odd chemist!

Nothing interested me more than doing experiments, and in all sorts of different fields. I read pamphlets on Indian disciplines in which the author stressed the importance of developing willpower. Fine, I decided to develop my willpower, because I found I did not have enough. So I began to practise some exercises. Then, one day, wanting to show a friend what I could do, I took a very sharp knife and, stretching out my hand, thrust the knife into the fleshy part below my thumb. Blood spurted out. I could feel myself go pale, but I did not flinch. My friend was dumbstruck; he stared at my bloody hand and did not know what to think. Yes, I managed to impress him, but what I had done was incredibly stupid.

It was at that time I started trying out all sorts of different trades. I enjoyed it, I was very curious to see what people worked at and how they worked. Obviously these work experiences did not last long, just a few days or a few weeks, because they usually took place during school holidays. When I was wandering around I would often find myself stopping in front of a blacksmith's forge. It impressed me to see how he shaped a piece of white-hot iron with great hammer blows and then plunged it into cold water to temper it. As I had always been drawn to fire, I asked him to hire me. He put me on the bellows to stir up the fire, and when he hammered, I hammered with him too. Sparks would fly, and I was amazed. Sometimes these sparks would land on my bare feet because I didn't wear sandals, and I got blisters. But I was much too proud to complain, and it was good for me to develop my willpower!

Do you know how much I was paid for my work? I made the equivalent of twenty cents a day, but at that time twenty cents was worth a lot, and I was happy to give that money to my mother. She would have never asked me to work; I willingly chose to do it. During those long hours spent at the blacksmith's forge, I was studying and reflecting when I was looking at the fire.

Another time I was hired to work in a sweet factory.[1] I was amazed to learn that the owner allowed us to eat as much as we wanted, so I ate so many sweets that first day! The other workers watched me with big smiles and I wondered why. They knew that this would not last long, and in fact I quickly lost all desire for them. When you have stuffed yourself with sweets for a day or two, you are so sick that you do not want another one for months. That is no doubt why the owner allowed us to eat them, because if he had forbidden it, each worker might have taken a dozen home every day, and he would end up with whole sacks missing.

I also got a job with a tailor, but I really did not like that. The only good thing about the job was sitting 'tailor-style' with crossed legs, a bit like the yoga lotus position. But I drifted off to sleep, because I really didn't find sewing all that exciting: it was never-ending! To add to that I would prick my fingers, blood would flow, and if I stained the material I would get my ears pulled. Then, I decided that this was really not the work for me, and at the end of the day I left, to the great disappointment of the boss, who had thought he could make a real tailor of me. Even that one day's work of sewing left its mark, for I learned how to thread a needle and make a knot, and I can still sew on a button or make a hem.

I worked with a carpenter, then in a cigarette factory, where I rolled cigarettes all day! I was also hired to work in a crayon factory. I have always enjoyed speed in work, and so in this job I worked out various tricks whereby I could go faster than the other employees, and the boss rewarded me for my speed.

I do not remember any of my other 'jobs' any more. But wait! During the 1914-1918 war, when I was a little older, I spent one summer working in an office. I had to write all the letters that they sent out. However, given that it was a sedentary job, and that it was hot weather, I would find myself overwhelmed by a gentle drowsiness.

You see, even at a very young age I had many experiences, and it was no doubt necessary that I should go through all this. I know very well that sometimes you think that here in the Brotherhood I am protected and far from the world, and that I have no idea of the difficult conditions in which people may live. In fact, I am more aware than most of you. Not only have I known extreme poverty, but I have lived amongst people who were very poor. I could see how they suffered at work and how much they valued having a few cents they had earned by the sweat of their brow.

I was also very curious to analyze the impressions I felt when walking in the streets of Varna, or in the park above the sea. I realized that as human beings were endowed with five senses, it was important for them to develop these senses in order to experience various sensations and emotions more deeply. So, as I walked, I practised that too. I paid great attention to everything that I saw, heard and felt. For example, what riches there are in fragrances! Those who do not know the scent of tuberoses or syringa are really missing something.

Perceiving all the subtle world around me opened up my heart to poetry. At that time, I read some poems and learned them by heart. I felt that they gave me a glimpse into the truths of the soul and much better than anything I heard in church. After so many years, I wonder whether I can still recite a few verses? Yes, maybe...

Lazourna ourna moïata doucha,
Lazourna ourna v'immorteli beli
Spi neïnata doucha.

It means:

'My soul is an azure urn,
An azure urn, where, wreathed in white everlasting flowers,
Her soul sleeps.'

This poem speaks of the beloved's soul in such a poetic way!

Then, one day, I too began writing poems, and I gave them to my friends to read. You know how it is: artists, creators, always want to display their creative works. They were mystical impressions, visions and prophecies. I filled entire notebooks with them, until I realized that this poetry writing was weakening me by making me too sensitive and therefore too vulnerable. I understood I had to find it within, to live it in my life.[2] I have no idea what became of the notebooks. I see that you would be curious to read them. Perhaps I should try to write a poem for you... at least, four or five lines.

There is so much to say about poetry and the effects it can have on the feelings of adolescents. Nerval and Baudelaire, for example, were geniuses who were able to attain extremely subtle heights and then to express these truths in their writings. However, some of these perceptions that they phrased so brilliantly lead those who read them into the twilight zones of the astral plane. It's true that these regions have a certain allure, that they are seductive, encourage daydreaming and allow the reader to escape the harshness of the physical world. But it is dangerous to linger there, as the mind grows dim and the will becomes paralyzed, which is harmful for adolescents, whose character is beginning to take shape.

A young student told me one day that she had to study surrealist poets for her examinations and that she did not understand them at all. Clearly, I did not have all the criteria necessary to make an informed judgment, but she gave me Tristan Tzara's poems to read, and yes, from a certain point of view they were completely unintelligible. And yet, even though they were unintelligible, I realized, as I started to read, that I was moving into the dark and chaotic regions of the subconscious; the images used were obvious to me. When you know the language of symbols, everything is crystal clear, and so it can be very instructive for those who want to study the subconscious. But I do not call this poetry, and it is even dangerous for very young people to venture into these shadowy regions. I have already spoken to you on this topic, when I revealed the higher and lower aspects of the sephirah *Yesod*.[3]

Often, when we are young and interested in people of remarkable genius, we want to be like them. I had read that Balzac drank vast quantities of coffee to keep himself awake all night while he was writing his novels; so, when I drank coffee – and I drank a lot of it in order to read far into the night – I identified with Balzac. And I wanted to be like Jean Jaurès because he was so eloquent. I also read the great tragedian Talma's biography, and I felt sure that if I took to the stage I would, like him, be able to bring audiences to their feet. We wish for so many things when young, when we have no idea as yet what we are really here for!

At that time I had school friends who got together to put on plays. One day they asked me to join their company, and that was how I took a small part in a Chekhov play. My character was considered a silent man, but in fact he was a chatterbox! So I was this chatterbox, and I think that's a part I have continued to play. I see that in France Chekhov's plays are greatly appreciated; he's an author whom I like very much too. He is so intelligent, so original, above all in the way he weaves together certain comic and dramatic aspects of life.

After a while, I felt that learning and acting roles was not what I was made for. So I left the group, though I still remained their friend, and I really enjoyed going to see their productions. This connection with my friends sparked my interest in actors and acting. Of course, there was a theatre in Varna and I was so tempted to go to some performances! As I had no money, I managed to sneak in without paying. I was unaware of doing anything wrong. If you are very young, love the theatre and the cinema and have no money, morality is not foremost in your mind. I always managed to slip in unnoticed, and you can imagine how much I enjoyed watching all the actors! Whenever possible I would go to performances several evenings in a row, so I saw the same play, but I was not at all bored, on the contrary. I noticed that the interplay between the actors did not produce the same effects from one evening to the next, even though they were saying the same words.

At that time, because of going to the theatre, I began to realize the power of words; I understood that words were like containers which had to be filled with one's own life. I realized that some actors tried very hard to touch the audience with facial expressions, gestures, tremors of voice or shouts but had no effect. Whereas others, without any gestures or vocal mannerisms, made me tremble. There was, in particular, an Armenian actor called Chartouni, who left me dumbstruck; he was truly extraordinary. As soon as he came onto the stage, whether he was talking or silent, whether he was looking at the audience or had his back turned, something alive and vital emanated from his presence. And as soon as he opened his mouth, we were captivated.

Of course, I was so young then that I was not able to explain this phenomenon. It was enough that I felt it. Later, I observed that this happened with other people, as well as myself. There are days when the slightest word vibrates, resonates and moves all who hear it, whereas on other days even the most beautiful speech delivered in a deep voice has no effect at all. What a world of reflections this was for me! For my tool also is speech, and I know that I will not be really heard unless I fill all my spoken words with my own life. This ability to communicate life depends on the state of the solar plexus. Go back and reread what I have told you about the parable of the wise virgins and the foolish virgins and you will understand. Yes, the oil that the virgins needed to fill their lamps is a symbol for the fluids held in our solar plexus.[4]

Of course, I really loved the cinema too, and so I would sneak into the hall unseen, just as I did with the theatre, and I would often sit through the second showing of the film. I longed to have a different life from the one I was living, which seemed so very uninteresting, and I lived all that I saw on the screen so intensely. I identified with all the characters, with their suffering and their joy. They felt absolutely real to me, more real than the people I met in my own life. Perhaps this is why many years later I had a reaction that still fills me with remorse when I think of it.

In Paris I had seen the film *The Bridge on the River Kwai*, which had just been released. One day, when I was taking the metro, I found myself in the same carriage as the actor, Sessue Hayakawa, who had been the Japanese general in the film. He was sitting directly opposite me. I don't know what came over me, but when I noticed him, suddenly I no longer saw the man himself sitting there but instead saw the hard, inflexible character he had played in the film, and I could not stop myself from giving him a terrible look. Obviously, he saw that look, he felt it and it disturbed him. He did not know what to do; he was almost paralyzed. I just went on staring at him… A moment later the train arrived at the station where I was to get out, and I left. It is hard to explain, but to some extent I was glad to have been able to express the feelings of indignation the character of this Japanese general had inspired in me.

And then, what did I hear the next day? One of our sisters told me that the evening before, Sessue Hayakawa had been invited to a party with other artists, and no one understood why he seemed so depressed and overwhelmed; he had kept himself aloof and hadn't said a word. 'Good Lord,' I thought to myself, 'was I perhaps the cause of this? Why did I look at him the way I did?' I was most distressed. I especially regretted that I hadn't spoken to him: I could have at least congratulated him on his acting ability, which was so good that I had identified him with his character. However, I was no longer the dreamy adolescent who sometimes confused truth with fiction. That was the moment I really understood that I needed to watch the way I looked at people.

Years later I was astonished to hear that Sessue Hayakawa had given up everything. Despite his great success and vast riches, he became a monk and lived in retirement in a Buddhist monastery in Japan.

It would be impossible for me to tell you all the books I read at this period. I read just about everything I came across, and one day I chanced upon *The Palm Reader* by Desbarolles. This became my passion, and I began to study as many hands as possible. I even stopped people I met in the street and asked to look at their hands. Without really knowing what I was doing and giving a quick glance at the hands, I would then make predictions. I don't know how but, according to others, these predictions came true. Once my knowledge increased, however, I no longer predicted anything.

On another occasion, I found a book on the powers of thought and how to gain them. Here again, I began practising by experimenting on my friends. Without them knowing, I would amuse myself by concentrating on sending them suggestions. I would order one of them to take off his beret, tell another to look for an object on the ground, or to stop a passer-by in the street. Those were the kinds of experiment I would do, just to see what would happen.

When I went walking in the park beside the sea I often found that there was no place for me to sit on a bench. So I would step aside, concentrate on someone who was sitting there and think, 'Come on, come on, up you get!' and a few seconds later the person would get up and leave. And all innocent and sincere, I would take the free spot on the bench! One day, when I saw a friend of mine on the street, I concentrated on his right foot so that he wouldn't be able to move forward. He was standing still and leaning against a nearby tree, and as I came up to him, pretending our meeting was quite by chance, he said, 'Oh Mikhaël, I don't know what is happening, but I just cannot walk.' 'Don't worry,' I said. 'I'm sure it will pass quite quickly', though, of course, I did not tell him that I was the cause of his problem. Once again, I concentrated on his foot and it was released.

Sometimes, standing at a little distance, I would begin to look intently at someone. They did not know that I was looking at them, and all I wanted was to see whether they had any reaction, showing that they felt something. I was always so pleased when I saw their head turn to the right or the left to see where this impulse they were feeling was coming from. It was a game to me… Of course, I haven't played this game for a very long time, but there have been times, when I have been in the underground or in the street, or somewhere, when I have looked at people without their noticing, so that I could send them rays of light and write something good within them. I still do that sometimes and I can see by their reactions that some people are deeply touched. Without knowing exactly what, they feel something, but many others remain completely unaware.

Meanwhile, the material situation of our family continued to deteriorate. It was quite clear that at least one person was taking advantage of my mother's inexperience in business and was cheating her, but we never knew who it was.

So, one day, I concentrated very strongly and thought, 'We need to know who the guilty person is. I want whoever is doing us this wrong to find their arm is paralyzed tomorrow.' The next day, I will not tell you who, but someone in our circle of friends actually had a paralyzed arm. It was a great surprise to me!

From the moment someone has learned to control thought and concentrate it, it is very easy to do certain things which appear extraordinary to the majority of people. I found books on hypnotism and once again I decided to experiment on my friends. I felt that some of them possessed an almost medium-like temperament, and these were the ones I chose for these experiments. I made them sit down and I stared at them… When they had fallen asleep, I would send them out into space. On their return I would ask them what they had seen.

Then I wanted to prove to my friends the existence of the etheric body, which sensitizes the physical body, whose double it is. When they asked me, and often their parents were there too, I sometimes asked one of them, perhaps a young girl for example, if she agreed to be put to sleep. I concentrated on sending her into a hypnotic sleep, then I would make a few hypnotic passes over her so as to withdraw her etheric body, which I put in the next room. Then the demonstration began. I pricked her lightly on the arm with a needle. She did not react; it was clear that she had felt nothing. Then, I would go into the next room with the same needle, and I would lightly prick her etheric body, which I had lifted away from her. Then, she let out a cry. All my friends were dumbfounded, and I was very proud that I could prove the existence of the etheric body to them. I did these experiments several times for them. One day, I did this to a friend, but at the end I had the greatest difficulty getting him back into his body. I was then so afraid that I stopped these experiments.

But I still continued other exercises. At that time, I was extremely shy. For example, if I had to go into a shop, I would pace to and fro on the pavement before I dared to enter, and then, when I had finally decided on what I wanted, I did not know how to ask for it and just stood there stammering. As for young girls whom I did not know, I could not even reply when they spoke to me, and if my sisters, who were much younger, brought their school friends back to the house, I would shut myself in my room until they had left.

One day, I decided that I could not continue with this situation; it was a sickness that I needed to deal with, and so I used autosuggestion. I fixed my gaze on a shining spot while I repeated that I had to lose this shyness, and then I imagined myself acting with confidence. In effect, I had to hypnotize myself and ended up by falling asleep. That was the way I conquered my shyness. Now that I have different knowledge, I would not suggest this method because it is damaging to the balance of the nervous system, especially when it is done so young.

It really would have been better, when taking on these explorations of the psychic world and the powers of thought, for me to have had a guide. Unfortunately, I had no one who could advise me and show me what was good and what was bad. And then, one night, when I was in bed, something happened which I have never been able to forget: two mighty individuals suddenly stood before me. I was not asleep, but at the same time I was not totally awake. I was in that half-waking state when I saw these two beings in front of me: one had a very striking bearing, and strength and power emanated from him, but his face was hard and his expression dark and terrifying. The other being was the embodiment of beauty, of gentleness; he was radiant and the look on his face showed the boundlessness of divine love. Immediately I knew that I had to make a choice between these two beings; I was greatly affected by the power of the first one, but in my heart and soul I was terrified by the awful violence I sensed in him. So I let myself be drawn towards the other one whose face radiated goodness and sacrifice, the face of Christ. And then I fell asleep.

When I awoke, I could not understand what had happened to me. I even began to question a little what I had seen, but that final sensation remained strongly with me, and I believe that I made the key decision of my life that day. The choice I made of the being who manifested love determined the orientation of the rest of my life. All those different psychic practices I had devoted myself to, successfully, I would be able to use later against the attacks of those who had decided to fight and harm me. It must be acknowledged that sometimes it is tempting: when people have really gone too far, why not neutralize them and teach them a lesson, especially when one has all the means necessary? Fortunately, I have always known that would be the worst possible solution.

Yes, now, when I think back on all those exercises that I engaged in when I was so young, I thank providence that I was helped to choose the path of love and not that of power. The other saving grace was that I was not at all malicious. I was just inquisitive and longed to understand and try out these experiments. All the same, without discernment, without a guide, given the psychic capacities I had, this could have turned out badly. You must not think that many of those who end up sinking into black magic consciously and deliberately choose to do so. Of course, this can happen, but there are certainly not many people who decide one fine day to become black magicians and do all they can to become one. Many of them perhaps had no evil intentions, but they were ignorant and foolhardy, they overestimated their strength, and especially their control, and they got carried away.[5]

All my later experiences showed me that the best solutions, the most effective and even the most economical – yes, the most economical – were always those of love. Strength untempered by love always causes damage. Unfortunately, the world is full of such forces. It is with love, and wisdom too, that we acquire the right to show our strength. Others in the visible or invisible world try immediately to use and exploit those who have brute strength and nothing else by turning them away from the path of righteousness.

What also saved and protected me at this time was my awareness that I actually needed to be guided and advised.[6] I did not believe, as many adolescents do, that I could be my own master. So, I worked unremittingly to remain linked to all those initiates living in the Himalayas whom I was meeting through reading certain books about India, and I begged them to enlighten me. At the same time, I continued going to church… The truth is that I went there just to hear the singing of the orthodox liturgy because, at that time, there was a truly exceptional choir in Varna cathedral. I did not need to hear what the orthodox priest had to say, because my soul had already been lifted heavenwards by the singing.

There was also a protestant preacher in Varna, who was remarkably eloquent. He would attract huge crowds, and I went several times out of curiosity to hear him, not just because he was so eloquent but because his sermons had real depth. However, he kept on saying, *'God so loved the world that he gave his only Son.'* Hearing him say this phrase over and over again became unbearable to me. And more importantly, how did people understand it in the constant repetition? Repetition is not explanation, and by dint of hearing it so often you no longer hear it. You must know the truths of Initiatic Science if you are to understand and interpret it.[7]

One day, a Jewish family moved into our neighbourhood. The father was a rabbi. We passed each other sometimes on the street, and gradually I became friendly with him. When he understood what I was interested in, he invited me to his home. He was a very deep, erudite man, and I asked him many questions about the Jewish mystical tradition. I learned a great deal from him. It was through him that I first heard the name Baal Shem Tov, who founded the hassidic movement in Poland in the eighteenth century. Baal Shem Tov means 'Master *(Baal)* of the good *(Tov)* name *(Shem)'*. I have great respect and admiration for Baal Shem Tov. I did not read his biography until many years later when I visited Israel* where he still has disciples. I was even invited to attend one of their meetings.

During this trip to Israel, I tried to visit as many of the places mentioned in the Bible as I could. I wanted to feel what had taken place there over past centuries, as it has been so important for the spiritual destiny of humanity. Of course, too many people have trodden this ground without the slightest respect for there to be any traces of the atmosphere of biblical times, of the patriarchs and prophets, of Jesus. It is in the etheric body of the earth that we must seek traces of their passage.

In Hebron, I went into the tomb of the patriarchs, and in this spot filled with a holy silence, I meditated for a long time. I hoped to find this same sacred atmosphere at Meron, near Safed, where I wanted to concentrate deeply at the tombs of Rabbi Shimon Bar Yochai, to whom tradition attributes the origin of the Cabbalah, and his son Eleazar. The site is very beautiful, set on a mountainside, but a great crowd had just been celebrating some festival, and I was astounded to find such noise and filth. There was no place at all where I could sit and concentrate. There were people eating, spitting, vomiting, slaughtering animals for sacrifice, and nothing but filth and rubbish everywhere. I had come

*in the spring of 1968.

to communicate with the spirit of the one called 'The holy lamp' and here I was in the midst of a disgusting spectacle. So, in my anger and indignation, I asked, 'Angel of air, angel of water, cleanse all this away!' A few hours later a torrential rain fell. The weather office had not forecast a storm like this and everybody was completely taken by surprise.

Before I returned to France, I wanted to meet a very old cabbalist who had been mentioned to me. He was the only one who really impressed me. He had white hair, a great white beard, beautifully sculpted features, a face from the Bible, the face of a prophet. And what depth of expression! He had a vast expanse of knowledge, and we spoke for a long time together. Then, at the end, he blessed me saying a few words, which, translated, were something like 'May the whole world follow you! May the whole world walk with you!' and his face was ablaze with light. I was much touched and filled with joy by these words. They were not just stating a hope, but it was a prophecy, as if he had seen and felt a magnificent future... I often think of this old cabbalist, and I hope he lives for many more years.

Throughout my childhood and adolescence, I was obsessed with the desire to learn. I felt limited, and I wanted to know and understand everything. I read endlessly. From morning to night, and often throughout the night, I kept on reading. Some days I would devour six or seven hundred pages. I would keep reading while I was eating so as not to waste time. Like all Bulgarian mothers, my mother used to make casks of pickled gherkins, peppers and celery. I would dip into these casks and munch away on the pickles and continue reading. How did I not destroy both my brain and my liver on such a diet?

It is true too that my family lived in such abject poverty that we often had almost nothing to eat, which led me to try an experiment that had a marked effect on me. I had only a small piece of bread with a scrap of cheese. I don't know what made me chew and chew each mouthful for such a long time that it melted in my mouth without my having to swallow it, but then I felt full of energy for the rest of the day. I often repeated this experiment. In this way I discovered that the way we eat is as important as the food itself, if not more so. That is why I have spoken to you over many years about the yoga of nutrition: I want you to understand that it is essential to eat your meals in silence, concentrating on the food, eating it slowly, chewing it well, and stopping from time to time to breathe deeply.[8]

All my analyses, all the explanations that I give you today about nutrition are based on this experience I had when I was fifteen years old, when I had to make do with the smallest amount of food. Of course, since then, I have gone more deeply into all the ramifications of this experience. Now, I know that nourishing oneself is a process which happens not only on the physical plane, but also on the psychic and spiritual planes.

At high school, I became more and more bored with the lessons. I found that the information they were giving me became like a barrier, a veil, between me and certain invisible truths which I had seen and which I wanted to go on discovering. I hardly studied at all, but because I still did not want to fail the examinations I would work during the last few days in an attempt to make up for lost time. This put a violent strain on my brain, and at times I was near the point of collapse.

So, one day, I decided that I could no longer go on like this and that I would not go back to school any more. I was fifteen years old, and when I told my mother of this decision, that I would rather go to work and earn some money to support the family, she was worried, and she did not really agree with me. But when she saw how determined I was, she finally relented.

Notes
1. See *The Mysteries of Fire and Water*, Izvor Coll. n° 232, chap. 6: 'A blacksmith works with fire'.
2. See *Creation: Artistic and Spiritual*, Izvor Coll. n° 223, chap. 4: 'Prose and poetry'.
3. See *Looking into the Invisible: Intuition, Clairvoyance, Dreams*, Izvor Coll. n° 228, chap. 3: 'The entrance to the invisible world: from Iesod to Tiphareth'.
4. See *New Light on the Gospels*, Izvor Coll. n° 217, chap. 9: 'The parable of the five wise and the five foolish virgins'.
5. See *The Book of Divine Magic*, Izvor Coll. n° 226, chap. 1: 'The danger of the current revival of magic'.
6. See *What is a Spiritual Master?*, Izvor Coll. n° 207, chap. 2, 'The necessity for a spiritual Master'.
7. See *Sons and Daughters of God*, Izvor Coll. n° 240, chap. 5, 'God so loved the world that he gave his only son' and chap. 7, 'The man Jesus and the cosmic principle of the Christ'.
8. See *The Yoga of Nutrition*, Izvor Coll. n° 204, chap. 1: 'Eating: an act which concerns the whole person', and chap. 2: 'Hrani yoga'.

5

The experience of fire

It took all the authority of Master Peter Deunov, who I met two years later, to get me back to high school and then to university. But for the time being, I was free... I went to work to earn money and the rest of the time I spent reading. I read everything that fell into my hands and, as can happen at that age, I was then very influenced by some materialistic thinkers: Moleschott, Ernst Mach, Ludwig Büchner and Ernst Haeckel... Even if, as in my childhood, I still experienced certain mystical states, I ended up accepting a material concept of the universe and of humanity, because, when looked at purely from an intellectual viewpoint, these theories can be most convincing. Little by little I no longer believed in anything, except in the laws of matter.

However, one day, by chance, I came across an essay, *The Over-Soul* by the American philosopher, Emerson. It was only a small pamphlet but it had an indescribable effect on me; I felt dazzled by light as if I had been struck by lightning. It was so long ago that I could not give you any very precise details of what he said, but I can still recall the idea that turned my world upside down. It was that everything in the universe is contained within the principle existing in all of us which Emerson called the over-soul. This over-soul reaches to heaven, lives in heaven, and is an emanation of God himself. In coming down to incarnate in matter, we have lost our awareness of this soul, of its existence in us, but if we seek to know it, if we identify with it, we come closer to our true being: our consciousness becomes heightened, its vibrations become more intense, and one day it will blend into the consciousness of the universal Soul, and we will be one with God and all creation.

Why was it that this idea, that each one of us possesses a quintessence of all that exists in the universe, struck me as if by a lightning bolt? No doubt because I already knew it; in that one flash I was in touch with a memory which had always been there, buried deep within my being. It was not some abstract idea, but something I lived intensely. And since the universe was contained within me, I had no need to ask for anything else; I just had to look and dig deep. Everything I have learned since then, everything I have understood and brought to fruition, has all sprung from this truth which I read in Emerson when I was sixteen years old. I had to explore this knowledge, these treasures buried within me, and bring them up into my consciousness. So, when I speak to you now, I am giving you fragments of my life. What I feel, what I think and what I breathe – it is with this that I nourish you.

Later, it is true, I sometimes asked myself how it was that this little booklet of perhaps twenty pages was able to turn my world upside down. It was then that I had the revelation of beauty. Yes, I saw true beauty, the beauty of light, the beauty of colours, the beauty of vibrations, the beauty of the structure and harmony of the universe, the beauty of God himself, and this has marked me forever. From that day I wanted to live in that beauty, which for me blended with the idea of God. I could waver no longer. How could I doubt what I had lived? I did not have the time to ponder on what I ought to do. Firstly, there was nothing to reflect on; I was living in light, and around me, people, animals, the earth, the trees, the stars, everything was transformed! I was content to walk forward without fretting over where exactly I was going, because of this strong sensation of the light permeating everyone and everything.

At such a time, I can tell you, there is nothing to reflect on: what is beautiful is beautiful, what is luminous is luminous, what is divine is divine. You do not need years and years to understand, for your consciousness is illuminated instantaneously. At that moment, your soul and your spirit are speaking, and the decisions you have to take are instantaneous and irrevocable. That is why, later on, my life could not have unfolded in any way other than it did. Obviously, just because we receive a lightning flash from heaven does not mean we are immediately transformed. No, the heavenly fire in us does not make us instantly omniscient, omnipotent and perfect. It gives us a vision; it sets our hearts and souls ablaze, and then it is up to us to work with it, so as to develop ourselves perfectly.

Certain aspects of all that I lived during this period of my life I found echoed in the books of great mystics such as Master Eckhart, Ruysbroek the Admirable, St Francis of Assisi, St Catherine of Siena, St Marguerite-Marie Alacoque, Jakob Boehme, St Teresa of Avila, St John of the Cross, St

Thérèse of the Infant Jesus and many others. Suddenly, you are dazzled, you feel, you understand. This cannot be explained – these raptures, these ecstasies that a soul experiences cannot be explained, and they have nothing to do with people's intellectual level: Jakob Boehme was a cobbler. Because I have experienced these states, I understand the true mystics, and I can also distinguish them from other states, those that are claimed to be mystical and which are, in fact, nothing but hysteria.

Shortly after my encounter with this essay by Emerson, I went walking one day in the hills around Varna and sat down to meditate. And what happened there? I was suddenly suffused with such brilliant light, flooded with such powerful currents of energy that I no longer knew where I was; I was swept away... But at that moment the organism defends itself to some extent, and so I fell into a semi-conscious state between fainting and sleep. When I came back to myself, everything was once again as it had been. I made so many efforts to try to regain this rapture, but I never succeeded; later on I experienced similar states, but never anything of such intensity. And that is probably a good thing, because the human organism cannot withstand such powerful vibrations. My experience was an exceptional one, a blessing from heaven. I knew in one instant, in a lightning flash, the splendour and the power of the divine world.

I do not know if you have read this essay by Emerson and, if you have read it, what effect it had on you. I have often advised people to read it, and they have all found it interesting, no more than interesting, and I was astonished. The experience I had was my experience, and if I talk to you about it, it is not to impress you, but to make you aware that you, too, have a higher soul – other philosophers call it the higher self. For the time being, you perhaps have no awareness of this soul within you, but if you think of it, love it, try to enter into contact with it, if you ask for its help, little by little you will feel it drawing closer to you. Otherwise, you know, its true abode is so high and far away that it will not be concerned with you. You may have difficulties and suffer, but it will not be anxious, it will not suffer, it is calm. Only if you turn towards your soul, if you call it, will it deign to look at you.

You will say, 'But how can that be so? It is my soul and yet it does nothing for me?' Why do you want it to do something for you when you make no attempt even to discover what it is? Understand me well, the soul that I am speaking of is of a different nature from the psychic principle that is usually called the soul but which is, in truth, the astral body, the body of feelings, emotions, sensations, desires and passions;[1] this soul, which we can call the lower soul, shares our daily life, is troubled, suffers and cries out. But what I am speaking to you about is your divine soul, which is pure light, knows neither trouble nor suffering and is very high and very far away; this is the soul we must strive to reach. The day that is achieved, what follows is the same phenomenon we call 'love at first sight'. Two people meet, and at that moment there is a kind of lightning flash, and that is all it takes; it is as if their souls are soldered, welded together. It is nothing at all like a love which grows gradually; even if this love is steady, deep and long-lasting, it cannot be compared with love at first sight. You will say that some experiences of love at first sight are no more than a flash in the pan. Yes, of course, but what I am talking about is the encounter between two true twin souls.

It takes a long time to prepare the physical body before venturing into certain spiritual experiences. That is why I had to work for years on myself to be able to receive the vibrations of the divine world without being completely floored by them. There are moments when you cannot bear so much beauty, so much light, so much love. I tell you quite sincerely that sometimes, even now, I am afraid. I am not certain that my body is able to sustain the power of certain currents. Accidents can happen that are just like when someone inadvertently touches a high voltage cable, is electrocuted and their heart stops. No one knows what it is like to suddenly come into contact with the power of divine love. Although somewhere in humans there is a mechanism like an electrical transformer that can lessen the tension, if no precautions are taken death can come as a lightning bolt.

Because I was too young and my mind was, therefore, not sufficiently formed and structured, I was not immediately able to interpret this lightning bolt from heaven that I received; the lightning flash passed through me and burned everything in its path. For weeks and months I wanted nothing else but to be able to live in that fire. From then on I searched for books which would enlighten me on this new path, and it was then that I came across a book by Paracelsus. I only remember that he revealed that the loss of a man's seminal fluids meant that he also lost a vital element, a very precious quintessence. I had never read or heard such a thing before, and yet so many men are driven to waste this quintessence in pleasure! I was most struck by this truth, and I took it seriously. What I did then, what I decided, I will not tell you, except to say that this discovery was a determining factor in my life.

However, I had been told that in order to control the sexual instinct, as well as all other instincts, you had to fight it, because instincts are the real enemies of humanity, and they must be fought. Religion said so, morality said so, and even sages said so. So I struggled, and the more I struggled the more I was tortured and torn apart, because it is exhausting to keep fighting against yourself, against something which you do not really know. So I tried other paths; I begged my heavenly friends to enlighten me, and I understood that I had to do things differently: not fight against my instincts, but have a high ideal and place them at the service of this ideal. For instincts are powerful life forces. If you try to eradicate them, you will either not succeed and become exhausted in the battle, or else, if you do succeed, it will not be much better, because you will have destroyed a part of your own life in the process.[2]

This is why, now, I can tell you that the high ideal is a transformer of energies. As soon as we place a very lofty ideal in our heart and soul, all our energies are forced to pass through it, and it re-orients them towards the heavens. The high ideal transforms these energies. How does this transformation take place? We don't need to know. For example, when we eat, we do not need to know in detail all the transformations taking place, first of all in the mouth and then in the stomach and the intestines, but we can feel that we have been given strength. The same applies to the high ideal; if we nourish it with our thoughts, our feelings, our desires, our instincts, it transforms them, and the energies produced by this transformation sustain our psychic life, our spiritual life, and our physical bodies too, for nothing is separate within us.[3]

But what helped me the most then, what saved me, was my love of beauty, this beauty of the divine world which had just been revealed to me. For that, I was ready to make all efforts, to accept all sacrifices. I entrusted myself to this beauty of light and purity as a refuge from seduction. Later, I read many other books by Paracelsus, for he wrote many. I always felt very close to him on many topics. Years later, I visited his birthplace at Einsiedeln in Switzerland. I was happy to be able to meditate there for a long time so as to be in contact with his spirit, because he had had a great influence on me in my youth.

Then, I found yet another book (though I can no longer remember either the title or the author) which explained the nature of the aura, the halo of light which surrounds saints, mystics and great spiritual Masters.[4] It described Buddha's aura, which was so vast that it extended for miles, and I imagined the extraordinary splendour of this aura, in which all those around him bathed. I, too, longed passionately to have an aura like that one day! So, I decided to concentrate on the light, as well as on all the colours that result from the breaking up of light through a prism. Only a prism can give us a hint of what true colours are, and so, using a prism oriented according to the sun's position, I began to study the seven colours of the solar spectrum.[5]

Colours act on the brain and, through the intermediary of the brain, on the whole body. Once I had succeeded in immersing myself in a colour, I could visualize it, imagine that I was swimming in it, that it was coursing through me. I discovered that, moving from red to violet and violet back to red, all the parts of the body, all centres were touched, and not one single organ was unaffected by the seven rays. Then, I decided to paint the windows of my room in order to further study the effect of colour. I began with red, then orange, and so on. I meditated in this space bathed in coloured light and watched, over several days, how this colour worked on me, then I washed everything and went on to another colour. I won't tell you what my parents and the neighbours thought of my experiments… but I carried on unperturbed. With the colour violet, I felt as if I was leaving my body. I invited friends in to see what effect this colour had on them, and they fell asleep. Flowers faded almost immediately; violet killed them.

How rich the world of colour is! I cannot begin to tell you all that I discovered, what I felt, what I experienced when I concentrated on colours. I was imbued with them; I intensified them within me and around me, then I projected them out into space. I longed for my aura to be, one day, as vast, vibrant and pure as that description I had read of Buddha's.

I have often spoken to you about the powers of the aura, but I am still not sure that you have really understood. To gain access to certain areas we must have a permit; as soon as we have that permit, the doors open. The same thing holds true for the invisible world: in order to access certain regions, we need a permit, and this permit is the aura, the colours of which it is formed. Think about this! Get into the habit of concentrating on the purest of colours, impregnate yourself with these colours, and one day you will feel that you are entering into the cosmic harmony, that you are touching the celestial hierarchies, and they will give you their qualities. Exercises with colours and the qualities that correspond to them are a key to the spiritual life.

All my life since then, I have continued to find great joy in colours, particularly in the colour hyacinth, as this has a very powerful effect on me. In my aura, I particularly sense the presence of both golden yellow and violet, and certain people have told me that they have seen them. Even children have seen them, yes, children. They may not yet have heard of auras, but they have a type of clairvoyance, and some of them have told me that they see gold and violet around me. Violet is so much part of me now that, each night, when I go to sleep, I see it appear. I do not do anything to summon it; it is just there, and so I sleep bathed in a violet light, violet of a particular shade which I do not think exists anywhere in the physical world. Why is it violet especially which appears at that precise moment? I do not know, but I go to sleep in a state of extraordinary joy because of this violet light.

Although I was always very drawn to books, as time passed I became more and more aware that I was not going to find true knowledge by reading books. I had to look for true knowledge elsewhere, and to do that I needed to leave my body. I always felt the need to go further and further, and so every day I spent hours in meditation and concentration exercises. Fortunately, I was never tempted to use drugs, and it is true that in those days drugs were not as widespread as they are today. But I used autosuggestion; I would put myself to sleep and, during this very specific sleep, I travelled through space. I cannot tell you exactly where I went, but I came back with clarity, an intuition and certainties that nothing could shake. Such experiences are in effect identical to those you can have during sleep.

You have certainly woken up some mornings with the feeling that you have come back from far away. Even if you do not remember what you have seen or heard, you feel that you have lived through something which has enriched your understanding. In the same way, true knowledge, initiatic knowledge, is gained on high, in the invisible world, and it is on high that I began to discover many of the truths I reveal to you today. But these journeys in the invisible were not without danger for me, for it is not enough to leap off into space; you must know the two paths, the one for venturing out and the one for getting back again. When I think again of my inexperience then, I realize that I must indeed have been protected.

I had also understood that only purity can give us access to those higher realms of the invisible world. So that started me off on another venture…

As religions throughout time have underlined the purifying power of water, I decided to do purificatory exercises by taking baths. I had discovered a book by Dr Kneipp*, and in my so-called laboratory where the jujube tree grew I began to apply some of his methods, in particular taking cold baths. But when I did these exercises, I did not just do them for a quarter of an hour or even half an hour, I would do them for hours on end. I was not moderate. That is why, when I talk to you now about the necessity for moderation and balance in all you do, I know what I am talking about. My God, I had no sense at all! And that is how, after spending hours in cold water baths, I found myself in bed with pneumonia. As usual, my mother took care of me.

But I, too, had discovered a way to heal myself which I often used afterwards. When I caught a chill, or had a cold and was feverish, I lit a wood fire in a bucket, sat very close to it, looked at it for a while and then went to sleep there,

---

*Sebastian Kneipp (1821-1877) – a German Catholic priest, who perfected a hydrotherapy method.

with a feeling of gratitude and love towards this warmth. When I awoke, I was healed. This was how I understood the curative properties of wood fires – how the living energy of trees can be transformed into health and strength. For it is not only the warmth which has the property of healing, but other elements contained in the burning wood. Obviously, fire cannot heal all sicknesses, but when I was close to it, I not only rid myself of toxins through perspiring, but I also received a real transfusion of energies.

I was so happy to have left school and to be free to do only those things that I liked! I was always looking for new exercises to do, and I came across a book by Yogi Ramacharaka on respiration. This book detailed the way to perform these exercises, the rhythms necessary, and I leaped headlong into them. Here I discovered that breathing can become a delight. We still do not know all the abundant riches that the Creator has put in air. Even I could never have imagined it if I had not had the experience. But one day, just as I was taking a deep breath, a fire suddenly entered me. Yes, I swallowed fire, a fire which penetrated right into my lungs. I was set ablaze and I knew what ecstasy was. What a feeling of light and joy! But I was not able to interpret what had happened to me. It was much later, when reading certain writers, that I understood that I had inhaled something which came from on high, a flame, an entity, a spirit, which then began to work in me. In different ways we can undoubtedly attract the Holy Spirit to dwell within us, and one of these ways is through respiration.[6]

I can testify that everything some books report about the quintessence present in air is true. This quintessence exists; we can nourish ourselves with it. It is such a powerful experience that it is almost impossible to bear. Do you believe me? Even if you don't manage to experience this, try at least to breathe with the awareness that you are receiving divine life, that through air the Holy Spirit may descend into you.

The Holy Spirit is fire, but it is carried by air, and we can attract it to us by respiration. But I was then so young and ignorant that I did not know that what had entered into me and filled my lungs with a delectable fire was something extremely rare. I lived these moments of ecstasy nearly every day, and I believed that anyone could live them too. I had no idea that it was so exceptional. I only understood this much later, especially when I, too, had to go through barren times of emptiness.

As with all mystics, there were periods when it was very easy for me to experience these ecstasies, and obviously I let myself be swept away without any restraint. But then, when a dry period arrived, which inevitably happened, I found it difficult to accept and felt completely dejected. I had rejoiced to excess, and then I collapsed into near depression. Once again, I had to learn balance, for even experiencing ecstasy requires moderation, and that was what enabled me later to confront unexpected events: I retained in my cells a store of energy which I had not wasted. Excessive joy is just as damaging to psychic and even physical health as deep grief.

This book on respiration by Yogi Ramacharaka explained well the results that can be obtained by following the given exercises, but it said nothing about the disorders and troubles that can face those who undertake the exercises without a guide or counsellor. I had no one to warn me of the dangers, and so here again I threw myself without moderation into doing these exercises for whole days at a time. This was how, when I was doing one of these exercises, I unintentionally awoke the kundalini energy.[7] What a terrible feeling it was, as if my brain was on fire. Fortunately, I understood straightaway the risks I was running, and I made gigantic efforts to put this force to sleep again – oh yes, what efforts I made! – and I succeeded.

If the kundalini energy is awakened prematurely, it exacerbates sexual desire. I was terrified by what I was feeling, and it took all the concentration of my thought and all my willpower to put it back to sleep. Kundalini energy is fire; it can awaken in people who are not very advanced from a spiritual point of view, and it can even awaken accidentally. It is an overwhelming energy, and those who have not prepared over time for its eruption inside them can lose their reason or even their life. The premature awakening of kundalini would have been the greatest disaster for me if I had not been able to put it back to sleep. Something told me that if I kept on striving to live in light and in purity, the time would come when it would awaken again without danger to me.

Nowadays, when occult sciences are all the fashion, there are many books being published on tantrism, but they are offering dangerous exercises to a public which has done nothing to prepare itself to understand and apply these methods. So I say to you too: be sensible, do not hurl yourself into experiences which will expose you to serious physical and psychic difficulties.[8] If you have not worked long and hard at developing self-control, if you have not purified yourself, instead of leading you upwards, the kundalini energy will go down and awaken other chakras on the lower astral plane, chakras that are not mentioned in Hindu books. And then, all that is dark in humans will be unleashed – not only the sexual instinct, but the need to dominate and to destroy will take hold of them, and they will become true fiends.

Childhood and adolescence are characterized not by wisdom, or even by qualities of the heart, which are acquired later, but by willpower. I had a particularly headstrong temperament. I loved tackling new experiments because I needed to surpass myself and to see how far I could go. Even if I was aware of the dangers, which sometimes happened, they would not usually be enough to stop me. That's why I continued doing breathing exercises for hours on end, day and night; I needed to keep alight within me that extraordinary feeling of living in fire.

Then one day, when I was busy with these breathing exercises, a friend burst into my room. He told me that the Rumanian army was marching on Varna. I replied, 'Thank you for warning me, but go away and leave me in peace!' And I continued with my exercises...

What I am going to tell you now requires a few explanations. Over the centuries, the Balkan countries were under the domination of the Ottoman Empire. In 1912, Bulgaria, Serbia, Greece and Montenegro united to declare war on the Empire in order to regain their independence. They won many victories: the Bulgarians went right up to the walls of Constantinople. When the time came to divide up the regained territories, a conflict broke out amongst the victors. Bulgaria claimed certain regions of Macedonia, which the Greeks and the Serbs did not want to give up, and so Bulgaria attacked them. Rumania came to the aid of the Greeks and

Serbs, and together they won. The vanquished Bulgaria was able to keep only a very small part of Macedonia. Then the Rumanian army began to invade the plain of Dobroudja*. The Bulgarians, who were not expecting this attack, suffered severe losses; trains filled with the dead and the wounded arrived in Varna. It was a terrible sight. And now the Rumanian army threatened the town...

After my friend had left, I spent a long time in my thoughts looking for the general of the army marching on Varna... When I felt as though I had found him, I concentrated on him with such intensity that I projected fire, I could feel flames shooting from my head, and with all the strength that I could muster I ordered him to make his army retreat... Two hours, three hours later, I cannot exactly remember, my friend, all excited, came back to me to say that a miracle had occurred: the Rumanian army had about-faced, and Varna was no longer threatened. Then, everyone was singing and dancing in the streets. Where had this Rumanian general received the order from to retreat? No one knew. And even I, myself, thought that it might have been by chance.

It was through these experiences undertaken when I was very young that I received the light, which has been with me ever since. I went into all these experiences alone and I lived them all to excess. I hardly slept at all, and because of the very difficult financial situation of our family, I was used to eating very little. I had become used to it, it was enough for me, and I was hardly ever hungry, but during the day

* Bordered on the east by the Black Sea, Dobroudja is divided between Rumania in the north and Bulgaria in the south. Varna is in this region.

I was often sleepy, and I had no idea why. I did not realize that I ought to have eaten more in order to be more awake and present. Of course, I must admit, if I hadn't been almost out of my body, which was my usual state because I had not eaten enough, it would not have been so easy for me to have access to the spiritual realms where I received so much other nourishment.

But I must make this quite clear: I advise no one, and particularly not young people, to deprive themselves of food on the pretext of gaining access to regions of the invisible world; they will expose themselves to the likelihood of becoming unbalanced rather than becoming enlightened. For me, these conditions were forced upon me; I did not seek out such deprivation, and if I talk to you of my experiences it is to make you understand that there is always something good to be found in the worst of situations. As for you, if destiny has placed you in conditions that do not require you to suffer this type of deprivation, do not, above all, make the mistake of forcing them on yourself.

And so, of course, the inevitable happened. Because of all the sleepless nights, the fasting, the reading and all the different types of exercises that I overdid, I gradually destroyed my health. I had become yellow and even green, and also very thin! But I could not change my way of living: I could not do otherwise than sustain this bright flame, this consuming fire. Everybody said that I had gone mad. And yes, certainly, I had lost my old brain and I was beginning to have a new one, but at what cost! By strength of will I kept on reading, and my mother, in total despair, threatened to burn my books, as she thought they were the cause of all these problems. She came knocking on my door, begging me to eat and to come out for a breath of fresh air. I would not open the door, and in the end she would sadly go away. I stayed shut away in this room, which was my kingdom. I locked the door, and no one was allowed in.

In the poverty stricken house where we lived, my room, too, looked very poor. But it was in this room that I began my apprenticeship in the spiritual life. Looked at in this way, despite appearances, I can say that I experienced there the most extraordinary and happiest moments of my life. Later, of course, I had other experiences, but to a certain extent I was prepared for them, whereas nothing had prepared me to experience, so young, this upheaval of my whole being. It is what we discover for the first time that leaves the deepest traces, traces so deep that I nearly died.

In fact, what happened was that one day I got a very high fever and became delirious. My family, friends, neighbours, everyone, expected me to die. My mother called in doctors, who had no idea how to help me. They gave me medicines which had no effect at all. And I, in the midst of my delirium, asked for books, books, bring me more books. I did not mind if I lived or got better; I thought only of reading all the libraries on earth. When they brought me books, I told them to place them close to my pillow so that I could see them and touch them. I read them in my thoughts; yes, I imagined that I was reading them, and that calmed me so much that the delirium faded. So, in the end, it was I who found the remedy. I remember that the book I always wanted by my side was Spinoza's *Ethics*! What was I expecting from this book, which I was quite clearly unable to read? I was at death's door, and all I wanted to do was to read. What madness! But it's true, books saved me; after having nearly killed me, it is they that saved me.

Notes

1. See *Man's Psychic Life: Elements and Structures,* Izvor Coll. n° 222, chap. 3: 'Several souls and several bodies'.
2. See *Sexual Force or the Winged Dragon,* Izvor Coll. n° 205, chap. 3: 'The Sexual force is essential for life on earth'.
3. See above, chap. 9: 'A high ideal transforms sexual energy'.
4. See *Notre peau spirituelle: l'aura,* Brochure n° 309.
5. See *The Splendour of Tiphareth – The Yoga of the Sun,* Complete Works vol. 10, chap. 11: 'The spirits of the seven lights' and chap. 12, 'The prism, symbol of man'.
6. See *The Mysteries of Fire and Water,* Izvor Coll. n° 232, chap. 18: 'The coming of the Holy Spirit'.
7. See *Man's Subtle Bodies and Centres – the Aura, the Solar Plexus, the Chakras,* Izvor Coll. n° 219, chap. 5: 'Kundalini force'.
8. See *Sexual Force or the Winged Dragon,* Izvor Coll. n° 205, chap. 5: 'The dangers of tantric yoga'.

6

Into the heart of the rose

The roses grown in Bulgaria are notable not only for their colour, their scent and the size of their velvety petals, but also for the length of their flowering season. The reason for this is perhaps the soil and the telluric currents there.* In some parts of the country, the air is fragrant with roses, and it is not without good reason that the Bulgarian rose is renowned worldwide. From my earliest years, I was attracted to roses and their perfume: I would breathe them in and remain for a long time just looking at them… Until, one day, I was smelling a rose whose perfume was so powerful and intoxicating that I left my body. I felt myself flying through space, where I discovered a world of light, beauty, inspiration and joy. From that time, I did all I could to repeat that experience.

Those who are driven by a powerful desire spontaneously, instinctively, find the methods they need to achieve that goal. So it was that I felt that roses could help me in my

*In the fifth century BC, the Greek historian Heroditus wrote: 'In this region wild roses grow, each rose having sixty petals, and their scent exceeds that of all other roses.'

meditation exercises. I have no idea what distant past, what knowledge buried deep inside me, gave me this conviction. When I was preparing to meditate, I chose a rose whose freshness, shape, colour and perfume would carry me the furthest and the highest. I considered it a heaven-sent living being which was sacrificing itself to show me the path, and I asked it to teach me how to obtain all the qualities it represented in the spiritual world.

Roses are beautiful on earth, but how much more beautiful they are on high, in the invisible world! For this being, which takes form down here, in reality lives in the subtle regions. The contemplation of a rose, the intoxication I felt from its scent, tore me away from the physical world. I then passed through the etheric plane, trying not to linger there, and continued without stopping through the astral and mental planes. And finally I arrived at the causal plane, where I found the rose, the true rose, which is formed by the beings of Venus called the *Elohim,* dwellers in the seventh sephirah, *Netzach,* on the cabbalistic Tree of Life.[1]

The rose is a gift that Venus gave to the earth. You will say, 'How can roses come from the planet Venus? The atmospheric conditions there render all life quite impossible!' I know that, but in Initiatic Science the planets are not just the physical material bodies that astronomy studies. In Initiatic Science planets are thoroughfares, intermediaries between cosmic currents and the earth. Through the intermediary of the planets, the earth receives currents, influences, of which God himself is the source. That is why, since time immemorial, qualities and virtues have been associated to the planets. All the planets are reservoirs of currents which travel through space and, according to their nature, condense on earth in different containers. Roses are the containers for the Venusian currents, the currents of love. When we draw close to them, we receive this love. Love is incarnate in roses; why neglect such a gift?...

Of course, on the surface a rose is nothing much, but in reality it has the power to put us in contact with the world of Venus; even a single petal is impregnated with its quintessence. In looking at a rose, loving it, we communicate our magnetism to it, and it communicates something to us in return; it links us to the beings that inhabit Venus's realm, who are more evolved than the inhabitants of earth. It is simple, it is a principle of magic: a rose is not Venus, and despite its beauty and its perfume, we should not dwell on it alone but rather see it as an intermediary between us and higher beings. It is these beings, through the rose, who help us discover true love, beauty and grace.

We link with the essence of the spiritual world through earthly objects. When we touch gold, which is imbued with the same vibrations as the sun, we communicate with the spirit of the sun. When we smell or touch a rose, we make contact with Venus, who gives us love, spiritual love, and our love becomes more poetic, purer, broader, more intense. Oh, how many things I have learned whilst meditating with a rose! I linked to its spirit and talked to it as to a living being. I asked it to make my soul like its soul, to imbue mine with its quintessence, so that my soul might become a flower in God's garden and bring joy to the heavenly beings who like to visit the earth. For these heavenly beings love to find flowers on their paths – pure and luminous souls. They take care of them and protect them so that they become even more beautiful.

Because I loved it, the rose would become alive. I had the impression that a sleeping creature was beginning to awaken on its bed of petals and was smiling at me, just like in fairy tales. Fairy tales are not just pretty stories for children, they are expressions of very real happenings in the inner life.[2] Thanks to the quintessences with which they are impregnated, roses very quickly put me in touch with presences which have stayed with me ever since. Once, when I inhaled the scent of a rose after having fasted for three days, I was flooded with a vortex of energies; I felt it enter me through every pore of my skin.[3]

If, at that time, roses already revealed many things to me, they have revealed even more as time has passed. So many little things lie hidden in big things! In order to discover them you must not dwell merely on their forms, but go beyond them to find the principle, the spirit. This is how, thanks to roses, I learned, little by little, to better perceive the essence of a living being so as to communicate with it better. And I so long to pass on to you too what I have learned!

At first glance a rose is simply a shape, a colour and a scent... but I did not want to stop there, so I tried to find what this form, what these colours and scents awakened in me. This is a good habit to develop: to be conscious of the effects that people and things have on us, so that we can become more sensitive and more understanding. But that still was not enough for me, and so I concentrated on the forces, on the intelligences that used a structure or a model to create the living being we call a rose. Then, I learned to apply this mental habit to all the people and objects I met.

And you, why don't you do the same as me? When you see a crystal, or a bird, or a face..., ask yourself what the invisible forces are that were involved in making it the shape it is. Nothing is more instructive than to look for the invisible that lies behind the visible, for everything is always prepared in the invisible before it manifests one day in the visible. A friend comes to meet you; don't you think your exchanges would be much richer if you tried to guess what elements presided in forming their face or gave them their particular bearing, their particular voice? There are so many things to discover beyond what we see!

The rose also said to me, 'You should not just dwell on what I look like, but you should also know of what quintessences I am made, how I prepare and distil them. Those who can learn to understand the way I work will be able to undertake the same process with what lies inside them, and then distil it to make fragrances that will perfume the atmosphere.' Will we really be able to sense them? Probably not straightaway, but in the meantime, you may be able to perceive certain psychic emanations. Have you never felt that certain vicious or perverse individuals emanate something nauseous, whereas when you are near others who are pure, loving and full of light, you believe you can smell the most delicious perfume?

It can happen that, when people come together to pray, the simplicity of their hearts and the intensity they put into their prayers reach certain regions of the spiritual world, and then the beings that live there respond by diffusing the scent of roses. Little St Thérèse of the Child Jesus certainly knew this truth and said that after she died she would send a flood of roses down to earth... I really love little St Thérèse.

It is difficult for me to put into words exactly what the sight of a rose awakens within me. I have the sensation of living with it, vibrating with it, and I am nourished by something that comes down from the divine world. In appearance it is quite small, but in me it is great, for it brings me so many things! It smiles at me, and I too look at it with great love; I ask it to enter deep within me to awaken other roses in my heart and soul, for it has that power. That is why I would like to give this advice to future mothers: during your pregnancy, from time to time look for roses, or even just one, and meditate beside them, asking them to influence the child you are carrying. The spirits of roses are beings that have agreed to incarnate here on earth to help people, and with what joy they answer your request!

If now I speak to a rose, saying, 'Oh beloved rose, who gave you your colour and your scent? Who taught you?', it will reply, 'It comes from a being people see every day who showers them with blessings, but to whom they show no gratitude. I am grounded in the fertile earth, but it is not the earth that makes me what I am; it is the sun, source of all life. It is the sun that gives me my colours and my fragrance; it is the sun that teaches me how to spread this scent.' A rose is silent, and yet so eloquent! Through its emanations, it never stops sending us this message: turn towards the sun and become like me. If we could measure the wavelengths that it emits, we would be amazed at the efforts it makes to influence us.

The rose still remains such a mystery! Its colour is that of spiritual love, its shape the expression of perfect harmony, its scent, that of purity. But among those who cultivate roses in their gardens or decorate their homes with bowls of flowers, how many have the slightest inkling of what roses represent? They use them to make the room pretty or as an aid to seduction. Why do they not look at them to discover the pathway to true love, a love that does not bind, a love that liberates? By simply touching one petal, we can link ourselves to those beings that agreed to be embodied in the rose so that they could inspire us and open unimaginable horizons for us. For those with an enlightened consciousness, a simple rose petal becomes the springboard for the greatest spiritual realizations. Whereas, without awareness, we pass by the most precious gifts, and become impoverished.

I like talking about roses, because this flower is linked to so many of the profound and poetic experiences I have lived! I feel that the beings working on it continue to give birth to and help blossom in me the same idea of beauty and perfection. I thank them, and I promise them that, in one way or another, I will do something for all the roses on earth, to improve their existence and contribute to their glory, even if they have already been glorified in the symbol of the Rosicrucians. And then those entities that take care of them are happy and say, 'Someone is talking about us; someone has noticed we exist.' Otherwise, no one notices they exist. Yes, they see the rose, but they are unaware of the intelligent beings that have created and worked on it. We must pay homage to these beings that work throughout nature, and listen to what they have to say to us.

That is why, when I bend down to roses, it is not just to smell their perfume but to listen to them as well. What do they tell me? That they are waiting for more and more people to understand them and to become translators of their thoughts, just as I am doing. Each rose is looking for a translator who understands its language. 'We have been consulting each other,' they tell me, 'and we believe that the time is coming when we will be much better understood.'

So, you see, the roses think I can be their interpreter and they want me to continue with my task. Once again, I tell you that what I am saying is not just poetic fancy, but a reality.

I am often given roses; they are placed on the table, and rose bushes were also planted in my garden. So, sometimes, when people come and visit me, I will give them a rose, or even just a fallen petal. I do it consciously by infusing the rose or the petal with spiritual energy. Those who have developed their antennae sense that this rose or this petal can put them in touch with the beings that created roses. Yes, the vibrations of even a single petal are those of these beings. An object, however tiny it may be, can still possess great powers, because what matters is the intensity of thought and feeling put into it, not the size of the object. While I am speaking to you, there are often one or more roses in front of me on the table, and everything I say is recorded on their petals. Some roses have such tender, delicate colours that I cannot help stroking them as if they were the cheeks of children.

The rose represents something so magnificent, so precious for me that when I want to send good thoughts to my friends, wherever they may be, I often send these thoughts as roses. When will they receive them? That depends on them. When a thought reaches them, they will certainly not know what it is, nor where it comes from, but suddenly they will sense that they are visited by a glimmer of light, a fragrance, peace, joy.

Even now, when I see roses, I find myself transported back to the time when I discovered the power they had to project me into spiritual realms. Since then, they have for me been linked to different events. I could tell you many of them, but here is one which immediately comes to mind.

It was at the Bonfin, on a day when I had been concentrating on the divine Mother. I had talked with her, I had made certain requests, and I felt filled with her presence. Then, I had to go to Nice, and Brother Jean* was to drive me. At the edge of the town, we were slowed down by traffic jams, and then we finally arrived at the Promenade des Anglais. It was August, the weather was hot and I had lowered my window. There was still a lot of traffic, and from time to time we had to stop. A car with several passengers in it stopped beside us, and in the car I saw a young girl who was smiling at me... Then, suddenly she jumped out of the car and came to our car. She was very pretty, her face was pure, expressive and intelligent, and through the lowered window she handed me a rose. Still smiling, she said something in a mixture of French and English which I didn't quite understand, then she quickly got back into her car. I was a little surprised.

The traffic started moving, but from time to time we had to stop, and this young girl continued looking at me, smiling at me. Of course, I too smiled at her. I was so happy to have been given such an answer from the divine Mother![4] Yes, for I knew that through this young girl, through her smiles, her looks and the rose she gave me, the divine Mother was replying to my requests. How did I know that? Because the rose, the symbol of Venus, is an embodiment of the eternal feminine and so, also, of the divine Mother. In the middle of a traffic jam, by what coincidence was this young girl

---

* One of the Master's first disciples: a former racing car champion, he was always most happy to drive him in his car.

there, like a messenger, with a rose in her hand? One minute earlier or later, we would not have met each other.

And that is not all; there is more. A few hours later, I was back at the Bonfin. What did I see on my doorstep? There was a magnificent rosebush in a pot, which somebody had left anonymously. This too was a reply from the divine Mother, which convinced me that she had heard me. Then, what heartfelt thanks I gave her!

I tell you nothing that I myself have not experienced. The longing for this heavenly beauty which had been with me since my adolescence allowed me to discover that, through roses, it was possible to make contact with spiritual beings and, there, in light, immensity and splendour, to feel joys that no human being, I think, could ever give me. I don't mean to suggest that it is easy to arrive at such a concept of love, let alone achieve it, but it is possible. How does it manifest? In many different ways.

I always hesitate to speak to you of such intimate experiences, because I never know how I will be understood, or even if I will be believed. However, sometimes, during the night, I am awoken by the sensation of presences in my room. These presences are etheric creatures of indescribable beauty. They are there, all around me, and they sing with such melodious tones that I feel my whole being expanding through space. They look at me, smiling with such great love. I too look at them. They are there, close to me, diaphanous but real and distant. What I experience is so divine, so intense, that all I want to do is look at them. Where do these creatures come from? I believe that once again the divine Mother is sending me her purest and most beautiful daughters, because she knows that it is this beauty, this love, which my soul longs for. So, there you are, I tell you this even though I would often prefer to remain silent. I tell you so as to help you, so that you can have a glimpse of what it is possible to experience.

Another day, it was in Paris. You know how it happens when you're walking along the main streets. You pass a crowd of people that you see without really looking at them. On this occasion, I was walking down the boulevard without paying particular attention to a young couple coming towards me. Just when we were going to pass each other, the young girl gave me a look, but what a look... I cannot remember whether she was pretty, I cannot recall her facial features; it was her look that struck me, a look filled with love, light and beauty; I felt as if all of heaven had come to me. Then, as if nothing had happened, they went on their way, and I on mine.

You will say, 'And you didn't come up with some pretext to stop them and begin a conversation with them?' No, why? I don't believe that the young girl was even aware of the look she had given me. It was not she who had looked at me. So who then? My twin soul. Yes, my twin soul had manifested through her. It had found this young girl, who after all had to have something exceptional if she was able to transmit a look which only my twin soul could give me. For several days, I lived in indescribable happiness; I didn't even think about the young girl. I had no desire to see her again; that would not have given me anything more – on the contrary. I thought only of the look, which came from elsewhere, and I knew as well that she could not have done it a second time. Nothing compares to a look...

You will say, 'But what is a look when our hands are empty?' So, do only hands count for you? Your soul can be filled with a look; doesn't that matter to you? When you hold someone in your arms, know that you are not holding very much. If I have told you about this episode in my life, it is only so that you can hear, at least once, that a look can contain all of heaven. Nothing can be compared to a look, and just by one look you can communicate with your twin soul.

Ah yes, the rose… I am aware of the privilege I had in being able to meet it so early on my spiritual journey. It inspired me with wonder and revealed to me the greatest and deepest truths. With the help of the rose, little by little, I entered those realms where harmony and order dwell. That is no doubt why, one day, I spontaneously picked up a compass and drew a circle that I divided into six equal parts. I had just drawn the geometric figure called the rosace or mystic rose, because it has the form of a rose.

Everybody knows this figure, and I have continued exploring all its riches over the years. I was fascinated by its perfect form, and it became a talisman for me. I hung it on my bedroom wall, and when I looked at it, it plunged me into a state of peace, harmony and bliss that nothing could disturb. I had buried it in my soul and watered it constantly with my love. Without my knowing, this symbol originating from a very distant past had surfaced in me. I kept drawing it over and over again, and it spoke to me. I even perfected a way to make it spin and then it vibrated, it radiated. What a wonder it was! Instinctively, I had understood that a symbol is like a seed, which we must sow and cultivate within ourselves by giving it water, warmth and light. Gradually I saw the flowers grow, and today I am still harvesting its fruits and being fed by them.

This figure of the mystic rose is made up of three parts: three flowers which overlap each other and which correspond to the physical, astral and mental planes. So it is a synthesis of the human being and their activities. When we follow the outline of one of the flowers, we take a different path from the ones we would have followed with the other two. The heart of these three flowers, the heart of the mystic rose, is the sun, our higher self. If we trace the outline of the petals, we alternate between moving away from the centre and coming closer in.

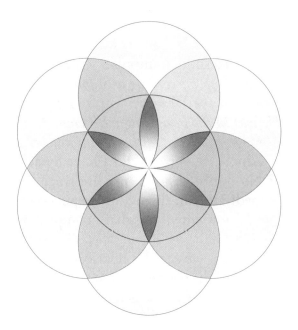

This triple mystic rose is also found in the physical body. Where? In the hand. Look at your hand: if you extend the directions of the lines drawn there, you will find that they make semi-circles. The biggest of these semi-circles is the one corresponding to the Saturn line. These lines are different for every human being, and each one possesses only some segments of the great cosmic rose. The structure of the universe can be read in the whole figure of the mystic rose: it is the perfect hand of God.

The mystic rose was the first symbol that I really worked with. At that time, I approached it without any special knowledge. I was so very young! Each time I studied this figure, I was flooded with a deep feeling of fulfilment. I identified with it, and I felt I was projected into that realm of awareness where the mystery of all origins is revealed. That is undoubtedly why, one day, when I had just drawn this rose once again, I felt there was still something missing. I searched and, on a sudden impulse, wrote underneath the first verses of the *Gospel according to St John: 'In the beginning was the Word, and the Word was with God, and the Word was God. He was in the beginning with God. All things came into being through him, and without him not one thing came into being.'* Why these verses? Did I have a particular link with them? No doubt. And all my life since then, I have continually meditated on them and deepened my study of them.[5] Today, I know why it was that I completed the design in this way.

And, here again, we see the relationship between this flower, the rose, and the geometric figure of the rosace. These first verses of *St John's Gospel,* which evoke the creation of the world, echo the first verse of *Genesis: 'In the beginning God created the heavens and the earth';* in Hebrew it is *'Béreschit bara Elohim eth ha-schamaïm ve-eth ha-haretz'.* The Hebrew word elohim is translated in English as 'God'. But *elohim* is a plural word and is the name of the angelic hierarchy which lives in the sephirah *netzach,* to which the planet

Venus belongs. The *elohim,* which the Christian religion call 'principalities', created the earth, and they watch over its evolution and the evolution of all people who live on earth.

You see, a rose can take us a very long way.

Notes

1. See *Angels and Other Mysteries of the Tree of Life,* Izvor Coll. n° 236, chap. 3: 'The angelic hierarchies'.

2. See *The Wellsprings of Eternal Joy,* Izvor Coll. n° 242, chap. 16: 'Opening the doors to the dream world'.

3. See *The Yoga of Nutrition,* Izvor Coll. n° 204, chap. 7: 'Fasting: 2. Another form of nutrition'.

4. See *Angels and Other Mysteries of the Tree of Life,* Izvor Coll. n° 236, chap 10: 'The cosmic family and the mystery of the trinity'.

5. See *'Au commencement était le Verbe',* Œuvres complètes, t. 9, Chap. 1: 'Au commencement était le Verbe'.

7
The universal symphony

I have always longed to learn music and to become a musician. From very young, I felt that music was the expression of divine perfection, and I was quite sure that if I knew how to work with it, music could transform not only me but also all those who heard me play. It reached a point when I dreamed of becoming the greatest virtuoso. I had read the legend of Orpheus and his lyre, whose song captivated gods and humans, tamed ferocious beasts and could even move rocks. I just loved this legend of Orpheus who had lived in Thrace! Unlike other initiates, he did not try to control by force but by the magic of sound, the magic of the word, the power of beauty. Since my country, Bulgaria, used to be a part of ancient Thrace, I was so happy to belong to the same country as Orpheus!

Obviously, I never thought of playing the lyre, but I passionately longed to play the violin. I imagined myself giving concerts before huge crowds, infusing my playing with something so unique that, on returning home, each one would be marked forever: the imprint I would have left on them would guide them to seek only beauty and harmony. But fate decided otherwise. We were so very poor that my mother could not buy me a violin. Sadly, I watched my friends going by with their instruments tucked under their arms on the way to their lessons, while I stayed where I was with only my dreams... The day I finally got the instrument that I had longed for so much, I was already twenty-three years old. It was clearly too late; you have to start very young, no matter what the instrument. I practised for hours on end, but my fingers no longer had the necessary suppleness.

Later, I had to conclude that even if I had been given the chance, I would never have been a musician. It was a good thing that I had all those obstacles, or I would perhaps have wandered down a pathway which was not really mine. Music has great power, it inspires all sorts of emotions and feelings, it gives wonderful impulses, but that is not enough. Emotions, feelings and impulses must be well directed, and a good direction requires a philosophy, wisdom. In order to help people, you must also and especially give them light, talk to them, explain... So destiny has directed me to a realm different to music: the realm of philosophy, Initiatic Science. However, in philosophy and Initiatic Science such as I envisage them, music is always present. Why? Because the universe itself is music; it is a construction founded on the laws of harmony, ruled by the laws of harmony.

If outer circumstances prevented me from becoming a musician, inwardly nothing hindered me from living in music. When I meditated, I tried to see the universe as one great symphony, and within this space that was already music I imagined etheric beings of marvellous beauty passing by singing. I had only one desire, that of joining them, and this desire often caused me to leave my body.

This was at the time when I had discovered those breathing exercises that I practised for hours on end… One day, when I was doing one of the exercises, I felt myself carried out into space, very high and far away, and suddenly I heard the whole universe singing: mountains, trees, seas, the whole earth, but also suns and stars – they were all singing. All creation was only music, and no human music could compare to what I heard. I say I 'heard' it, but in fact that is just a way of speaking. This music is not heard with physical ears, but with the soul and spirit.

Poets or philosophers such as Pythagoras and Plato have called this symphony of the whole universe 'the harmony of the spheres' or 'the music of the spheres.' Everything in existence emits sounds, but obviously not sounds in the sense we usually understand the word 'sounds'. In order to perceive them, you must leave the physical body. The music of the spheres is the synthesis of all the languages creation uses to manifest. In nature, we distinguish not only sounds, but colours, movements, fragrances and forms, because our sense organs give us a differentiated perception of things. But, beyond our five physical senses, we have other organs capable of synthesizing all these perceptions, and in certain extraordinary moments it is possible to grasp creation as sounds, colours, forms, movements and fragrance all at once.

What I experienced then was both marvellous and terrifying. I have no idea how long the experience lasted. It was probably only a very short time. I felt that I stretched out to the dimensions of the universe, I myself became the universe, I expanded indefinitely in space, and I had no idea where all this was going to lead… So, suddenly, I was afraid! I was afraid that I would dissolve, that I would be pulverized, that

I would be annihilated… and then I returned to earth. I am quite sure that I would not have survived, if this state had been prolonged. So I came back to my body, because it was not the time for me to leave; I had still not even begun my work. Since then there have been moments when I have regretted that I willingly brought this experience to its end for I have never been given another chance to live it again, but it is impossible for the unequipped physical body to bear the power of such vibrations for long. Even if the soul has distanced itself from the body in such a moment, it still remains attached – it only detaches if it is allowed to go too far – and the intensity of what the soul lives has a very strong effect on the organism. Only angels, who have no physical bodies, are able to bear such vibrations.

It is true, I then felt great regret at having voluntarily brought this experience to an end, but at least for a few moments I lived, I saw, I heard the whole universe singing together in such magnificent and sublime harmony that… But no, it is not comparable with anything that can be heard on earth. Higher beings allowed me to live this brief moment so that I could have an inkling of what heavenly harmony is, and now that one memory fills my soul, enough to maintain, support and feed the whole of my spiritual life. Even though it was so brief, and even though it is given only once, this experience, which is one of the most rare, yet most rich, is more than enough for a lifetime or even for several lifetimes. For this music, yes, let's call it music, because there are no other words for it, touches not only our sensitivity. It is also a word of wisdom which shows us the direction to follow, a word which inscribes divine law on the soul of anyone who is privileged to hear it at least once. Now I hear it in other ways.

This experience of the universal symphony, which I had so early in my life, has remained like an imprint, a seal with which my soul has been marked, and it has pushed me ever since to search for harmony always and everywhere.[1] Once you have heard the whole of creation's voices singing together, you can never forget it, and it makes you long for just one thing: for this harmony to be achieved here on earth among all people. Having heard the music of the spheres just that one time convinced me that we must live with the awareness that we are participating in a choir, in the great cosmic choir.

So many men and women love gathering together to sing![2] They feel that creating this harmony together in a performance has wonderful effects on them, but they also feel that it projects them into a higher dimension of existence. How is it that all these men's and women's voices, which seem so different when you hear them individually, are attuned so marvellously when they sing together? However, when the rehearsal or the concert is over, they all go home to resume their pathetic preoccupations, their old feuds, their grudges. Harmony is gone, and so too is life; yes, life as well, because disharmony is death. Even if they sing magnificently, they have still not really understood what it is to be a choir. If they understood, they would go on singing together even when they have left the choir.

What does this mean? That throughout our lives, wherever we are, even if we are alone at home, we must sing in the choir, see to it that our voice, that is to say all that we emit as thoughts, feelings, desires and emotions, vibrates in harmony with all of nature and with all humanity. It is then that we feel life springing up within us. That is why belonging to a choir is an opportunity not just to spend time in a pleasant fashion, but also to work consciously at learning to submit our individual life to the law of universal harmony. Even those who cannot sing need to work on harmony, for the least harmonious vibration on earth puts us in contact with the great cosmic harmony.

Cosmic Intelligence has given a particular note, a unique sound, a voice, to all beings so that they can form a symphony in the universe. You will say that you cannot hear these voices. Yes, of course, and I, too, do not hear them as I did when it was given to me, just once, to hear them all that time ago. But, do you not feel happy just thinking that the whole of creation right now is singing? And doesn't that make you want to join your voices in this anthem? My wish for you all is that, one day, you too will be given the chance to hear this music of the spheres, even if it is only for a few seconds as it was for me. You will never forget it, and you will carry the longing for this moment with you always and everywhere. What you will have lived then will always guide your steps along the path of harmony of hearts and souls.

Notes
1. See *Harmony and Health,* Izvor Coll. n° 225, chap. 2: 'The world of harmony'.
2. See *Creation: Artistic and Spiritual,* Izvor Coll. n° 223, chap. 5: 'The human voice', chap. 6: 'Choral singing'.

8

Meeting Master Peter Deunov
The revelations of Psalm 116

It was a day when I had to go to Sofia. I made use of the time to go to some bookshops. With the money I had earned I was happy to be able to buy a few books too. In one of these shops I spent a long time looking through the theosophical books of Leadbeater, Annie Besant, Helena Blavatsky and several others. At one moment, the owner of the bookshop approached me; he looked at me kindly, then he showed me some small pamphlets, saying with a smile, 'This is what you ought to read.' I was taken aback: what were these little pamphlets? Furthermore, the author had a Bulgarian name, Peter Deunov. How could a Bulgarian be compared with these prominent people, the theosophists who had lived in India and met great Masters? All the same, I took his advice and bought the pamphlets as well as two or three other books.

By the time I caught the train back to Varna – and I have no idea how it happened – I had lost all the books, and I only had the Peter Deunov pamphlets with me. So I read them, and what a wonderful discovery that was for me! Who was this person, who spoke with such authority, such clarity and such wisdom? I said to myself, 'I must go and see him.' Was he perhaps the Master I had been looking for?

Some time later, I found that the owner of the bookshop in Sofia, who had suggested I read these books, was, in fact, a disciple of the Master. Providence had arranged our meeting. His name was Golov. The booklets he had suggested were part of a collection called *Sila i Jivot* which means 'Strength and Life'. I was seventeen years old, and I was so ignorant that I did not think this title was very impressive. I had no idea then how greatly my comprehension of the word 'life' was to expand in the future.[1]

As soon as I had finished reading these pamphlets, I wondered how I could meet the Master. What a surprise it was to discover that he lived in Varna! He had been living there for a while in exile, having had to leave Sofia because of accusations levelled at him by the hierarchy of the Orthodox Church. Some bishops, who saw him as a dangerous heretic, had sought King Ferdinand to order his departure from Sofia, where he had established the White Brotherhood. He had left for Varna accompanied by a few faithful disciples.

After my first visit to the Master, I started to attend the lectures he gave at the London Hotel where he was staying. I had not yet been to him to ask him to accept me as one of his disciples. One day, I decided to ask for a meeting with him, and I went with a boy and girl of my age who, like me, wanted to follow his teaching.

When we found ourselves before the Master, there was first of all a moment of deep silence. Then, with feeling and all the sincerity in my heart, I said to him, 'Oh Master, will you allow us to follow you?' Once again, silence fell, and something holy hovered in the room. I will never forget the countenance of the Master as he looked at us intensely and deeply… Then, with deep seriousness and much love, as if he alone really knew the importance of this decisive moment, he answered, 'Who can prevent you from following me? No one.' And that was all; he said not another word. Once again there was a silence, in which I felt that I was in communication with his spirit. Currents of energy coursed through me, as if he were opening doors and windows in me, as if he were commanding the spirits of light to take care of us.

On the table there was a Bible, and I noticed afterwards that the Master always had a Bible near him. He picked up the Bible and began leafing through it as if he was looking for something. We stood there, feeling quite small and a little anxious. We had started out on a path with no idea of the ordeals that lay ahead of us. The sister died very young. As for the brother, I cannot speak about what happened to him.

The Master searched for a moment in the Bible, and then he pointed out a psalm for each of us, saying, 'Read this, it is for you.' He gave me Psalm 116. I read and reread that psalm so very many times! I even learned it by heart. Since the Master had given it to me, it meant that my whole life was in it. How could I not understand that it foreshadowed the terrible ordeals that lay ahead of me?

'The snares of death encompassed me;
the pangs of the tomb laid hold on me;
I suffered distress and anguish.
Then I called on the name of the Lord:
"O Lord, save my soul!"'

Nine years after my arrival in France, these ordeals, written in the psalm that the Master had given me that day, came to pass.

During that first year when I met the Master, he invited me sometimes to come and see him. One day, he said to me, 'The path is open to you; you have all the conditions to make progress. Heaven is with you and it will give you much. But a time will come when the whole of the Black Lodge will rise up against you to block your path.' At that time, I was far from understanding what the Black Lodge was and how great its power to harm. I smiled and said, 'I will pass through.' What he said in reply was something that I have treasured in my memory ever since. And then I asked, 'When will this happen?' 'In the twenty-sixth year.' I thought he meant by this that it would occur when I was twenty-six, but when I reached that age I only had a knee injury. It was very painful, and I was disabled for a long time, but it was only a knee injury.

Years later, when I was looking back on all the events of my life, I remembered these words of the Master. I did the arithmetic; he had told me of these tests in 1918. Twenty-six years later, in 1944, he left his body. I had been in France for seven years, and it is true that, from that moment, the worst period of my life began. I reached rock bottom in 1947-1948. Finally, in 1950, the sky began to clear.

During this dark period when I was opposed, threatened, and finally, because of lying accusations, sent to prison, I remembered those words of the psalm and the prophecies of the Master. *'The snares of death encompassed me; the pangs of the tomb laid hold on me...'* One particular night, I was seized with such anguish as I had never known before, a mortal anguish. If I did not die at that moment, it was only because my faith and my trust in the Lord, my love for him, never left me. I clung desperately to the following verse, the verse of help and deliverance: *'I walk before the Lord in the land of the living.'* In the depths of my distress, I said to myself that after this torment I would truly know what life – true, eternal life – was.

'I walk before the Lord in the land of the living.' When I had read this psalm, after the Master had told me that this was for me, I had been most struck by the beauty of this verse and also by its mysterious quality; what was this land of the living? I had learned this verse in Hebrew, and I even had it engraved on a thin sheet of gold I always carried with me.

I am not in the habit of telling you what I have lived through; it is not necessary, I may well not be understood, and God knows what else people may imagine! Yet, I believe that some of you will understand me, as will others who come later. It is for them that I speak, as it may clarify things for them and help them one day. For at a certain moment in the soul's evolution, after years of work and purification, it must pass through certain regions still unknown to it that can only be called hell. This ordeal is part of all initiation.

During that night when I was gripped by this mortal anguish, something happened which I have never been able to explain. Perhaps I was meant to die; perhaps I was even already dead. I was plunged into hell fire, a terrifying fire: I had flames in front of me which resembled no fire on earth; it was the sight of death in all its horror. I felt my hair stand on end. I wonder it didn't go completely white that night. And I cried out, *'Oh Lord, save my soul!'*

Then, exhausted, I fell into a deep sleep. Sometime between one and two o'clock in the morning, there was a noise, as if someone had knocked on my door. This noise woke me, and then I felt myself surrounded by luminous presences, very powerful beings, who worked with me and on me for the rest of the night. And suddenly, resurrection. I had arrived in the land of the living! I then realized that this day was the Master's birthday. He was born on 11 July in the morning.

In the spiritual life, death is always followed by resurrection. We die so that we may come alive again. From the Egyptian and ancient Greek mysteries right up to Christianity, we see how many religions speak of death followed by resurrection! After the god Osiris was killed by his jealous brother Seth, his wife Isis gathered together all the pieces of his body and brought it back to life with the help of the god Anubis. In the same way, Athena rescued the heart of Dionysus, whose body was boiled and eaten by the Titans, and she brought him back to life. The preparation of the philosopher's stone is also based on the principle of death followed by resurrection.[2] How then should we interpret the death and resurrection of Jesus?[3]

After many years of trials, I too could say, *'Oh Lord, you have delivered my soul from death.'* Finally, I was walking in the land of the living. What is this land of the living? It is the sun. Yes, the sun, but an aspect of the sun we do not yet know. Everything we see on earth and in the sky is only the tiniest portion of reality – outer shells or burnt out clinkers. Reality is the immensity of the invisible world. You will say, 'What? The universe is so vast; look at the solar system and then beyond at all those galaxies and nebulae!' Yes indeed, but all that is nothing compared with all we do not see.

In a past long gone, astronomers were initiates, and when they spoke of Jupiter, Mercury, the Moon, Venus and so on, they were thinking of the beings who lived in these regions, entities who have their own qualities of character and have a particular work to do in the universe. Contemporary astronomers have lost this knowledge, and they attach only material realities to these names. They look at the planets, study the atmosphere, the degree of humidity, the features that stand out, the elements they are made of, and then they declare that there is no life to be found on them. And in the same way, they have no idea what the sun really is.

The sun is the *'land of the living'* mentioned in the psalm, and one day we will live in this land of the living. But even now, there is nothing to prevent us from leaving the valley of tears and death, which is for the time being the place where we live, and projecting ourselves into the land of the immortals. All enlightened consciousnesses already live in the sun. As soon as we start to live in light, we are living in the sun; our feet walk on the earth, but our head is in the sun. Because we wish to live forever in this land of the living, we try each morning to draw closer to it. By going to watch the sun rise, we begin to direct our steps toward it.[4]

Notes

1. See *Harmony and Health,* Izvor Coll. n° 225, chap. 1: 'Life comes first'.
2. See *The Philosopher's Stone – in the Gospels and in Alchemy,* Izvor Coll. n° 241, chap 11: 'The regeneration of matter: the cross and the crucible'.
3. See *Sons and Daughters of God,* Izvor Coll. n° 240, chap. 10: 'Jesus, dead and resurrected?'
4. See *Sunrise Meditations,* Brochure n° 323.

*Mikhaël, aged 11,
with his mother*

*On his arrival
in France, 1937*

At the Bonfin (Fréjus), before leaving for India, 29 September 1938

Sunrise at the Bonfin

The meeting hall at the Bonfin

The incident of the kitten, Villeneuve (Switzerland), 1958
Chapter 15, page 343

At the Bonfin, 1971

At Vidélinata (Switzerland), 1975

At Izgrev (Sèvres, France), 1976

Aerial view of the Bonfin, July 2007

At Blagoslovénié (Quebec, Canada), 1985

9
'Frantsia', France

In Varna, during the summer, there were evening concerts in the large park overlooking the sea. On those evenings, I would go to the deserted beach, stretch myself out on the sand and listen to the music floating down from above. The orchestra played overtures to Wagner's operas, *Lohengrin, Tannhäuser* and *Parsifal,* but I also remember Franz von Suppé's *Poet and Peasant* and other pieces that are not played much nowadays. Night fell, fireflies darted around me, and I gazed at the starry sky dreaming…

Do you know what I dreamed about? France or *Frantsia;* I would say this name that sounded so poetic, and I had such a longing to visit it. Was it an intuition about the future? At any rate, given the times, the age I was and the conditions I lived in, it was impossible. So, I went on dreaming of this country I imagined to be so magnificent, and particularly Paris, with its avenue with the heavenly name of *Champs Élysées,* 'Elysian Fields.' What a marvellous place that had to be! And when I thought about it, I felt real spiritual joy.

My dream came true twenty years later, in 1937. I came to your country to see the World Exhibition, but it was not for a visit of just a few weeks. Having been a teacher, I was then a headmaster, and now Master Peter Deunov told me to leave Bulgaria for good and go to France*. He saw very clearly that the Second World War was coming, and he also felt that Communism was going to control the Eastern European countries, and it would threaten all expressions of religion and spirituality. He asked me to go to France to preserve his teaching, which he suspected would be forbidden in Bulgaria. And that is exactly what happened: for decades the Master's disciples were not only forbidden to gather together, but they also had to hide his books to prevent them being confiscated and themselves from being prosecuted and sentenced.

So it was at the Master's request that I came to France to keep his teaching alive. Of course, he did not order me to go, as a true Master never forces obedience and submission from his disciples. I felt that what he asked me to do was for the good, and so I accepted. I was, however, aware of the difficulties awaiting me. I knew a little French; I could read it, but I could not speak it, and I was leaving a small country where the life I had led had not prepared me for such a big change. You have no idea what Bulgaria was like at that time. How was I going to live in France? Was I ready for it?...

When I arrived**, it was easy to tell by my accent that I was a foreigner. If people asked me where I came from, I realized that most of the time they knew nothing about Bulgaria, nor even where it was; they confused it with

---

* A second volume, *Auprès du Maître Peter Deunov – Éléments d'autobiographie 2*, will cover the period 1917-1937.
** 22 July 1937.

Rumania or Serbia or some other neighbouring country, and each time I had to explain. Since that time it has become better known, thanks to its roses and its yogurt... Then there was that business with the Bulgarian umbrella,* and the attempted murder of Pope John Paul II.**

As soon as I arrived, I began to explore Paris. I spent a lot of time walking along the streets looking at the houses, the monuments, the shops and all the people. Everything was so new! I wanted to see everything: Notre-Dame, the Eiffel Tower, the Arc de Triomphe, the museums and so on. One day, friends took me to Luna Park. Perhaps you do not know what that is, as the park has been gone a long time, but it was an amusement park at Porte Maillot. Great crowds of people came to enjoy themselves there. For example, there was a stall where you could shoot at a target on the wall. There was a bed with a woman lying on it, and if you hit the target, the bed would flip over and the woman would fall out onto the ground. She would then get up, readjust the bed, lie down once again on it, and the whole thing would begin again. There was also the 'laughter palace', with its corridors where great gusts of wind would whisk off hats and blow skirts up in the air. There were also swings, which would pause in mid-air just when people were upside down... I was really amazed at the inventive spirit of the French. I had never seen such things in Bulgaria.

Then, there was a ride called the 'butter plate', and that was really interesting. This 'plate' was a round wooden

* In 1978 an official of Bulgarian television was assassinated in Paris by a cyanide injection from an umbrella.
** in Rome, in May 1981 – the Bulgarian secret service was said to be involved.

platform, big enough for several people to stand on. Once they had climbed onto it, the plate began to revolve slowly at first, and then little by little it went faster and faster. What happened then? Those who were standing near the edge were subject to the intense centrifugal force; they were thrown off balance and hurled off the platform, whereas those who were in the centre stood steady, as the centrifugal force was weak due to the effect of the centripetal force. They were not knocked over.

I looked at this for a moment and then I said to my friends, 'You see, this butter plate, which is only there as amusement for the general public, deserves a little more attention from us. The physical laws in play here are identical to those that govern our psyche.' They were astonished and I explained to them: 'People are like this butter plate; some of the psychic regions within us are at the fringe, others are nearer the centre, and our consciousness determines where we stand on the platform. If we walk near the edge, among pleasures, passions and intrigues, we become prey to forces which make us lose our balance, and we fall. If we want to be safe and balanced, we have to seek our inner centre. Meditation, reverence and prayer are methods which allow us to find this centre, this point in us where nothing can shake us.' How many things can educate us! Oh yes, you see, even the butter plate at Luna Park.

Paris was really a school for me, something unique. I was amazed by it all, I marvelled at everything, which sometimes made the people I met smile. But what can I say about the Elysian Fields, the Champs Élysées? The people who named this great avenue after the place where the souls of the blessed live, according to Greek and Roman mythology, certainly wanted to make the whole world dream. They certainly succeeded with me, as I cannot tell you how much I dreamed of this place. That is why I was surprised and disappointed to find cafés, shops, and all sorts of people milling up and down without the slightest idea that they were desecrating ground whose very name was holy for me.

But the most important thing for me was to learn to speak French accurately and as quickly as possible. So, I decided that the cinema, among other things, would be a good school for me; in films, we hear people talk about a variety of different topics, and that was what I needed. Six months after my arrival, at the request of my friends, I gave my first public lecture.

What an event for me to address the French for the first time in their own language! At that time, I was living in the home of Sister Stella,* and that morning, after she had gone to work, I turned on the tap of my wash basin and found there was no water. I went down to check the tap in the kitchen sink, but I forgot to turn off the tap in my washbasin. Then, I went out… On my return, the water which had been turned back on was flooding the apartment, and I began mopping it up. When Sister Stella came back from work, she found the flood, and me on my knees mopping up. She was most distressed, but I just started laughing and said, 'No, no, don't be distressed. Water is love and abundance, and so this flood is a marvellous omen!'

I continued to give lectures. Sometimes I could not find the word I wanted and so I would ask the people in the room, 'How do you say this?... How do you say that?...' and the answers they gave me were sometimes funny, as they did

---

* One of the first disciples of the Master. She was his secretary for a good forty years.

not correspond at all to the word I was looking for, and so everyone would burst out laughing. Now, of course, after so many years, I can express myself much better. Not perfectly, according to some people, and that is true. But others say that my speech is not as lively as it was in the days when they could feel, apparently, the physical presence of my thought as it searched for the words it needed to be understood. So you see, you can never please everyone.

More and more people came to hear me. The room was not always big enough to hold everyone, and some people would be seated on the stage. The audience would be a very mixed bunch, and so I had the chance to make all sorts of interesting observations. One day, after the lecture, a pretty young woman, elegantly dressed, came up to speak to me. As soon as she opened her mouth, I saw how very superficial she was, and so I asked her what attracted her to the topics I was talking about. She told me that a friend had made her come by telling her that she would learn a lot of useful things. In fact, she had no real desire to learn, but she came, and continued to come regularly. Out of curiosity I asked her why she came. 'Oh,' she said, 'you are dressed so tidily and your collar and cuffs are so white!' My collar and cuffs! I was dumbfounded. She was completely uninterested in what I had to say. I waited so that she could say at least one word about what she had heard, but clearly she had forgotten everything… and had she grasped anything? Only my collar and cuffs had made an impression on her. As if there was something surprising that I should give public lectures looking moderately presentable!

So, I found myself in the situation of the minister in an anecdote. Yes, once there was a minister who, on Sundays, did his very best to move his congregation, but whatever he did he always had the same frozen, indifferent faces in front of him, and he was very disappointed. Then, one day, he saw right at the back of the church a poor fellow sobbing. 'Aha!' he thought happily to himself, 'at least I have managed to touch someone!' At the end of the service he ran to the door to greet his flock and to talk to the man, who was still wiping the tears from his eyes. 'Ah, my good man, what was it that touched you so deeply in my sermon?' 'Oh Minister, I used to have a goat which I loved so much, but a few days ago it was eaten by a wolf… I was so sad because when I looked at your little scraggy beard and heard your voice, you reminded me of my dearly loved goat!' So there you are; the secret of my success was entirely due to my collar and my cuffs.

Another time, I saw a very pretty young girl arrive, who was to take part in the Miss Europe or Miss World contest, I forget which. She wanted to marry a very rich man, who did not love her, and her mother – who was the one I had most to do with – came to see me. She believed that I would agree to use some magic spells (and I cannot even speak about it, as they were so improper) to influence this man. She promised me a huge fortune if I was successful. Obviously, I refused to do any of the things suggested. So, neither mother nor daughter ever came to any more of my lectures. I assure you, if I had satisfied all the requests of this kind that both men and women asked of me, I would have been a billionaire long ago. When will people understand that you should never use the spirits and powers of nature for a personal goal and, in particular, to win the love of someone?[1]

Among the people who came to my lectures, there was a quite likeable woman whose main preoccupation was to attract artists of all sorts to her salon: poets, musicians, opera singers, actors of stage and screen. One day, she invited me to one of her receptions. I arrived in the midst of very distinguished people. They all knew each other, and as I was the stranger, she had to introduce me. What did I hear her say? 'Ladies and gentlemen, we have the great honour today to be graced by the presence of a great initiate, a very great magus, an outstanding clairvoyant. He has just arrived from Bulgaria and he will reveal extraordinary things to you; he will predict your future, and so on.' What a surprise for me! I had accepted her invitation because, for someone in a foreign country, it is always interesting to meet new people. But here I felt I was caught in a trap. This woman had not warned me of the role she wanted me to play.

When she had finished her presentation, there was silence. The guests were clearly all waiting for me to speak and make those sensational revelations she had promised. And I, I said not a word. Everyone went on looking at me expectantly, but I stayed silent… Truly, I did not know what I should do. Finally, I said, 'I am most honoured, Madam, to have been invited here by you. But I am surprised, as I never imagined that you would want me to make sensational revelations. I have nothing special to say, except that I am most happy to make the acquaintance of your friends.' And that was all I said. What a disappointment! They began whispering and fidgeting amongst themselves, and many of them left very discontented. Others remained, and I had some very good conversations with them. That was what I came for, not for anything sensational.

Then, of course, this woman, who had been irritated by my behaviour, which had made her lose face, asked me why I had acted in this way. She told me I had certainly lost the good esteem of some of those people, whose company could have been very useful for me. I replied that I did not value the esteem of those who confuse spiritual life with show and that she, too, needed to learn this lesson.

Yes, it was a very instructive time for me. In Bulgaria I had just worked and studied in the shadow of my Master and I had never put myself out in public. And then, what I discovered surprised me; I felt I was not at all suited for what many people expected from me. What did they think the spiritual life was?

Sometimes, after a lecture, men and women would come and introduce themselves, telling me that they were initiates. They would even tell me what level they had reached – the seventh, eighth or ninth degree of initiation – and they wanted to know what degree I had reached. I would then have to explain to them that a true initiate never talks about such things; the true initiate remains secret, obscure and hidden like the old man in the ninth tarot card, the Hermit. This old man, wrapped in a great cloak, walks in the night; he has a staff in his left hand and under his cloak he reveals a lamp, which he holds in his right hand. The cloak he wears is prudence, the staff is willpower and the lamp is wisdom. But often I could see that these people did not understand, so I would end by saying, 'You think you are initiates? That is all well and good, but don't go telling that to everyone. Let others feel it for themselves from your behaviour and by what emanates from you.'

At that time I was introduced to my friend Krebs, who was a most unique individual. I do not now remember how he came to hear of me, and he too came to listen to my lectures. He had a passion for the violin, and he was researching the making of Stradivarius violins, particularly the varnish used to coat the instrument, whose composition had been lost. This research was a true passion of his and he spent all his great fortune on it. He imported wood from distant parts and from particular types of pine trees, and a room in his apartment was practically filled with a huge violin he had had built; he would climb inside it to study the laws of acoustics. For this he was in touch with many members of the Academy of Sciences, and his desk was piled high with sheets of paper covered with mathematical formulae. It was at his home one day that I met the physicist, Auguste Piccard, that genius inventor who had made the first balloon capable of reaching the stratosphere, as well as the bathyscaphe.

I was very fond of this friend, and I would sometimes go to visit him in Montmartre where he lived. He was already very old when I met him; he had a moustache and long white hair. He looked a bit like Saint-Yves d'Alveydre, and much more like Barbey d'Aurevilly, the author of a collection of short stories, *Les Diaboliques.* One day, I told him that. He laughed and replied, 'Yes, perhaps I do, and it doesn't displease me.' He was very tall, and always dressed in black with a black bow tie. When we walked together along the roads of the district, he would talk about his research, about his disagreements with the physicist, Louis de Broglie, I no longer know what about. We must have made a striking picture, he with his white hair and black clothes and me with my black hair and much lighter clothes, for people would often stop just to look at us.

He was a man very aware of his own worth. In daily life, he would very rarely let others talk. Yet, he listened to me, and when he came to my lectures he would sometimes go away sadly. One day I asked him the reason for this, and he replied, 'I used to think that I knew a lot of things, but when I listen to you I realize that I know nothing.' In fact, we did not know the same things. I would have been absolutely unable to follow him in his research, but he had lived unaware of some of the truths of Initiatic Science, and it was too late for him to regain lost time. I do not know why he took it into his head to fight all the black magicians in Paris and throughout the world. I warned him that it was dangerous: it is not that easy to be victorious over black magic. And then one day what happened? He died suddenly. I was very sad… Some time earlier he had given me a magnificent present. In Geneva, one year he had taken part in a competition with various stringed instrument makers, and the violin he had made won first prize. This violin had a truly exceptional tone. No doubt, because I had told him how much I regretted not having learned the violin when I was a child, he gave it to me. I was most touched by his gift. Sadly, I was incapable of playing it.

Obviously, Paris gave me the extraordinary opportunity to discover and read many books. Out of curiosity, I went two or three times to auctions at the Hotel Drouot. I saw a magnificent library of beautifully bound books for sale. And at what a price! Whereas the books that I looked for often lacked a cover, the paper was all yellowed and the edges of the pages tattered.

I often went to the bookshops in the Latin Quarter. I would glance through the books that were on the bookshelves for a brief moment and then I would ask the owner, 'Have you got any other books apart from the ones I see here?' 'No.' 'Are you sure? You don't have others tucked away in an attic?' 'Well, yes, of course, but they are just rubbish and no one would be interested in them.' 'Show them to me, anyhow.' And so, I would stay for hours and hours rummaging through them in darkness. How much dust I swallowed! I would come out tired and creaking in all my joints, because I had had to be bent over or on my knees, but I would be so thrilled when I had managed to find a rare book! When I went back home in the evening, I would be staggering with weariness. I think that sometimes I even walked while I was sleeping. Luckily I had a sort of inner radar, which stopped me from bumping into all the lampposts on the pavement!

One day, in one of these bookshops in the Latin Quarter, when I had explained to the bookseller what kind of books I was looking for, he said, 'Follow me.' I went upstairs, through dark and dusty corridors, and he introduced me to an old lady with white hair. She had a fine, intelligent face, and when she understood what I was interested in, she showed me all the books she had in her keeping. I spent a long time there.

Just as I was about to leave, this woman, whom I did not know, started to speak to me about her husband, a very well-known esotericist called Paul Vulliaud, who had written on the Cabbalah. He had also done a translation of a book of the *Zohar*, the *Siphra di-Tzeniutha*. Then, she asked me several questions, and I told her that I had been in France a short time and that, at the request of various friends, had given some little talks in a room in the Club de France on the Boulevard Saint-Germain… and that some of these talks had been printed into pamphlets, and so on. She asked me to bring her these pamphlets, which I did the next time I visited her. She looked through them for a moment and then said she would like to show them to her husband. I wondered what this man, who had written many erudite works, would think of my badly printed pamphlets, which were barely presentable. When I returned once again, she said, 'My husband would like to meet you, but, as he is very weak, he hardly ever goes out these days, and so he wishes to invite you to our home.'

I was a little anxious about meeting Paul Vulliaud: what would he think of these little pamphlets I was almost ashamed of? What would he say to me? But when I saw the way he welcomed me, I was quickly put at ease. He was only interested in the ideas, and he said to me, 'This is just what I am looking for.' We met several times and we had long conversations. He told me a lot about esoteric people whom he knew or had known, and he put me in touch with some of them. It was all most interesting. But what struck me the most was his face and his attitude: he looked so much like Master Peter Deunov; he had, like him, a beard and white hair, but, above all, he smiled like him and made the same gestures. Oh, I was so happy to meet someone in France who reminded me of my Master! We understood each other immediately and we had such a good friendship.

Unlike many other esoteric people, Paul Vulliaud was not proud about his very great knowledge, nor did he use it to crush other people. He would put the presumptuous in their place, but his energy went into enlightening and supporting all those who were sincerely looking for true knowledge. Sadly, I was not to know him for long because he was already very old and sick. I wanted so much to meet other people of his quality! I had been introduced to several famous authors who were spiritually minded and whose books I had read, but what did I see?

Opium addicts, morphine addicts, cocaine addicts… Not all of them, of course, but how many of them, instead of working on themselves, used drugs to enter the subtle mysterious worlds they wanted to discover! They found something, but you do not reach the higher realms of the invisible world through drugs, and they were destroying themselves.

I also really wanted to persuade some of these cabbalists, astrologers, magi and alchemists that it is not enough to read books and to practise certain systems and formulas to achieve results, but it was a very difficult task. I met an alchemist who has since become famous. We would meet at my house or his, and this man was so preoccupied with his research that he lived in the greatest poverty. Even though I did not have much myself, I helped him, and I also recommended him to some of my acquaintances. He was very learned and I liked him a lot, because he was also a very good man. He wrote books and later on he was asked to speak about alchemy on television. He told me that he was looking for the philosopher's stone, but the way in which he was searching for it was never going to be successful. The philosopher's stone has to be found first of all within, before it can be found on the physical plane, and to discover it in oneself demands some quite exceptional qualities.[2]

I was not particularly keen on being invited to gatherings, but sometimes when I was invited I would accept, and then I would have conversations with all types of people. One day, a young woman came to ask me about love and about certain erotic practices. I do not know why she put these questions to me and I did not ask her. I no longer remember what answers I gave her, but I do know that she left very happy with my explanations.

Some time later, during one of these gatherings, a writer began to revile me for no apparent reason in front of everyone. I asked him what wrong I had done to him, and he told me that this young woman who had asked me those questions had left him. He had engaged in sex magic with her, and after she had heard my explanations, she realized how dangerous these practices were. So I said to him, 'Sir, I had no idea that this young girl belonged to you and that you had rights over her. I did not know why she was asking these questions. If, without knowing it, I rescued her from your underhand dealings, what have I done wrong? The sun is allowed to shine, and those who don't have a hat are in danger of sunstroke. You must have a hat…' And from that moment, he did not want to say another word to me. Some years later he came to see me; life had given him some lessons and he had understood.

For a short while, a certain Parisian club kept sending me invitations to attend their meetings and to give talks. I received their programmes, and on one of them it was written that I would speak on such and such a subject on such and such a day. But it was pure invention. I had never agreed to do so and, in fact, had never been asked. When they saw that I did not reply, they sent me even more invitations, and these were even more alluring: the meetings would be held in a specific hotel, and people of high society would be there as well as famous writers and scientists. To be polite, I replied that I would think about it. But I had already thought about it, I knew I would not go. I never got in touch with them and so they finally dropped their invitations.

The truth is that those kinds of gathering were not for me and I never felt comfortable attending them. I willingly admit that it is a weakness on my part, but I am not made for that sort of thing. It has always felt superficial to be speaking about the spiritual life in a room, or some public place, in front of people who have only come out of curiosity. The only thing which interested me was to undertake consistent work, in depth, with the same people, as I had begun to do as soon as we had a house in Sèvres.*

During my first years in Paris I read a lot, but I was also able to listen to a lot of music, and that was a truly great privilege for me. One of the first people I met after my arrival was the sister of a very famous singer at the time. This singer was herself the wife of the director of the *Opéra Comique*, and so, thanks to her, I was given free tickets to attend all the concerts I wanted, and I was able to go to the opera. Not only did I experience the greatest joy at listening to the music, but I also tried to analyze the different effects that music had on me. With the criteria I had, I made some most interesting observations. I would often close my eyes so that I could notice which centres were activated in me by the different resonances of the instruments and the singers' voices, and also which vibrations can awaken certain psychic faculties. I cannot list all the composers and performers I heard. I had always wanted to hear Adelina Patti, but by the time I arrived in France she had already been dead for a long time. However, I was able to find, to my great joy, some very rare recordings of hers… I think at this time I must have seen all the operas of Mozart, Puccini and Verdi… When I travelled in Italy, people would stop me to say how much I looked like Verdi, whereas other people thought I looked like Garibaldi. When I went to Spain, there were those who took me for Fidel Castro! People's imaginations are quite remarkable!

* Izgrev, headquarters of the Universal White Brotherhood since 1947.

Obviously, I wanted to know about the life of all these musical geniuses, how they worked and what struggles they had. And so, I read many biographies. From all these books, I remember, in particular, one anecdote about Paganini. He was giving a concert one day before a crowded room. After each piece the audience clapped loud and long. But in the first row there was a young man with a sombre face who never clapped. Paganini noticed him, and, as he was very easily offended, this did not make him happy. At the end, when everyone was clapping and demanding an encore, he said, 'I will not play unless the young man sitting there in the front row will come to speak to me.' So the young man was brought to him, and Paganini said, 'Everyone here is happy to hear me and showed their appreciation, everyone except you. What is it that you don't appreciate in my music or in my performance?' 'Oh Master,' replied the young man, 'I am a musician and I thought I had talent, but when I listen to you I realize that I am not much good. I am overwhelmed by my mediocrity and that is why I am not able to show you my admiration.' 'What is your name?' 'Vincenzo Bellini.' 'Good, come and see me, and I will see what I can do for you.' When I tell this little story, I don't know why I am so moved by it. I expect it is that I cannot help being a little sentimental.

Thinking back on all these shows, all these concerts I attended at this time, and all these books I read, I sometimes ask myself whether I did not waste my time a little. However, I did learn many things, and as it says in *Ecclesiastes*, *'For everything there is a season, and a time for every matter under heaven.'* So, there is a time to gather all this knowledge by turning towards the world, and then there is a time to turn inwards and extract the quintessence of all that we have seen, heard and read.

Just because we follow a spiritual teaching does not mean that we should neglect the masterpieces of world literature, the philosophical works, the novels, the poems and the plays. Even if I read much less these days because I do not have so much time, I have, since my youth, always kept an insatiable curiosity for books. And when I go into a house, if I can do it discreetly, I look at the bookshelves. I look at the titles of the books and that teaches me about their owners. Yes, displaying your library of books is like standing naked in front of your visitors. And the same thing applies if you have no books at all.

Those first years in France were very rich for me, rich in encounters, rich in discoveries. I did not have all the responsibilities that I bear now and I was freer to go to bookshops, libraries, museums... I spent hours at the Palace of Discovery! And do you know that I even went to the Faculty of Medicine? I got to know some students, and, as part of their studies required them to dissect bodies, I asked if I could come with them to do some dissection. The anatomy of the human body is such a miracle! I wanted to look at these organs closely, to see the heart, the lungs, the liver and the intestines, so that I could understand some things which I am not going to speak about at the moment. My friends got permission for me to go with them, but it was very difficult for me to stand the sight of their work! I very quickly gave up the idea of dissection.

I was therefore very happy to be in France, and particularly because I was where my Master had sent me, but my situation became complicated. Officially, I had come to Paris only for the World Exhibition, and so I ought to have gone back to Bulgaria. I had to keep renewing my visa and I was always threatened with being expelled from the country. I went to the police headquarters so many times and I spent so many hours waiting in those corridors! Fortunately, there were people who supported me throughout these proceedings. It was clearly my destiny to remain in France, but it was not without difficulties!

When the war came in 1939, the situation became even more complicated because I was a foreigner in your country.* As it was for all the French, it was hideous for me to see France occupied and German tanks in the streets of Paris. There was so much suffering… Among the people who came to my lectures, some were Jewish, and it was heart-rending to see them come with the yellow star sewn onto their clothes. Fortunately, they were never troubled.

I used to be visited by mediums and clairvoyants, who told me their predictions: how long the war would last, who would win, and so on, and then they would ask me about the accuracy of their predictions. I would reply, 'If you are not sure about what you are saying, why would you be confident in what I tell you?' Other people asked me if they should leave Paris to find shelter elsewhere. I said, 'No, stay where you are, as you would be much less safe on the roads.' Some people trusted me, but others left and never came back.

During this period, I had to tell my friends so many times that they needed to conquer their fear, particularly during the bombardments. Near our house at Sèvres, there was a battery of Anti-Aircraft Defence cannons that fired every night, and the whole neighbourhood would be woken

* A complicated time, as Bulgaria was allied with Germany.

with a jolt each time. So, I explained to my friends that before they went to sleep, they should already have the idea firmly fixed in their mind that at some time or other during the night they would be woken by the bombardments. In this way, they could overcome their fear more successfully and would also experience the shock to their nervous system less painfully. Fear can only be conquered when you call consciously on the will; otherwise it is easy to fall into a panic reaction, which can be more dangerous than the danger itself. I have experienced this myself.

Sometimes I had to go to Paris, and when I came back to Sèvres by train I would come out of the station to be met by gunfire. Believe me when I tell you that I would walk calmly without the slightest fear. But, one day, when I came out of the station, I started running to avoid the splinters of shrapnel that were falling all around. Until, suddenly, I realized that this hurrying had released a fear in me which kept increasing. Unhappy with this observation, I stopped dead. I summoned my will to help me regain my calm, and I succeeded, though with some difficulty. I realized that by running I had released the fear that lurks at the base of all human beings, and that made me think. It is not that those who are called courageous never feel fear, but they have learned to control it.[3]

One day I was told that I was suspected of being an Oustachi.* Me, a member of a terrorist movement? It was a very serious accusation, but my God, what a grotesque

* The Oustachis were members of a Croatian nationalist society that was formed in 1929. Using terrorist tactics, they were the authors of the plot to murder Alexander I of Yugoslavia in Marseille, in 1934, where a French minister in his entourage was also killed.

one! I had never been this type of revolutionary. As often as possible, I explained to those who wanted to listen that the only revolution in which I was interested was the one people were capable of creating within themselves. I was working on this revolution within myself and had been doing so for years, striving to install true order, divine order within myself. I added, 'If any of you want this, too, I am ready to give you all the methods you need to revolutionize everything within you.'[4] I do not know if they understood me, but to be accused of belonging to a terrorist organization such as the Oustachis was extremely dangerous for me.

How many times over the years I have had to confront the police and bureaucracy! Sometimes I was summoned; other times they came to me. They were always interested in my profession; they watched what I did and tried to understand who or what I was representing. Summons after summons, visit after visit – what reports they must have filed on me! Sometimes, I would even find it amusing, as it gave me the opportunity to have a little conversation with those who were questioning me. One day, I finished by saying to one of them, 'Frankly, your questions astonish me.' 'Why is that?' 'I wonder how many times it will take for you to understand who I am. How many more years will it take for you to be sufficiently informed? As for me, I can tell you in five minutes who you are.' I said this to an open and sympathetic man, who laughed; we spoke together for a short while and then we parted good friends.

Some years later, Bulgaria began to be interested in me. There, they were asking questions about their compatriot who had succeeded in creating a Brotherhood in France where they sang in Bulgarian, and who published books translated into several languages, which attracted many foreigners. One day, I received a letter from the Bulgarian ambassador to France saying that he wanted to meet me. I was a little astonished, but I agreed. He came in a car down to the Bonfin with three people, one of whom was introduced as the driver. I invited them to come and take part in our meeting with all the Brotherhood. Evidently, they were surprised and happy to hear such good singing in Bulgarian and how well the Bulgarian formula was said before and after meals.

At one point, my attention was caught by the way the man who had been introduced as the driver was looking at me. I had noticed his intelligent and determined face immediately, when I shook his hand, but now, seeing his sharp and piercing look, I understood that he was a man used to observing, to scrutinizing, and that he had come here to examine me, too. So, I decided to give him a little lesson, and I began to look at him in such a way as to make him understand that I was able, like him and perhaps better than him, to look into the hearts and minds of people. From that moment, it was over, and he lowered his gaze.

Several times I looked in his direction. Now that he understood that I had seen through him, I wanted to have a good exchange with him, for, in truth, he was rather likeable. But he kept his face averted, and so it was not possible. Without doubt this man was an operative in the Bulgarian secret service, and he was doing his job... When I meet people, I never dwell on what they do in society. Whether they are bakers, masons, university professors, policemen, ministers – or even secret service agents – it's all the same to me. I look for their heart, their soul, their spirit, so that I can give something good to them. But I couldn't do it with this man; he was not expecting to meet someone capable of resisting him as I did. I will never know what kind of report he made on me.

For twenty years I had studied and worked beside Master Peter Deunov without knowing what he was preparing for me. He never told me and he hid it from others. When he made the decision to send me to France, he warned only his secretary, because he could foresee the opposition and jealousy that this would arouse, but it was impossible to hide my absence and its goal for long. The World Exhibition, which had been the pretext for my departure, lasted only for a while, and soon criticisms started to arise. What had I come to do in France? It was quite impossible that the Master would have chosen me, such an insignificant human being, to propagate his Teaching. Some people claimed they wanted to come and help me in my task, and the Master had to stop them. When he was no longer there to protect me, some of them did come, and I became the object of all sorts of intrigues and scurrilous slanders... Before I left, the Master had dictated two letters to people he knew: one was a Polish woman, whom he asked to welcome me, and the other was a Bulgarian, whom he asked to help me find lodgings. I was to give them these letters on my arrival in Paris. I delivered the first one, but I could not deliver the second, as the Bulgarian to whom it was addressed was no longer there, so I kept it. This was fortunate, because after the Master's death, all sorts of stories began to circulate about me, and it was the only proof that I had left Bulgaria at his request. At least ten years had passed already... If it had not been for his request, I would never have come to France.

I was not at all surprised by these attacks, despite their wild assertions; indeed, I was almost expecting them. Each time a person is chosen to fill a position, to carry out a mission, there are always people who will spread criticisms, and then they will try as hard as they can to find others, who have their own motives, to join them, so that together they can fight the one chosen. Why should I be an exception? But whatever happens, the one important thing for me was to show myself worthy of being the Master's choice and deserving of the trust he put in me.*

Notes

1. See *The Book of Divine Magic,* Izvor Coll. n° 226, chap. 1: 'The danger of the current revival of magic', and chap. 15: 'Love, the only true magic'.
2. See *The Philosopher's Stone – in the Gospels and in Alchemy,* Izvor Coll. n° 241, chap. 10: 'The philosopher's stone, fruit of a mystic union'.
3. See *True Alchemy or the Quest for Perfection,* Izvor Coll. n° 221, chap. 5: 'Fear' and *The Wellsprings of Eternal Joy,* Izvor Coll. n° 242, chap. 8: 'Forging ahead fearlessly'.
4. See *Freedom, the Spirit Triumphant,* Izvor Coll. n° 211, chap. 8: 'Anarchy and freedom', chap. 9: 'The notion of hierarchy', and chap. 10: 'The synarchy within'.

* See Appendix I, p. 459.

10

No prison can confine the spirit

'You have spoken the word of God, yet there has been a file of accusations drawn up against you, and you have been thrown into a prison where you have to wear the uniform of a detainee... Is that enough to prove that you are indeed guilty, and are you persuaded that you are a criminal? No. If I were to find myself in such a situation, I would transform the prison into a palace, I would keep in touch with my friends, I would bring light to the prisoners and set their hearts aflame. If you are a bearer of truth, the one who protects you will come close to you, and you will talk together during the night. In the morning he will be there to defend you. And the governor of the prison will be there in the same way. You may be imprisoned, but you will feel free.'

I do not know when or where Master Peter Deunov said these words. He was no longer alive when I was incarcerated, and yet I have the impression that he was there in prison with me, so that all that was promised in these few lines came true. I lived there two terrible years*, but it could

---

* from 21 January 1948 to 7 February 1950. Originally, the sentence was for four years.

have been for much longer had it not been that at certain moments the governor and some of the guards protected me: were they influenced by the Master's spirit? And, although newspapers were writing articles about me as a dangerous criminal, in prison I was praying, meditating, advising, and bringing cheer to the detainees, who would tell me all about their lives. I also had conversations with the guards and the prison governor.

If you haven't experienced detention yourself, it is almost impossible for you to understand how difficult it is to bear the bad food, the heat, the cold, the promiscuity, the cigarette smoke, the threats, the shouts and the brawls. The hardest thing for me to bear was the disgrace. In such a situation, so as not to feel totally destroyed, I had to look within myself for something stronger than everything, and that something is thought, spirit. If we manage to do that, we discover true freedom. I was kept in prison for two years, but I can say that for those two years I was freed. The more limited I was physically, the more I learned how to find freedom. Each day I would work on my thoughts and my feelings so that I would not be impatient or angry or full of hate, because thoughts and feelings are the real prisons, and we alone can deliver ourselves from these prisons.

The Master had said, 'If I were to find myself in this situation, I would transform the prison into a palace.' A king can walk freely from one room to another in his grand palace, but if he has not learned to control his thoughts and feelings, you could say that, in effect, he is locked in a tiny cage. He comes surrounded by ministers and generals, his servants bow respectfully as he passes, but if you could see what was happening inside him, you would see that he was wearing a rough garment stamped with his prison identification number. A prisoner who, on the other hand, has learned to put the power of the spirit into action leads the life of a prince.

I would not wish any one of you to have to go through the terrible experience of prison just so that you, too, could have the chance to test the powers of the spirit. Try, however, to strengthen yourselves, for no one can pass through life without having to undergo some unfair and difficult situations. Cosmic Intelligence, which wants to make human beings free and powerful, is implacable. It has given us willpower, heart, mind, soul and spirit, but what have we done with them? Not much, and faced with ordeals we feel weak and powerless. In order to discover the value and extent of what we possess, we must be forced. So, we must accept that we will face ordeals and accept the idea that this is how we will find true freedom, true wealth.[1]

To a certain extent, I had already been warned of what I would have to go through. For some months earlier I had been having dreams, the most important of which were concerned with the four elements. In one I was jumping from rock to rock as the ground fell away from under my feet. Sometime later I dreamed of floods: filthy water swirled over everything, but I managed to cling on to the branch of a tree. Another time I was caught in a tornado and I looked everywhere for shelter. The last dream was about fire; everything was burning. I found these images very clear because, symbolically, the four elements relate to our psychic life and to the ordeals we will have to confront in our lives.

The ordeals of the earth are like earthquakes; they confirm our stability, our endurance and our willpower. We are shaken up, to see whether the foundations of our pyramid are sufficiently sturdy. The ordeals of water are those of the emotions; we are plunged into the black torrents of hatred and treachery, yet our love must neutralize all these poisons. The ordeals of air are produced by tornados and hurricanes: will our intellect lose all sense of direction or will it continue to see clearly and reason correctly? The ordeals of fire are the most fearsome; they burn all the impurities which prevent our soul from merging with the prime Cause, on which all life depends. In order to find God, we will have to pass through the purification of fire.

I am always warned in one way or another of the dangers that lie in wait for me. Either I pick up the feeling of what is ahead, or someone else warns me. I do not know why it is, but I am not a person who pays much attention to such things. I do not take precautions; it is just not in my nature. One day, someone told me I was foolhardy. Yes, that is indeed possible. Then, of course, when I do find myself in deep trouble, I chide myself for not having been more prudent, but by then it is too late.

Some time before my arrest and imprisonment, I had the strong feeling of an impending threat: there were signs in the behaviour of certain people around me that could not be mistaken. But, one evening, near midnight, someone telephoned me. He told me everything about a plot that had been hatched to ruin me: I was to be the victim of a conspiracy in which false witnesses would be ranged against me, and I would be accused of rape amongst other perverse actions. This person said, 'You are in grave danger, and your status as a foreigner really complicates matters. There is only one way to save yourself: flee. Leave France as quickly as possible!' In fact, I could leave, but I did not do so. Sometimes there are situations where it is very hard to know exactly what to do. What was the best way for me to carry on the work entrusted to me by my Master? I decided to stay, whatever the consequences might be.

As soon as I crossed the threshold of the prison, I realized how important it was for me to take precautions, so that all the violence, coarseness and ugliness there would not penetrate my being. Neither my faith nor my love must be weakened in any way at all. I had to follow my path. I worked even during the night so that the fetid air I was breathing would not contaminate me. I could never let down my guard, and what I experienced there, what I saw and heard, taught me more than any crime novel or film.

Even in prison there are ways to be useful, and, as far as possible, I tried to help my companions. Each morning we would go out into the courtyard for some fresh air and exercise. Some people ran around and then would go back exhausted. Others would just walk around, but it did not do them much good because they did not really know how to walk. So one day I suggested that I might give them some pointers. I explained that the most important thing was to find an appropriate rhythm, then to move their arms, and to breathe correctly. At first, there were not many takers, but after a while the numbers grew.

I observed these men pacing up and down their cells like animals in a cage. They kept going over and over the same questions. Why had they been caught? Who had betrayed them? How were they going to get out of there? And they kept feeding their desire for revenge. It was obvious that some of them, when they were freed, would go right back to their old ways of stealing, violence and murder. So, to others who were willing to listen to me, I began by saying, 'Why do you want to make other people responsible for the situation you are in? If you are here, it is because you had too much self-confidence. You believed too much in your own ability; you built up these great plans in your mind that you believed no one would be suspicious of, or that if they did suspect you, you would be clever enough to get away with. But, despite all your precautions, you did not succeed, and you got caught. If you had doubted yourself just a little, if you had thought, "I might make a mistake, I might not have thought of everything, I might not be as cunning as I need to be", you would not be here in this prison. Next time, doubt yourself a little, and this will protect you from making any more foolish mistakes.'[2]

What can be said about the effects of prison on detainees? Others have written about this at length, but I want to dwell on a topic which I have not heard raised very often. It is not unusual for people to be aware that they should be punished for their faults; something inside tells them that they deserve some sort of sanction, but it also tells them that they should make amends. The justice system pays little attention to the second half of their feelings as it thinks it is sufficient merely to put them in prison. So, when they are penned up within the four walls of their cells, they are haunted by the memory of what they have done, and they keep playing, over and over again, in their minds, the words and images of their crime. Even though they may not be willing to acknowledge this, many live obsessed by the evil they have committed, and they struggle with being locked up and powerless. What they need, in order to find themselves on the right road once more, is the chance to clear their conscience by giving them conditions which allow them to make restitution for their faults. A guilty conscience cannot be soothed permanently just by hearing cheerful words of understanding, or even through medication. If we want the guilty to find a new direction to their lives, we must, as far as possible, give them what they need to make amends for their crimes.

The greater part of the conversations among the detainees always revolved around money, and for many of them it was clearly this obsession with money that had led them to prison. They could not imagine anything more important than money, it was their god, and it was those thoughts of money which kept them imprisoned, not their cell walls. Watching them and listening to them, I felt great compassion for them. One day I decided that I would try to awaken in them the idea (no matter how faint) of the existence of a different god than money. I used only the simplest of arguments and began by asking questions that I would let one or other of them answer.

I would ask, 'Do you think there are any good and honest people on earth?' 'Honest people? Absolutely not. There is nothing but injustice everywhere.' 'And how about you, are you fair?' 'Oh yes, of course I am a good man.' 'Fine, that's a good answer. And what about beautiful people... do they exist?' 'Oh yes, we have certainly seen women who are really beautiful.' 'And are there intelligent people?' 'Yes, there are those too.' 'So, you agree that there is goodness, beauty and intelligence. And have you met any strong people?' 'Oh yes, I've still got the marks where a tough fellow beat me up once in a brawl.' 'And you agree that there are still other qualities whose existence you would acknowledge?' 'Yes, more or less.'

'Good. Now let us imagine that all these qualities, which you have agreed exist, were stretched out and amplified to infinity... The result would be what we could call God: the sum of all qualities and virtues expanded and amplified infinitely. We cannot deny this reality since each one of us possesses some small portion of it. If this Being, who believers call God, did not exist, where would these qualities and virtues have come from? You can deny the existence of a God who is pictured as an old man with a big white beard, who writes all our sins down in his notebook, but you could not deny that these virtues exist.' At this my companions became quiet...

I then added, 'This Being, for whom you have never given the smallest place in your life, is, in fact, the one Being that you search for above all others.' 'But that's not possible!' 'Yes, indeed it is. You, tell me what brought you to this prison?' 'I loved a woman who deceived me. I was so angry that I beat her and left her seriously wounded.' 'Aha! So what you were looking for was love.' I turned to another one: 'And what about you?' 'I wanted to wipe out a competitor who had taken the position I wanted. He got to make all the decisions on how things should be, and I no longer had any power.' 'I see. So you were after power. And you, my bank robber friend, wanted to be rich. So here we are, with love, power and riches, which, just like beauty and knowledge, are God and come from God. We are attracted by the unlimited, by the infinite, and in one form or another we are still looking for God. The only trouble is that the ways and means we use to reach God are not always the best, and we should learn to choose different ones.' I have no idea how much they understood of what I was saying or whether they remembered any of it.

To tell the truth, I do not think that reasoning alone can prove God's existence. The arguments used are so very weak! It is almost an insult to the Lord to imagine that any rationalization, no matter how skilful, is capable of proving his existence. How can you prove the truth of light to a blind person except by giving them sight? I am not concerned with trying to prove that God exists, nor that beyond our physical world there is another one which we cannot see. I just make the existence of God and the invisible world the implicit basis for all my work, and it is on this basis that I build.[3] When I talk to you, I do not ask myself whether or not you have faith. And it is because I act in this way that one day the existence of God will no longer be in question for you. You will have no doubts, and you will begin to communicate with the realities of the invisible world. You ask, 'But what about those leading questions you asked the prisoners?' Those were just to encourage them to think a little…

Among these men who found the whole concept of God to be quite foreign to them, there was, however, one man who told me that every evening, before he went to sleep, he would say a prayer. I was amazed to hear this, and I told him so, because I knew that he had committed some serious crimes for which he had expressed not the slightest remorse. He told me that this habit came from his childhood; his father would make him say his prayers every evening, and he had never forgotten that. It did not hinder him from becoming a thief, and he added that he would really like to be free of the habit, but, somehow, he just could not shake it. This would suggest that good habits are as hard to get rid of as bad ones. He would certainly have been a worse criminal if he had not prayed.

One day an inmate said to me, 'I detest you. I absolutely cannot stand you.' 'Why is that? Have I harmed you in any way?' 'No.' 'And have you seen me doing anything harmful to anyone here?' 'No, on the contrary, but it is just your very presence that upsets me.' 'I see, and why do you think that is? Can you explain it to me?' He was unable to come up with the slightest explanation. So then I asked him, 'Could you at least tell me who you enjoy being with here?' His reply floored me. When I heard which prisoners were the ones he appreciated, brutal men without morals, I was very glad to know that he found me so disagreeable; it was as if I had been given a diploma!

It is important for you to understand this. It is not necessarily anything to do with your behaviour that makes people like or dislike you, but it is because of who you are, what emanates from you, and whether or not that vibrates in harmony with what these people really are. Sometimes, and this is a dreadful fact, if you do something good to someone who feels this instinctive antipathy toward you, you will not only fail to change their feelings toward you, but you will become even more unbearable to them. I can tell you that I have had more than one occasion to meditate on this particular aspect of human nature.

But, amongst the inmates, there was one to whom I felt most sympathetic. He had got it into his head that when we both got out of prison we could become partners... to commit some crimes, of course. While we were still incarcerated, he gave me some lessons so that I would know what to do when the time came. I listened to him, and it was all most instructive to me. Compared to him, in this field, I was clearly an absolute ignoramus. He showed me, for example, how to use my thumb, index and middle fingers to lift up very heavy loads without dropping them. This was obviously a very useful trick for a burglar.

In the beginning, none of the guards wanted to engage me in even the briefest of conversations. They had been given strict orders. There was to be no contact, no conversation (I was even secretly spied on), in case I should hypnotize them and escape. The newspapers had portrayed me as a magician, and magicians, you know, are capable of making anyone fall asleep. But when they began to realize that this odd magician was totally harmless, some of them became less wary and suspicious and instead became not only interested in me but even sympathetic toward me. Not only were they not afraid to speak with me, but they would also seek me out to ask questions and to ask me for advice... and that is fairly unusual in prisons! So as not to compromise their position, they would summon me out of my cell on the pretext that the clerk needed to see me. People began to notice very quickly that I was always being called to see that blessed clerk! One of the guards actually showed me some photos of his fiancée so that I would give him my impression of her character.

One day, the prison governor summoned me. The reason? The guards were frequently changed, and one of them, who was particularly spiteful, had thrown my Bible onto the ground. I had dared to reproach him severely for this act. He submitted a complaint and I was summoned. Everybody thought that I was going to be sentenced to solitary confinement in the terrible, dark dungeon where people often fell ill. Surrounded by three of the guards, I stood before the governor. When I explained what had actually happened, he smiled and sentenced me to three months without tobacco or wine. When I got back to my cell, my companions were most disappointed, because I had been in the habit of giving them my portion of tobacco and wine, and now, poor souls, they were to be deprived for the next three months!

Now I have to acknowledge a weakness on my part. However great my love for people, no matter how degenerate, there were moments where I was very near to losing all patience. Whilst I was meditating or reading, my cellmates on all sides were behaving like mad men. I tried to tell myself that they were children incapable of controlling their energy, but at such moments, how I envied hermits, who lived alone, listening to the voice of silence, that rich, eloquent nourishment for their soul. I would think, 'Oh what luxury to be able to go to the mountains or the forests to taste peace and to converse with the luminous beings of the invisible world, which is all harmony and heavenly music; what delight!' But then I would realize that I was behaving like a thief, grabbing hold of a good thing that for the moment was unattainable, and I said to myself, 'You have to find the forest and the clear mountain lakes right here where you are.' So, I would focus all my energy on the beauty of the Teaching, and on the power of the egregor* of the Universal White Brotherhood. The result would be that I no longer saw the ugliness that surrounded me, I no longer smelled acrid tobacco smoke, I no longer heard the shouts and noises around me, and the look on their faces shifted from animal to human. Everything was transformed thanks to the magical influence of this thought.

In the coldest weather, even with the windows open, I was able to feel a beneficial warmth, because my head was full of the truths of the Teaching, and they acted as central heating. Everybody else was shivering, teeth chattering with the cold, stamping their feet to try and warm them, whereas

* a psychic collective being formed by the thoughts, wishes and fluidic emanations of all the individual members of a collectivity working together towards the same goal.

I sat cross-legged on my bed, praying and meditating. I have always been particularly sensitive to the cold, and the open window was right above my bed, yet I never became ill. I was protected by the Teaching and the idea of the Brotherhood, which were always present in my head. I felt as if I were linked by an unbreakable chain to this great family spread not only throughout the whole world but also on other planets and throughout space to the stars and beyond.

So, this is what I say to you. Whatever happens, if you feel completely at the end of your tether, at the bottom of a chasm, stripped of all you possess, if your house has been burned to the ground, if everyone has abandoned you, if you have been betrayed by your friends, rejected on all sides, never ever forget that you belong to another world, where none of these miseries can hurt you, that you are linked to it by your soul and your spirit. Send up signals for help. Do you feel as if no one sees you and no one will come to your aid? You are mistaken: in truth, there are thousands of beings who are there watching over you.

Picture in your mind's eye the ocean at night and little boats travelling on the waters. If their occupants feel they are in danger, they send up distress signals, flares of light, so that they can be seen in the darkness, and then rescuers can come to their aid. That is what I did during those long nights in prison. By sending out the light of my faith, my love and my hope, I called on heavenly beings to help me. How important are human beings with their judgments and condemnations in comparison to the heavenly beings? When we can attract the attention of these entities, they are capable of opening all the doors and windows within us to let their peace and their joy come in. It is so very simple for them to see us and come to our aid. Even if they are busy with mighty projects, the waves produced by fervent prayer immediately catch their attention. They do not see those who complain, who are rebellious, hateful, or who display any other negative emotion, because these people are deep in darkness, buried in obscurity. But, if these people send up light signals towards heaven, if they separate themselves from the darkness, then they will immediately be noticed.

The luminous spirits we succeed in attracting become our friends, they never leave us; they persist in sticking with us just as much as those spirits of darkness we find so difficult to shake off. Why should not friends be as persistent as enemies? They come to support us, to bring us understanding, to advise us, and if we pay attention to their advice we are always inspired. That is why we should never despair, even when we are in the worst situations, because, one day, things will turn to our advantage since we have been so very inspired.

When you are attacked from all sides, when you watch those whom you thought you could count on being dishonest, disloyal and unbalanced, there are times, it is true, when you wonder if it is worth carrying on. What could I do, confronted with the lack of understanding of those who thought they were protecting society by locking me up? However painful it was to have to bear such accusations and betrayals, it was far worse to find that, after a while, these accusing voices were heard not only in the outside world but also within myself, and they ended up invading consciousness itself. These inner voices tormented me over and over again saying, 'Even if you have not committed any of the crimes that you have been accused of, you must be guilty in some way or other and deserve blame.' So how was I to deal with this torment, if I was not to allow it to destroy me?

I ended up by finding this exercise: I recalled all the moments of light, of inspiration, of spiritual joy that I had ever experienced and said to these inner voices of doubt and despair, 'It is not possible that I should have been able to live such moments and at the same time be guilty of the things you are accusing me of.' And then these doubts would go away. Not surprisingly, they would come back again after a brief time. However, until the day when they were completely vanquished, I was able to combat them by using the memory of those solemn moments lived at the very heart of the spirit.

In truth, the worst thing would still not have been doubting myself, but doubting the Teaching, the philosophy of the initiates, the path to be followed or my Master, who some time after my arrival in France had written to me: 'Keep going forward with faith and love. Do not be afraid.' Why should I not have doubts about myself? It is what forces us to progress. There is nothing more dangerous than believing you are infallible. That was why, during this period, I spent a lot of time looking back over my life to see the tangled web woven by all the various threads that had brought me to this point. One of the good things that can be said about prison is that there is no shortage of time! And so I would go back in my mind to see all the people I had met, and I would analyze all the impressions they had made on me, the kind of relationships I had with them and what had ensued because of them. I understood how important it was, because it gave me some indicators for the future.

It would be very useful for you, too, to do the same thing yourselves. Take the time to go over the events you have experienced, look at the way you handled them, examine the people you met, those who brought good things to you and those you found difficult. Even if these people are superficially different, you will find, if you study their emanations, that they have something in common. So, if you get into the habit of sensing and analysing their emanations, when you are faced with strangers you will have something to rely on. You will find the same thing is true for the events that occur in your life: so often the same things are repeated (though in different forms), and if you have not really studied them closely, if you have not learned the lessons, you will find yourself again in the same situations, and you will still have no idea why.

Life is subject to a sort of periodic movement: everything repeats itself, but never in exactly the same manner, and so it is up to us to develop our discernment. But it is also important to be cautious and not stir up any old memories from the past as you go over it to learn its lessons. It is never good to stir up the dregs. Everything we have ever experienced is recorded and filed somewhere within us. You could say it is like having bottles of chemicals stored on shelves. These bottles need to be handled with care, and you should avoid opening some of them for fear of being asphyxiated.

It was also at this time in prison that I decided to seriously study my astrological chart. Both in Bulgaria and in France, many people had asked me to do their horoscopes, and they were all satisfied with what I had said, as they found it helpful. But when I looked at my own chart, nothing seemed to correspond to who I was, nor to what I had experienced or was experiencing. After some years, I decided that this could not be my chart. I even thought that it must belong to some very mediocre fellow, or to someone even worse than mediocre! I asked myself, 'How have I been able to transform myself as much as I have? It's true that I have worked over the years, I have made all sorts of efforts, and I had a Master. But even so, this just doesn't fit'. This disturbed me a great deal; there must surely be something missing that I did not know. So I wrote to my brother Alexander in Bulgaria asking him to question my mother, and this is what I learned.

When our village in Macedonia was ravaged by fire, we were not able to retrieve anything from our home, which had been completely destroyed. We lost everything, including our identity papers. So when my mother and I moved to Varna, we had to get new ones. My father went to ask for them, and the papers were drawn up according to his statements. The date he gave was inaccurate: I was born in January and he feared that, when it was time for me to go to school, I would not be enrolled in the class he wanted. So he said I was a year older than I really was. I had had no knowledge of these facts until I heard this news. Why was it that I did not know my real birth date until I was nearly fifty years old? So that I should not know in advance the ordeals that awaited me and do something to avoid them.

So when I was in prison, some people who had learned of the place and false date of my birth had done my chart and concluded that I was indeed this criminal who had been sentenced to prison. When I was released, I met one of these people, who said in a most contemptuous way, 'Well, with a chart like yours, you were very lucky to have been let out of prison. Let's wait and see what is coming next for you…' I replied, 'What have you done to check my true birth date? I, myself, found it out only very recently. The chart you have been looking at is not mine.' Astonishment crept over his face, but I could also read a certain fear there as well.

There is no point in going back over all these events to ask myself whether or how I could have avoided them. Since, at the time I was warned of the plots against me, my friends on high had not inspired me to flee, there was nothing for it but to meet these ordeals head on. I have always had the greatest trust in these friends; they knew that even if the dishonour inflicted was, for me, worse than death, I would come back to life once again. Yes, when you are reborn, you are more alive than if you had never died. And I was not the only one to benefit from this new life. You, too, have benefited.

Often, during this time of my life, I felt held in the hands of God, just like a block of stone in the hands of a sculptor. What do sculptors do? They take a hammer and tap on the chisel to begin to release the forms within. God does the same thing with us, and we need to accept that and say, 'Lord, I thank you for chipping away all this unnecessary material. I thank you for sculpting me into a beautiful piece.' Yes, in the middle of the greatest suffering, we can, we must, give thanks.[4]

In these terrible conditions in prison I understood how grateful I should be to heaven for having prepared me in my youth to endure such hardships. If I had been raised, as a child and adolescent, in ease and comfort, how would I have been able to bear what I was obliged to live there? Obviously, I also read a lot, and books were a great support to me. Fortunately, I had already learned to look within myself for what was lacking in the outer world. Each hard situation in life is like being shut up in a prison, and all of us have within us the power to free ourselves.

Sometimes people ask me, 'Why is it that you, who developed those powers of thought when you were very young, did not use these powers in your defence to neutralize your enemies?' True power is never about using such abilities against others; it allows us to become more and more invulnerable to attack, to be able to change the stones hurled at us into precious jewels. True power, true greatness, consists in having knowledge and power, yet not using them for personal benefit. Heaven, which has allowed us to gain these gifts, watches us. We must use this knowledge and power only for our own spiritual growth or that of others, as opposed to controlling others, reacting to attacks or seeking revenge. Is not that the example Jesus gave us?[5]

The truth is that life is a school in which we are all enrolled, and in this school we do not know who are the teachers and who the students. Children, even beggars, can teach us, but above all it is our enemies who teach us. Sometimes it would be so easy to respond to attacks or slanders, but not all such ways of reacting are necessarily good. I have always felt the danger in lowering myself to the level of my attackers, because I would become as dirty as them. In my response to the situation I always want to work from the highest level, not to join my enemies in maliciousness and wickedness. Victory won on that level is, in fact, a great personal loss.

At any rate, it is almost impossible to defend oneself against unfair accusations. A short while after I left prison, a friend came to tell me that he feared for my safety. Apparently in Paris there were people who were convinced that I was a monster, and so they wanted to do away with me. I have no idea how they did it, but they had made hundreds of copies of the banknote that carried the face of the astronomer, Le Verrier. Somehow they had replaced his face with mine, and below it they had written 'Michaël Ivanoff, more dangerous than Hitler'. They were distributing these notes throughout the streets of Paris. Hearing this, I burst out laughing, because it was so grotesque. My friend said, 'You ought not to laugh, for these are genuinely crazy people.'

Crazy or not, when they are convinced that you are guilty, when they want you to be guilty, there is nothing you can do about it; everything you say will be used against you. I have found myself in such situations so many times! But one day when someone was busy accusing me of leading people astray, seducing women, breaking up families, pushing people to commit suicide and so on, I just listened to what that person was saying. If I had tried to justify myself, I would never have succeeded, so what was the point in wasting my time? After a moment, I looked at him with a smile and said, 'But you haven't even scratched the surface! I have done much worse things, and you have no idea what I am capable of.' The speaker just stared at me, completely dumbfounded, and no more was said. So that's another way to avoid being injured when you are unjustly accused.

It is with love that we take revenge on our enemies; when we treat them with love, we heap coals of fire on their head.[6] I know that one day all those who have done me harm will be so ashamed of their actions that they will come to ask my forgiveness. Some of them have already done so, and others who have already left the earth are doing so. I feel their presence near me, their sorrow, as they beg me to forgive them.

I could tell you in detail all the ordeals I had to endure in prison, all the attacks levelled at me, and how, even years later, after I had been totally vindicated,* many attempts were made to destroy me, but it would not be very useful for you. If I speak about these things occasionally, it is to show you the methods I used to deal with them and the conclusions I drew from the experiences.

Clearly, I would never have chosen to undergo the ordeal of prison, but it was no doubt inevitable, and I had experiences there that I would not have had anywhere else. They were a test for me. I was forced to summon all my inner strengths, to organize and control them and to project them heavenwards. You can be quite sure that I would never have dared speak to you as I have done over the years if these difficulties that I had to overcome had not educated me – my goodness, how they taught me! – proving to me that the spirit can triumph over everything: no prison can confine it.**

Look at the trees in the forest: they are all crowded together, and if one of them wants to spread out, it is hindered by its neighbours. So the wise tree decides that if it shoots up toward the sky, it will find freedom. Why not follow the example of the tree? Each time we feel that we are cramped by people or circumstances, we, too, need to shoot up higher and take refuge in the world of light, at the side of

* in September 1960.
** See Annexe II, p. 464.

God. Even if we are alone, sick, exiled or in prison, we have complete power over our inner worlds. 'I would transform the prison into a palace,' said the Master. It is my soul that I need to transform into a palace, because it is the soul that has the power to be either a prison or a palace.

And it will not do any good when we are suffering to lay the blame on the Lord. Since he has given us all we need to conquer the problems, it is clear that the Lord does not want us to live in the midst of such ordeals. Sooner or later conditions will improve, and it is then we will really benefit from the work we have done. We will find ourselves in a new situation, and in a much better position, by having developed new strengths under difficulties.

Master Peter Deunov asked me to come to France in order to save and make known his Teaching. To fulfil this mission, I would have hoped I would be spoken of in better terms, because what good is a message if the messenger is seen spattered with mud, sullied and dishonoured? But I had to accept events as they occurred, trusting that in time heaven would step in to re-establish the truth.* I had to bear it, I had to drink the bitter cup, all the while waiting for heaven to make itself known. Psalm 91 says:

> *'Those who love me I will deliver...*
> *When they call to me, I will answer them;*
> *I will be with them in trouble,*
> *I will rescue them and honour them...*
> *I will show them my salvation.'*

* See Annexe III, p. 470.

The psalm does not promise us that we will be spared but that, at the end, the Lord will welcome us into his light.

If we work conscientiously at the task entrusted to us by heaven, there will always be events that will reveal the truth and put the situation to rights. Otherwise, whatever we do, we will not succeed. There, too, I am speaking not just about me, but also for all of you. Whatever the difficulties, we must carry on until heaven intervenes, because it knows the exact right moment, and after that you will see events unfold in a totally different direction.[7] When spring comes, nature is transformed! When the divine world steps in, it is like the coming of spring: warm breezes are felt everywhere, and all the good seeds we have sown begin to sprout.

Notes:
1. See *The Wellsprings of Eternal Joy,* Izvor Coll. n° 242, chap. 3: 'Suffering is a stimulus'.
2. See *Love Greater than Faith,* Izvor Coll. n° 239 chap. 3: 'Constructive doubt'.
3. See *The Faith that Moves Mountains,* Izvor Coll. n° 238 chap. 5: 'Faith always precedes knowledge', chap. 11: 'God is Life' and chap. 12: 'God in creation'.
4. See *Le rire du sage,* Izvor Coll. n° 243, chap. XII: 'Remercier, source de lumière et de joie'.
5. See *The Book of Divine Magic,* Izvor Coll. n° 226, chap. 16: 'Never look for revenge' and *The True Meaning of Christ's Teaching,* Izvor Coll. n° 215, chap. 7: 'Father, forgive them; for they do not know what they are doing' and chap. 8: 'If anyone strikes you on the right cheek...'
6. See *The Tree of Knowledge of Good and Evil,* Izvor Coll. n° 210, chap 9: 'The real weapons'.
7. See *Love greater than Faith,* Izvor Coll. n° 239, chap. 7: 'Never abandon your faith in good'.

11

A year in India:
February 1959 - February 1960

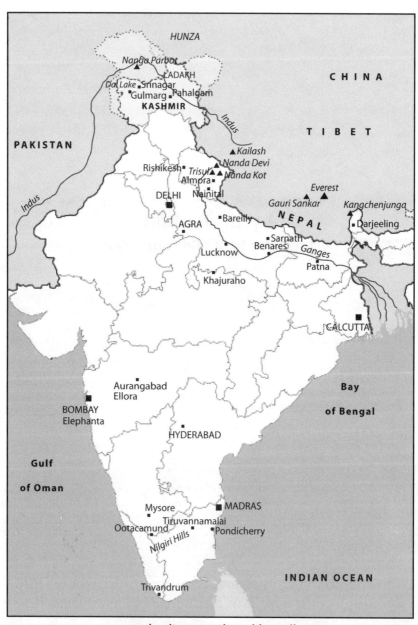

Main sites mentioned in India

To travel to India… That is the dream for an increasing number of Westerners, because they think the country represents the height of spirituality. They have read several books on Hinduism, Buddhism, the different yogas and spiritual Masters, and so they imagine that, as soon as they set foot on Indian soil, they will be led immediately to the great initiate and sage who will give them enlightenment. And without any previous preparation they set off… just like that. Even if they have heard about the widespread poverty, the lack of hygiene and the dirt, they often have no idea how difficult it is for Westerners to bear. Some people say that when one is looking for a spiritual Master, material conditions do not really matter. Agreed. But what do they think it takes to find a Master? Even if they believe that they have found one, are they sure that they will be accepted? And what will they do when they sit in front of someone who spends hours in silence? Are they able to enter into communication with him during this silence? If, as they often state, they have not been able to find any real spiritual nourishment in the West, they will not be able to find it in the East.

Whether in the realm of religion, philosophy, literature, music or architecture, India has enriched world culture with splendid treasures that are worth becoming acquainted with. But, poor Europeans, they dive into all these traditions and practices, thinking that by doing them they will achieve something that Christianity was unable to give them! For a start, they will be presented with gods in all sorts of strange forms that they will not know how to interpret: Kali, who dances with a necklace of human skulls around her neck; Avalokiteshvara, with a thousand arms and eleven heads; Indra, who reveals herself in the form of rain; Ganesha with an elephant head; Hanuman, the monkey, and so on. The Hindu pantheon is an impenetrable forest in which Westerners are liable to get lost, if they are not familiar with the world of symbols.

Let me be quite clear: I do not underestimate the value of India's religions and spirituality; far from it. All I want to do is to warn Westerners, who go off to that country, their heads full of illusions that they will come back enlightened, just because they have been blessed by a few yogis and have visited various holy sites. I have met many of these 'pilgrims' on their return from India, and they told me that they felt lost. This is not surprising; when we have not yet given our lives meaning, it is always risky to imagine we will find it by leaving the traditions and culture we were born into. Before leaping into such adventures, we must give it some reflection. Occasionally, I have been able to verify how wise some Hindu yogis are. They ask Westerners, 'Are you Christian?' 'Yes.' 'Well, stay Christian.' They know that culture and traditions are like native soil for trees. What a lot of time it takes for an uprooted tree to become re-rooted in a different soil!

All religions come from the same source, their differences coming from the fact that they have arisen in different eras among people with different mentalities. This is the first thing to take into consideration, because people do not find it easy to adapt to different ways of looking at things. I repeat that the Hindu tradition is extraordinarily deep, rich and full of poetry, but apart from a few exceptions, Westerners who venture in are often in danger of getting lost. Or else, they may just dwell on appearances, on forms, on superficial exotic details, which show no respect for all those bygone great spirits who worked so hard and long, searching for ways to leave the fruits of their experiences to their people. Do not imagine that the wise men and the spiritual Masters of India feel very honoured when they see all these Christians leaving their own religions, disguising themselves as yogis with shaven heads and orange robes, muttering a few Sanskrit words as they recite mantras while burning incense sticks.

Since my return, I know how impatient you are to hear me talk about my stay in India. Of course, I will do it, but my intention is not to impress you by telling you all the things I experienced there. I find that you are already assigning too much importance to what I might say, as if I am going to bring you something more precious, more essential, than I did during the years before I took this trip. You may not believe me, but if this experience in India was very rich for me, it was because it underlined for me the value of our western tradition. Since my return, this value has become even clearer, because now I can really compare the two. I am not going to say that the western tradition is superior but that Westerners can find all they need for their spiritual development in it.*

As soon as I arrived in the country, I wanted to understand Indians as they are now, their physical appearance, their mentality and their bearing. Using all possible modes of transport, I travelled the length and breadth of India, from Srinagar in the Himalayas to Trivandrum in the extreme south, where the soil is such a vivid red, and from Bombay to Calcutta. I moved in all groups, I encountered great Masters, but I also met politicians, bankers, professors, craftsmen and beggars. I observed how people buy and sell, how they feed themselves and dress, how they sleep and pray. I also tried, mentally, to go back in time to see what the life of this nation had been, its customs and practices.

It really is something extraordinary to look at street life in Indian towns, and I spent many hours walking and observing the vividly colourful crowds. In all the countries of the world I visit, the sight of the crowds in the streets always

---

*Before he left for India on 11 February 1959 the Master left this message:

'Beloved brothers and sisters of the Universal White Brotherhood here at Izgrev in France, I command the spirits of nature, the birds, the trees and all other things to carry out the charge I have given them, that they should be powerful conductors of inspiration and protection for you all.

'May the sunrises, conducted by invisible beings that surround you and speak to you, lead you on the upward path of divine evolution.

'Be united by the love that binds and makes all actions, all words and all thoughts fruitful!

'I am not there and yet I am with you always.

'A higher Being than I takes you under his protection.

'Live your life on earth divinely!

'Hallelujah!'

makes me think the same thing: these men and women all have their own unique existence, their own history, their own problems to be resolved, their own suffering and their own loves. They come and go as individuals focused on themselves, but in reality there is one Being who sustains them all, because this Being lives in them. And I always try, at least in my thoughts, to give them something good from my heart and soul.

There is little value in telling you about India, because so many travellers have given much better descriptions than I am able to give; but obviously, just like all others who go there for the very first time, I was immediately struck by the vast amount of poverty, alongside extraordinarily lavish wealth. I saw immense palaces, whose outbuildings housed and cared for hundreds of horses, and yet outside the walls of the palace great crowds of beggars were dying of hunger. In Bombay, New Delhi, Lucknow, Calcutta and Madras, I went into fabric shops just so that I could admire all the wonderful abundance of silks in the most iridescent colours. They were so splendid! I do not think you could find anything to equal them here in Europe. And when I left these enchanted grottos, the majority of the men and women I encountered were dressed in rags. One wonders why there are so many neglected areas of the world.

Everybody has heard of the widespread poverty in India, but it is one thing to have heard about it and quite another to see it. One day, in Calcutta, I had to cross a bridge. On both sides lay the sick and the suffering, beggars sitting or stretched out on the pavement. Some of them were probably already dead. Hands reached out to me as I passed, and I gave all the change I had in my pockets. And even doing this I had to try to control myself. I was so overcome by the sight of such destitution, such suffering, such abject misery that when I got to the end of the bridge, I wept.

Besides the sight of such poverty, the noise was most difficult for me to bear. At the beginning of my stay I was really shocked to find that Indians, so religious and so mystical, never stopped making a noise, even in their temples and ashrams. One has to go to the forests or the mountains to finally find silence. I was present for the celebration of Independence Day. Everyone was out on the streets, endless lines of children, adults and elderly people walking or driving by. Many of them had little trumpets that they blew incessantly. What pandemonium! The celebration continued for three days and nights!

When you notice certain character traits, those of patience and acceptance of hard conditions, you feel that Indians are very old souls; yet, on the other hand, they are like children: they love noise. At any rate, they do not seem at all disturbed by noise, and this is what often made staying in hotels so painful. At one or two in the morning, I was often woken up by comings and goings and talking in the corridors. Once, having been patient for a while, I went out of my room and saw three or four merry fellows engaged in lively conversation. I said, 'European culture is at least better in that after ten o'clock at night everyone stops making a noise so that people are able to sleep undisturbed. Have you any idea what the time is now? You show no respect and no love.' I expected them to argue with me, but not at all; one of them threw his arms around me and apologized, promising that they would not start up their loud conversation again. And, in fact, from that moment on, they did not make any more noise.

In the hotels where I stayed, some people, once they got to know me a little, thought of me as some kind of yogi, albeit an odd one, because, in their opinion, a yogi can tolerate anything. Ah well, that proves that I must not be a yogi, because I do not tolerate everything, and especially not noise. But they were very nice to me and accepted me for who I was.

One day, out of simple curiosity, I went into the hotel kitchen. And what did I see there? I saw rats calmly wandering around. From that moment on I decided that, whenever possible, I would prepare my own meals. They were very helpful with this too and let me do my own cooking. They said that I was a *brahmachari,* which is the name given to celibate men who are consecrated to God's service. And, do you know which vegetable I loved the most in India? It was the turnip. Yes, indeed, I have never eaten such tender and tasty turnips.

Thanks to their ancient culture, Indians instinctively know how to recognize those who have devoted their lives to spirituality. They spontaneously go up to them and ask for their blessing. How often I was stopped, not only in hotels, but on the streets, in buses, by men and women asking me to bless them, something that had never happened to me in Europe. They would even get down on their knees in front of me. I was most uncomfortable with this, and to begin with I would try to lift them up. Finally I gave up, because I saw that this behaviour was part of their traditions. But I never got used to it. Some people would ask me questions and wanted to invite me to have a meal with them, or even to come and stay with them for a few days. Very often I had to invent reasons to avoid all these invitations.

Among those who stopped me in this way, I discovered sometimes that some were very important people. They offered to lend me their cars so that I could go into town to see its buildings or go to famous sites in the surrounding countryside. I was really most surprised to note this respect, this reverence even, which so many people, from all backgrounds, gave me.

Even if one is forewarned, it is still astonishing to see how closely Indians live together with animals. They accept them as though there is no clear boundary between the human kingdom and the animal kingdom. It is true that, from one point of view, these boundaries do not exist, and it is also true that, for them, animals like the cow, the monkey, the snake and so on still have a mythic, and therefore sacred, character. This is why they allow cows to wander down streets, disturbing the traffic. Snakes are also part of the daily scene: no matter where you are, you will find a man with a bag full of snakes; he plays his flute music to them, and they rise up and sway to his tune.

As for the monkeys, they invade the temples, where they cause all sorts of damage and leave filth everywhere they go. It is rarer, but it appears that in some temples rats are fed and protected as holy beings. Monkeys, however, are to be found everywhere, not just in temples but throughout the town, where they leap onto the merchants' stalls, snatch up fruit and then hurl it at the heads of passers-by. I was told of an incident in which monkeys snatched a baby and took it high up a tree; all the parents could do was to offer them food, so that they would come down and bring back the child.

As for the city of Bombay, it is invaded with crows; on trees and rooftops, their non-stop cawing is unbearable. Foreigners complain about it, but it doesn't seem to upset Indians at all, and they do not chase them away. One day I was so irritated by them that I threw a few pebbles to make them keep their distance, and then an amazing thing occurred. When, later, I left the hotel to walk in the forest, they followed me. As soon as I left the hotel, it seemed they recognized me, and they accompanied me to the forest. What happened there is another story. Crows are highly intelligent, and it is worth taking the time to study them better.

I walked a great deal in the forests of India, but I always needed to stay alert. One day I saw a whole troop of monkeys hurrying toward me. They weren't very big, but their bite can be dangerous, and there were a great many of them. One of them in particular came very close, hissing in a menacing fashion. I stared directly at it and shook the stick I held in my hand, and it turned tail, followed by all the rest of them. There were said to be a few tigers in this forest, but I never met them. Perhaps they thought that I was more ferocious than they were and so, being afraid of me, dared not show themselves! When I was in Kashmir I was warned that the spot where I liked to go was infested with snakes, very small snakes that were extremely poisonous – one bite would ensure a rapid and terrible death. Once again, I never had the chance to see even one of these tiny snakes. Walking in these forests I was amazed to discover all sorts of berries and wonderfully sweet fruits, which kept me nourished the whole day.

When I was an adolescent, before I met Master Peter Deunov but was looking for my path in life, I read books that spoke of wise men and mighty beings who lived in India, particularly in the Himalayas, and I had got into the habit of linking in thought to them. When I finally travelled to India, I had no idea what I was going to encounter. I no longer needed to find my direction as I had found that a long time ago, but I needed to test myself. Yes, I had a certain idea about myself and my work, and I needed to find confirmation of it. So for a year I visited many ashrams, I was received in sanctuaries that were forbidden to strangers, and I went to great Masters, some well known, others not. Among these great Masters I was privileged to meet was Neem Karoli Maharaj Babaji. Before I left France, I of course knew about Babaji, who Yogananda Parahamsa mentions in his *Autobiography of a Yogi*. I did not know if I would be able to meet him, because he moves from one place to another all the time, and there is never any forewarning of where he is going to stay. For years people have looked for him, but with no luck; he is also very difficult to find as he often disguises himself, sometimes as a beggar in a crowd or as a traveller. It would be hard to recognize him as a yogi if you were to meet him quite by chance on the road.

I really wanted to meet Babaji. So, when I was in Almora, I sent him a message through my thoughts, and he replied by coming himself to meet me on 17 June. He sent one of his disciples to bring me to his home. When I had told Dr. Bindu of my desire to meet his Master, this great clairvoyant told me that it would happen on 17 June.

You want me to speak to you about Babaji, but the real essentials can never be spoken. First of all, he says nothing about himself and no one even knows his age. Old people, who knew him when they were children, have assured me that his face has not changed at all. But let us leave aside the question of his age. To look at him you would not see any difference between him and other yogis. He wore a garment so old and threadbare that one day I offered him a new *dhoti*. I had chosen it very carefully, and when I brought it to him he thanked me but would not accept it. On the occasions when he was willing to be approached, he had a very simple, easy manner; he would often receive me in an unceremonious way, stretched out on a sofa. But the most striking thing about him was his expression, a deep and wonderful look full of love.

I was astonished by the welcome he gave me. His look and his smile reminded me so much of my own Master. And we had such extraordinary exchanges in deep silence! On 21 June I met him once again, and then we left Almora together, by car, to go to Bareilly. At Almora, where I had stayed for some time, I left behind my friends: Dr. Bindu, Anagarika Govinda (who was a great specialist in Tibetan mysticism) and his wife, Li Gautami.

I had long talks with Babaji, but I still had many questions to ask him, and as he had to leave he put me in touch with one of his disciples, who lived in the mountains at Nainital, where another of his disciples took me by train. Nainital is a very beautiful spot, most picturesque with its five temples built on the peaks, and it is there that Babaji has his ashram. When I arrived I was greeted by a man, who was about thirty-five years old, called Hanuman Baba. (In the epic of *Ramayana,* Hanuman is the king of the monkeys, minister to the god, Rama). He had a magnificent, pure and intelligent face, and he emanated something very spiritual. There were no introductions, but I knew then that Babaji had alerted him of my arrival; my travelling companion took his leave, and Hanuman Baba led me into the house, where he gave me the room normally used by Babaji when he stayed at Nainital. I stayed there for a while. The window looked out on snow-capped mountains; in the distance I could see the summit of Nanda Devi, and so during this visit I was able to meditate every day in front of a most magnificent view.

I stayed for quite some time at Nainital, and it gave me the chance to study and to have some very interesting experiences. First, I met every day with Hanuman Baba, who was a most unusual being. Babaji had put him through a very strict discipline, yet it seemed that he could bear it very easily. For several years he had had to stop speaking, and not a single word passed his lips; he used a slate to write down whatever he needed to say. He was also required to sleep in a sort of dark hole with just enough room to lie down. Why? Because, in darkness and absolute silence, there is no stimulation for the five senses, and the yogi tries to deaden the senses through meditation. When the five senses stop functioning, they no longer absorb psychic energies, and this allows other senses to awaken, thanks to which the yogi begins to see, hear, feel and touch the fluidic elements of higher realms.

Every morning, for his work, the silent disciple would go to town where he had a job in an office. Returning at five o'clock he would perform his duties at a small temple nearby. Then he would come to see me and would answer my questions by writing on his slate. I spent hours with him; I would speak, and then he would reply in writing. He knew English very well, and sometimes we would stay together until two or three in the morning. His daily food was just a half litre of milk, and yet he was full of energy. He wore only one garment, winter or summer, and he walked with bare feet so quickly that it was difficult for me to keep up with him. Guided and taught by Babaji, he had awakened the kundalini energy, which had reached the *ajna* chakra in his forehead.[1] The yoga exercises he showed me revealed his high level of attainment, and I learned a great deal from him. At the request of Babaji, he taught me some exercises of *shabd* yoga, the yoga of the word, and I was able to note their effectiveness.

Hanuman Baba often took me to visit his garden, where he grew all sorts of plants, but especially medicinal herbs. He had other plants that he told me had the most extraordinary properties: one of them would enable you to live for weeks on end without food, another to be impervious to cold for days on end in the snowy Himalayas. I did not test these plants myself, but it is possible; I believe in the power of herbs. One day he showed me how to make a paste from the root of one plant and the red leaves of another. He ground them together by rubbing them on a stone, and then that mixture would be put on the forehead, between the two eyebrows, to awaken the third eye. I noted the name of these plants, which I could give you, but it would be difficult for you to find them. Hanuman Baba told me that many yogis and *sadhus* passed through Nainital and that they had given him much of his knowledge about plants and drugs, which he had used to develop his psychic powers.

Before this trip to India I had, of course, read a great deal about the practices of yogis. It is clear that the main aim of these practices is to make the physical body come under the control of the mind. Nothing must resist it. And Hanuman Baba confirmed this to me, saying that for yogis everything or practically everything was possible. For example, there is a practice that they call *thoumo*. Through concentration and breathing exercises over a long period, yogis can awaken the *muladhara* chakra[2] at the base of the spinal column. When they awaken this chakra it is as if a fire is lit in their body. Then, little by little, the fire rises up the spinal column through the *sushumna* channel, setting alight the other chakras, and the whole body is set ablaze. This allows the bodies of certain yogis to give off such heat that, when they have been plunged into the icy water of a lake and then wrapped in wet linen, they are capable of drying the linen with their body heat. How many years does it take to be successful in this exercise? I think there are better ways to spend one's time than doing this kind of thing.

Other yogis practise eating the raw intestines of animals or even their excrement. Still others, after having eliminated urine or semen from their bodies, are able to reabsorb these liquids back through the same orifice.

Basically, these yogis, or *siddhas,* believe nothing is impure, and it seems to me, on reflection, that all Indians are influenced to a greater or lesser extent by this philosophy. That is why they have completely different ideas from Europeans about filth. I often thought this as I watched them accept, without disgust, situations that I found truly revolting. In many towns (Rishikesh, Benares, Patna, and so on) I would walk along the banks of the river Ganges. The Ganges is a sacred river, certainly, but I could never bathe amongst all the excrement and bodies of dead animals that could be seen floating in it. When I went to visit the caves at Elephanta, an island not far from Bombay, at the entrance to one of the caves I saw pilgrims take a bowl of stagnant, greenish water with great reverence and then drink it. I had to control myself not to call out, 'Don't drink that!' They believe that these caves are holy places and therefore pure. I have no objection to that, but the water itself is polluted, and microbes do not respect holy places. There is so much to say on the subject of what is pure and what is impure![3]

One day, Babaji sent me a message. He asked me to meet him at a place that I would reach after a long bus journey.

Meanwhile, he himself had to go farther, and so he got a message to me at a bus stop. The buses in India are in such a dilapidated state that when I got off the bus I tore my trousers. Fortunately for me, I found a tailor in the village who could do the repairs, while I waited in a little hovel. It was there that, when the repairs were done, the tailor told me where I should meet Babaji and that he would drive me there by car himself. Just hearing the name of Babaji would make everyone do all they possibly could to help. On yet another day, when someone was driving me to him, we had to stop to fill up with petrol, and they refused to accept our payment.

The meeting place Babaji had arranged for me was at the home of a banker. When I arrived, there was a whole group of young people singing and laughing. I was placed beside Babaji for the meal, and afterwards the two of us spoke together for a long time. We then took off in the car, once again with me at his side. There was something so subtle, so delicious that emanated from his being that, at one moment, I placed my hand on his knee. He then began to sing in some unknown language. Yes, Babaji sang, and we exchanged looks filled with light and love.

But I do not think it is all that important to speak to you about these meetings with Babaji, because I do not want you to expect extraordinary actions or manifestations on my part. Only by our own efforts are we able to attain knowledge and powers. We should not glory in the knowledge and powers of a Master. His knowledge and powers are his and his alone; it is he who benefits from them and uses them. What do I gain by basing my prestige on the value of another, whether it be my Master, Peter Deunov, or Babaji? What counts is what I am, what I know and what I can do…

I have been told that some people question whether I have met the great Babaji. It is true that there are many Babajis, because the word means 'little father'. They think that I have only met some yogi with this name. And even if that were true, what difference does it make? I am who I am, and the person I met was of exceptional greatness. Let's not look for the reasons why it was that he came to see me, whereas others have looked in vain to meet him over dozens of years. Some people wept as they told me of all their years of searching. At any rate, whenever I said his name, those who knew him had no end of marvellous stories to tell me about him.

I remember, in particular, two men, one a professor in New Delhi whom I had asked to explain the Sanskrit alphabet and the other a man who had a great temple on his land (where Gandhi died after being stabbed by a fanatical Hindu). Both these men were inexhaustible on the subject of Babaji. It even happened that people who had made a vow of silence took me in and broke their vow just to speak to me of him. In Kashmir, when the minister I was staying with understood that I had seen Babaji, he flung himself upon me to embrace me. Everywhere I was offered places to stay. I realized that, in India, the mere name of Babaji was a key to open all doors, and if I had the chance to meet so many people it was because the word had spread that a French *sadhu,* who was travelling through India, had had several conversations with Babaji.

But I had not gone to India to be invited and entertained everywhere. What I had appreciated above all with Babaji was to feel that here was a being in whom love dwelled. This was such a different experience from the many other Masters and yogis I met, most of whom were basically working on gaining power. They ruled over their disciples as if they were gods dealing with slaves; they did not even look at those who approached them and fell at their feet. It is the custom in India to prostrate yourself before your Master, but even so...

In Benares I was told to go and see a yogi who apparently had great powers. I found him surrounded by disciples. His face was beautifully proportioned, but I was struck by the pride and coldness he showed to those who approached him. We started to talk, but the minute I opened my mouth he began to contradict me. After a moment I said to him, 'I did not come to see you because of your knowledge or your powers. I am looking for people who, having knowledge and power, do not use it to dominate others but are capable of showing love, goodness and gentleness.' He was furious and said to me, 'If you had any idea who I am, you, too, would prostrate yourself before me.' I laughed as I answered, 'And if you knew who I am, maybe it would be you who would prostrate yourself before me. I am willing to believe that you are powerful, but those who have true power do not flaunt it; they let others divine it for themselves.' And I left him.

I had to see him the next day because, before he had become vexed with me, he had suggested that I should come to meet his own Master. When I got back to the hotel, I thought that he would never forgive me for having humiliated him before his disciples. So, during the night, I concentrated and with my thoughts tried to make him understand and accept certain truths that he really needed to know. I had no idea what the result would be. The next morning I was totally surprised because when we met he welcomed me warmly, apologizing for his attitude the day before, and we were able, at last, to have a good conversation.

Then, he took me to his Master, who was a lovable old man of great gentleness! I wondered why this disciple had not tried harder to be like him. What had he learned from him? But it is true that disciples do not always resemble their Masters... He was a pure, liberated being, freed from all human greed; one felt that his only reason for being on earth was to help others, and it was even said that his body was transparent. I sat in front of him, and for a long time we just looked at each other in silence. I would have liked to hold him in my arms. He was wearing a garland of flowers around his neck, which he took off and placed on me, and I took great care of this necklace. As he could not speak English, he asked one of his disciples to translate what he wanted to tell me. He then spoke some magnificent, prophetic words which I cannot repeat as I do not even want the spirits to hear them. These words must remain hidden and secret until the moment when they come true.

In Calcutta I visited the ashram of Ananda Mayi Ma. She was a truly remarkable woman and one could feel the presence of the Holy Spirit in her. She was not well educated, but pundits, politicians, would come to see her, and she always gave them good advice. She welcomed me with such love, and what a look we exchanged! But there too, there was so much noise!

At some distance from Bombay, at Ganeshpuri, I visited the ashram of Nityananda Maharaj, who I had been told was a renowned clairvoyant. I arrived there, in the midst of a great crowd. Nityananda was seated, scantily clad, and I sat down in front of him. He closed his eyes and, after a long while, he looked at me as if he had come back from a very great distance and said in English, 'A pure heart; peace is in his soul, and all powers are given to him.' I must say that I had some doubts about that statement. All powers? But I understood the way in which he meant it. Then he spoke a name which I no longer remember now, the name of a sage who had lived in India in the distant past; according to him I was the reincarnation of that man.

Later, when I returned to Nainital in the mountains to rejoin Hanuman Baba, I asked him about the person whose name Nityananda had spoken. He went to find a very large book and showed me a picture in it. It was of a man sitting in the lotus position, who had hovering above him a cobra with seven heads. These seven heads indicated that he possessed all powers. When we parted from each other, Hanuman Baba gave me a rosary of one hundred and eight shells, because one hundred and eight is Babaji's number. It was a royal present.

When speaking about me, Nityananda had said, 'Peace is in his soul', and that is what matters most to me. Peace and harmony are all I seek, and not only in me and for me, but so that I can bring them to others. It takes a lot of self-study and self-analysis to understand how difficult it is to achieve this peace, this harmony, throughout one's being, right down to the smallest cell.

One day, in fact, I was in Bombay, and I had meditated for a long time with some great *sadhus* I had met. Afterwards, when I put my hands on some objects, I felt how very stiff they were. Why? This made me think. So I worked on loosening them, thinking as I did so that in future I must look after them more carefully. You may wonder, 'Is that really so important?' Yes, it is, because the energies that are emitted from your fingers will be different, depending on whether your hands are tense, fidgety or relaxed, and the effects they produce will also be different. We always leave a subtle fluidic mark on everything we touch, and on the people we contact, whether near or far.

When I greet you, for example, I always try to put something good not only into how I look at you, but also into my hand, so that I can give you some particles of my life and my love.[4] It is much easier to control the look in my eyes than it is my hands, but my desire is to bring you nothing but blessings with my hands. We can relax our hands without necessarily having to keep them still. If you see me sometimes stroking an object, or a fruit, very gently, know that I am doing an exercise; I am relaxing my hands. And you too should try to practise it.

When I was on my way back to Nainital to see Hanuman Baba again, I visited the ashram of Sivananda at Rishikesh. He welcomed me most warmly. That is why during our conversation I felt able to say to him, 'All day long the loudspeaker is blaring and there is not a moment of silence here. Why don't you use your authority to encourage your disciples to be quiet for some portions of the day, and also encourage them to wash themselves and not leave filth everywhere? Their behaviour is repulsive; they throw rubbish around and spit no matter where...' I thought he would be angry at this but, as he was not, I continued, 'At your gatherings, you ask the disciples to come up onto the stage to sing or recite a poem, and at that very moment you begin to speak to other people. Why? Some of the listeners will focus their attention on you rather than on the poem or the song, and the others will not listen to you at all. I would never allow such behaviour among my disciples.'

He listened to what I said and, since he did not show the slightest irritation, I added that although I knew it was an age-old tradition, it was still shocking to me to see disciples prostrating themselves before their Master as if before the statue of some impassive divinity. I stayed only a short time at Rishikesh, and I do not know what happened after my departure.

The truth is that I also met this behaviour in ashrams for Westerners, and it makes me question what they were doing there. When they go back home, they will boast about having gone to India and give the impression that they are great spiritual beings and much more, that is, of course, if they haven't completely lost their minds. I remember a rich American woman, who was most likeable, and she told me that her need for a spiritual life had drawn her to India. She had asked me to come to her home so that I could explain to her the difference between the teaching of Buddha and that of Jesus. It is true that in this country, because of the dirt, there are many flies, but how on earth could one explain the difference between the teaching of Buddha and that of Jesus to someone who never sat still and walked up and down the room, brandishing a flyswatter to kill the flies? I put up with it once or twice, but after that I found reasons not to accept her invitations.

Although I had stopped making predictions, in my adolescence, by reading people's palms, I never stopped being interested in palmistry, because the hand is a resumé, not just of the person, but of the universe. Many palmists say that our hands hold the science of all sciences, and they base this belief on a verse in the book of *Job: 'I will put a sign on everyone's hand, that all whom he has made may know his* *work.*' When I was in the big cities of India, I would go to the book shops and libraries, and in Calcutta I came across a book called *Samudrika Shastra,** which gave me information on various points that have been completely abandoned by Western palm readers. There are so many details and subtleties that have been lost. For example, there is much to be learned just from studying the thumb!

Nothing in the hand is there by chance. How should the fact that fingerprints are absolutely unique to each person be interpreted? A hand is a book to be read; every detail is significant: from the length of fingers to their direction in relation to the palm… The lines that cross the palm can be deep or superficial, thick or thin, straight or curved, broken or continuous, and everything must be carefully noted. There are also points, chains, crosses, cuts, squares, arcs and embossments, which all have their various meanings. In the book I read, it said that Buddha's hand and the hands of other great sages carry symbols such as crescents, temples, swastikas, lotuses and the tree of life… I used this book as an aid in studying my own hands. Some time later, in the town of Ootacamund,** I met an astrologer who was also a palm reader, and I was sorry not to have been able to extend my stay in order to talk with him. I think he was someone who would have been able to discover many things by his study of hands.

I spent a certain amount of time in Calcutta, and there I found a book on Jesus, one I had seen before when I was in a monastery in Ladakh. In order to read it, I had to go each day

* the name for palmistry in India.
** in the state of Tamil Nadu in the south of India; can be found on maps with its abbreviated name Ooty or by its Tamil name Udhagamandalam.

to the monastery because the monks would not allow anyone to take it off the premises. I read the book in an
English translation. It states that a very young man, called
Issa, had come to India with an entourage of people from
Palestine. For several years he had followed the Brahmin
teaching but had ended up in conflict with it, as he took
exception to the Brahmins' attitude to the caste system, to
their rigidity and their lack of love, the result being that
the Brahmins became furious and persecuted him. A few
years later, he went back to Palestine, and the story from
then on was identical to the one we know from the Gospels
about Jesus, right up to his crucifixion. But it did not stop
there: it said that Issa, who had survived the torture of the
cross, came back to India accompanied by his mother and
the apostle Thomas and lived in Kashmir until he died at
a great age.

One day, researchers will reveal to the world how things
actually unfolded and tell us the truth about Jesus' life. I
leave this field to them, as history is not my calling, and I
have other subjects which interest me a great deal more. Let
the specialists dedicate their time to researching manuscripts
and archaeological sites! As for me, I concentrate on
principles, and what I say comes from what I know of true
Initiatic Science. I leave it to others to find confirmation in
the historical accounts of witnesses.

When I went to southern India, I went to Madras
where I visited the Theosophical Society, set in magnificent
grounds with parks reaching right down to the sea. I went
to Pondichery to the ashram of Sri Aurobindo, whom I
would love to have known, for he was a remarkable man,
but he had died a few years before. As everyone knows, a

Frenchwoman succeeded him. She is called Mother. Each morning, before sunrise, she would come out onto her balcony before a crowd of people, who contemplated her reverently. She would greet them with a gesture and then go back inside.

One day there was a festival. On this occasion she sat in a room and, one by one, those who wanted to passed in front of her. She gave a handkerchief to each one of them. I was among the crowd and, when I found myself in front of her, as she handed me the handkerchief I looked deeply into her eyes with much love. As she spoke French, I wanted at least to say to her that I was happy to meet her and to come to her ashram. But, at that moment, I do not know what happened, but she started to shake, and I saw a kind of fear in her eyes as her limbs, and even her jaw, began to tremble. When I saw that, I too was afraid. She was looking so alarmed that I wondered if she was going to faint. What a scandal that would have been! Those close to her would have thought that I had not respected this woman whom they all saw as a divinity. That was why I took the handkerchief without a word and quickly left the room. Why did she begin to tremble when I looked at her? From that moment on, I felt that I was no longer a welcome guest.

Further south, at Tiruvannamalai, I went to the ashram of Ramana Maharshi, about whom Paul Brunton had written in his book, *Secret India,* that such a light emanated from him, such love, such joy, that the colour of his skin was like gold. Unfortunately, Ramana Maharshi had also died by the time I visited his ashram, but his disciples were still there. They were truly like their Master, full of love, full of light, full of smiles, and they welcomed me royally! They kept their Master's room as a sacred place where no one was allowed to enter, but they did allow me in to meditate for as long as I wished, and I was able to communicate with his soul. What unforgettable memories I have to this day of that ashram! Years later, I met Paul Brunton, who came to see me at the Bonfin, and it was such a pleasure to talk with him.

For some while after that, I lived in the Nilgiri mountains and, in particular, at Ootacamund. Not far from the town was a great forest of eucalyptus trees, and I would often go for a walk there. These trees were immense, with huge trunks and thick foliage, and the atmosphere was so imbued with their scent that, after a short while, it was almost overwhelming.

Not far from where I was staying, there was a rajah's palace; he was not there at the time as he spent most of his time at Hyderabad. I spoke several times with the palace caretakers, and they allowed me to visit it. I was astounded by the luxury everywhere. The furniture had all come from England, and the most precious materials were used for the living rooms, bedrooms and bathrooms. I have never seen crystal chandeliers of such beauty. The gardens were also magnificent, and from there you could look out on the jungle.

Years previously, I had read Helena Blavatsky's book *The People of the Blue Mountains.* These blue mountains are the mountains of Nilgiri (*nil,* 'blue' and *giri,* 'mountains'), which she made famous in her account of how two Englishmen one day discovered a quite extraordinary population living there. These inhabitants, though small in number, are made up of two tribes, the Todds and the Mouloukouroumbs. There is an enormous difference between them, the Todds being tall, beautiful and very benevolent, while the Mouloukouroumbs are short, ugly and endowed with uncanny, harmful powers, being able to kill just by darting poisonous glances at an individual. Only the Todds can command the respect of the Mouloukouroumbs, who fear them and withdraw from them. But there is no need for me to go into the details as you can read the book yourself.

I went, along with an interpreter, to the Todds' territory. The first thing I saw was a man stretched out on the ground with his back exposed to the sun. My guide told me that this was a priest. He got up and kept a certain distance from me. I came closer with my interpreter so that we could speak together, but he drew further back. He was undoubtedly fearful that I would touch him, which is against their rules (a priest must not be touched), but that was not my intention.

I was very happy to see these people, who still possess a certain mystery. Both men and women behaved with great reserve. They did not push strangers away, but you could feel that they did not appreciate being regarded as some sort of curiosity. Thanks to my interpreter I was able to talk with some of them. I saw their homes, their temple (which was shaped like a beehive) and also their buffaloes, which had fascinated those who visited them.

You cannot say that the Todds have a religion, in the sense that we use the word, but they worship their buffaloes, which they view as their teachers, because they say that their Masters, the *rishis,* manifest through these animals. When they need to make a really important decision, they perform secret ceremonies during which they question their buffaloes. To Westerners, who are ignorant of certain aspects of the animal kingdom, such behaviour seems quite mad. They do not know that souls travel and can take possession of an animal's body. Obviously, an animal has an animal soul in its body, but the body is like a building, a home in which different souls can co-exist, for a short while at least. So an animal can be inhabited by a human soul or even by a higher being. This explains why, in some religions, animals are raised to the level of gods and are worshipped.

Instead of criticizing or ridiculing such practices, it would be better to study them and to admit that the animal kingdom is a mysterious realm, certain aspects of which we might not understand. The Todds believe, therefore, that through the mediation of their buffaloes, they are taught by the souls of a higher evolution. They also worship the sun, and when asked where they go after their death they answer, 'Our bodies go into the ground and are transformed into grass to feed the buffaloes. Our souls go to the sun, where they enlighten and warm all beings.'

I would have liked to go into the land of the Moulou-kouroumbs, except that I could not go into the jungle without a guide, as I would have got lost. No matter how much money I offered, I could not find one person willing to go with me. They all said, 'No, no, Sahib, these are dangerous beings; we are afraid of them, and they have even killed some of us,' so that was confirmation for me of what Madame Blavatsky had written.

I have a particularly lovely, poetic memory from my time in Ootacamund. One day, on the street, the sight of a little girl of six or seven caught my attention. She was dirty, clad in rags and sitting beside her mother, who was just as dirty and badly dressed as she was. The two of them were sitting eating something; I do not know what it was, but it did not look particularly clean either. The little girl

had a pretty, slim face, but what was most striking were
her hands, so I stopped to look at her: the way she took
the food with her fingers and raised it to her mouth was so
very expressive, refined and delicate! Where had this child
picked up such an awareness of gestures? I was completely
captivated by her, as I had never seen anyone eat like this.
She had a little wooden spoon, and when she took some
food from the plate, her gestures were so gracious! One
would have said she was a princess, but there may be no
princess in the world able to eat with such grace. How I
wish that I could put as much harmony and poetry into my
gestures when I am eating!

To tell the truth, I was often struck by the elegance of
Indians' hands. Many men and women who were not particularly good-looking and whose features were quite coarse
still had elegant hands with slender fingers, indicating
something spiritual about them. I even saw it amongst
beggars who made very delicate movements with their
fingers. But this little girl whom I saw in Ootacamund was
truly exceptional, and quite often I find myself thinking of
her again.

I had plenty of opportunities to observe children in India,
as so many of them were living on the streets. It was not
known if they had parents or, indeed, any adults to take care
of them. As most of them did not speak English, I could not
question them. But one day I had a long conversation with
a young man. It was near Benares, the town where Buddha
had begun his teaching.* There were temple ruins where
archaeologists had done some digs. The site was accessible
to tourists, and a young boy of about twelve was to conduct

* Sarnath.

the tour. Of course, he had been told what to say, but he did it in such an intelligent way, and with such impeccable English, that I was most impressed; the historical events, the names, the dates, he gave them all in such a natural way as if he had always known them. I asked him some questions about himself and his family. He also belonged to a very poor family, who lived far away. What would become of him later?

I often think of these two children, but I met many others. And I would ask myself how many of these children, who were so good-looking and seemed so talented, would be able to rise above this poverty, misery and filth. Most of them were lively, happy, smiling, but what kind of life awaited them?

One thing, amongst many others, of course, which particularly struck me during that year I spent in India was the presence of little altars in people's homes. Rich or poor, Hindus keep a place in their homes for a few pictures, a few statuettes of gods. Some do not even have a home, as they live outside beside the road, on the pavements, but they will make an altar there, with cardboard boxes or wooden crates and a few pictures, before which, at various times during the day, they prostrate themselves and pray. How often, in the West, do our homes have a place dedicated to God?[5] And, contrary to what is happening in Christian churches, which are frequented less and less, Hindu temples are never empty.

In most of the temples I went to, I would see the symbol of Shiva represented, the *lingam,* an upright shaft on a horizontal support. Hindus prostrate themselves and meditate devoutly before it, and the women often come to place flowers on it. Sometimes I asked them about this symbol, and I realized that most of them had only the most superficial understanding of it. They went no further than seeing the upright shaft as a representation of the phallus, the organ of procreation, the masculine principle. I said to them, 'No, you haven't described it all; underneath that upright shaft there is a horizontal base, which represents the feminine principle. The masculine principle is spirit, which works on the feminine principle of matter. All creation is the result of this work of spirit on matter. In this symbol your rishis have united the two principles to show you that creation can happen only when both principles are there, not separate but united.'

This union of masculine and feminine is very clearly depicted on the outer walls of some temples, for example, at Khajuraho, where centuries ago suggestive erotic scenes were sculpted. There, it is men and women who physically unite, whereas the symbol of the *lingam* represents a process of the spiritual life. It is within ourselves that these two principles must be united; until then, we are incomplete. If initiates are complete beings, it is because they have realized within themselves that union of masculine and feminine, and so they have no need to look outside themselves for their complementary principle. That is why they are liberated beings, free and creative.

Years after this trip to India, friends invited me to Greece. They suggested I should go to see Mount Athos, and so I went there, but only with brothers, for that is something else again! Over the centuries, many monasteries were built on the mountain, and the Orthodox monks who lived there had so thoroughly rejected anything and everything that could remind them of the female principle that not only could no woman set foot on the land, but they had even banned all female animals; they were not even allowed to own a she-goat. What kind of spiritual life can they possibly have when they hold such shrivelled concepts? Of course, they have some wonderful works of art in these monasteries – frescoes and pictures –, but the main impression that I took away from my visit was one of great boredom and sadness. When we decide to exclude from our field of consciousness one of the two principles of creation, what life remains?[6]

We can live a life that is pure and chaste, without having to exclude women and female animals. How can we not see that all of nature speaks to us of these two principles, the masculine and the feminine, which join together in the work of creation? There are even plants whose shape is the symbol of the *lingam*. At Sri Aurobindo's ashram in Pondichery, there were flowers which were the exact representation of it, and I saw cobras putting their heads into them. I was amazed at the intelligence and workings of nature.

Clearly, these Hindus I met in the temples were a little surprised to have someone from the West come to give them explanations about the symbols that were part of their age-old traditions, but they listened to me most attentively. I also spoke about the kundalini energy and chakras. These words were very familiar to them as part of their spiritual heritage, but once again I saw that they did not know very much about them. So I said, 'You paint a red spot between your eyes on the *ajna* chakra, which is the centre of clairvoyance and spiritual sight. But if you concentrate on it, you must also concentrate on the *sahasrara* chakra, which is at the top of the head. Since the *ajna* chakra, the centre for spiritual vision, is receptive and feminine, you need to

245

work too with the *sahasrara* chakra, which is emissive and masculine. By uniting these two principles, you become a living *lingam*.' Yes, indeed, there are so many things to know and to understand! It is not enough to bow down or to lay flowers before the symbol of Shiva in temples, or to paint a red dot between your eyes.

I have given you more knowledge on so many topics than most Hindus possess! That is why, if you want to develop the two principles in yourself, if you want to awaken the chakras, you do not have to go to India. All the exercises we do in the Brotherhood have exactly the same goal, and they present no dangers for you. In contrast, the techniques taught by yogis, and which certain Westerners believe they can do without any preparation, can often lead them into dead ends, with all sorts of psychic and physical troubles to follow.

Wherever I went in India, the presence of the *lingam* met my eyes, reminding me of the reality of these two principles that I have worked with over so many years. The symbolism of the *lingam* is identical to that of the Hebrew letter *shin* ש. When I was in Kashmir, meditating with the peaks of the Himalayas before me, I had more revelations about this symbol. Perhaps these revelations had been predicted in advance. At the Bonfin, before I left for India, on the feast day of St Michael, while I was giving a lecture after the meal, someone took a photo. When I was shown this photo it was astonishing for me to see the letter, *shin,* shining above my right shoulder. Was it just an effect of the light? I understood so many things about the two principles when I was meditating before those Himalayan peaks! From then, I have never stopped talking about them, so that you, too, can take part in my discoveries, and so that I can share with you my wonder at the splendours of nature that lay before me. One day all this will be revealed to you.

Near Srinagar, in Kashmir, there is a lake* formed by a river. Chalets as well as boats for trips on the lake are available for tourists. When I went there I had no intention of tarrying but just wanted to go a little further to the peaks, which are covered in magnificent forests. However, when I saw the lake, I stopped in my tracks: in places, it was covered with lotuses of all colours and impressive size; as for their leaves, they were so wide that you could have tucked a baby up in them. I had never seen such a sight as these huge flowers of such subtle variation of colour floating on the water; it was truly magical, and I stayed contemplating them for a long time. Lotuses, which begin life at the bottom of a lake or pool, come into flower on the surface of the water, and the purity of their petals, their luminous colour and their perfume have nothing in common with the mud of their origin. It was then that I sensed why, in the East, this flower is a symbol of spiritual growth; it can be interpreted as the passage through the lower levels to the higher levels of consciousness.

In Kashmir I also went to Pahlgam and as far as Gulmarg. One day, after I had done some concentration exercises, I went out for a walk in the mountains. And there, what was extraordinary was that I was able to go great distances at that altitude without feeling tired. I felt as if I were flying; my feet hardly touched the ground, and my body felt weightless. I was astonished to be able to walk and climb so quickly and with such lightness! It was the first time that such a thing had happened to me. It was as if I were levitating.

* Lake Dal.

Alexandra David-Neel, who lived in Tibet, writes in her books of similar happenings with Tibetan lamas, who could cover enormous distances and even move over and above rivers and lakes. She herself said that she had once had such an experience. I was lucky enough to meet Alexandra David-Neel in Lyon. She really was a quite extraordinary woman!

What I experienced that day in the mountains was very interesting, but it happened without my wishing it, and I never did anything to relive that experience. It would take too much of my time and energy, which I would rather dedicate to more useful work for the benefit of the whole world. Levitation is a natural phenomenon that occurs when there is a change in vibrations, a reversal of polarities. It is a state that some mystics can experience quite independently of their willpower, but it can also occur as the result of exercises and concentration, and that is really of no great interest. I am not interested in the displays of fakirs and yogis. Cosmic Intelligence has given human beings this extraordinary power of thought, and it should not be used to show off to the general public.

It was at Gulmarg that I contemplated Nanga Parbat each day. I would dearly have loved to go to the summit of that mountain and many others in the Himalayas! But I was not equipped to do so, and I never went above five thousand metres, as to go higher would have been dangerous. But, in thought, I was able to project myself to all those peaks, and I would stay there for hours on end, in the untouched snow, in communion with the great spirits who live there.[7]

Before leaving the region, I wanted to go to where the Hunzas lived and meet them. You have, perhaps, heard of the Hunzas. They became instantly famous when it was discovered that their exceptional longevity came from a diet that was based on apricots. I had been given a small book about these people, who live in a valley in Kashmir.* Before I had even begun reading it, I just looked at the photographs and was truly struck by the resemblance between these men and women and the people of Macedonia. And then, when I read the preface, I found that they were the descendants of soldiers of Alexander the Great, who had led his army as far as the Indus; some of the soldiers had deserted the army and settled in this valley. In this book about the Hunzas, I was greatly surprised to recognize certain costumes and traditions that I knew from my childhood in Macedonia. During my visit to India, I had hoped that I would be able to visit them, but it was too far, right up in the north of Kashmir where the roads were very bad, and conditions did not allow me to do so. Now, I regret it.

I am sad, too, that I was not able to go to Mount Kailash, because the Chinese had just forbidden access to Tibet. But people who had been able to go there before gave me herbs and relics from this mountain, which is regarded as even more holy than Everest, which I had contemplated from Darjeeling.

Darjeeling… When I arrived there, I was surprised and delighted by how the women were always smiling. More than any other town in India, the women here, whether young or old, had joyful faces, even though they were overburdened with work. These were the people who carried luggage along the train platforms. It really made me feel most uncomfortable to allow them to carry my suitcases, which were very heavy, but they insisted, and so I gave them

*In the north of Pakistan. Nowadays this region, called Jammu-Kashmir, is split between India and Pakistan, and the Hunza territory capital, Baltit, is controlled by Pakistan.

double the money they asked for the job, to their great amazement.

Darjeeling is renowned for its tea. Until I went there, like most Bulgarians, I drank only coffee, but during this trip I grew to appreciate tea, as the custom had been widely spread through the British influence. People who wanted to meet me would say, 'Do come one day and take tea with us!' and I would accept their invitation. I have a lovely memory of one woman who, after she had served me, went into the garden to pick a flower from the lemon tree, which she placed most delicately in my cup. But, of course, even this memory of lemon-scented tea is dwarfed by my memory of the view from Darjeeling of Everest, Gaurisankar and Kangchenjunga…

A one-year trip is clearly not long enough to see all that India has to offer: the great diversity and richness not only of its many people but also of nature and the monuments. I went to the caves of Ajanta, famous for their paintings and sculpture. I also went to Ellora and the sanctuaries carved out of the rock. At Mysore I walked in the magnificent zoological gardens. I cannot list them all.

But I would like to mention Agra, where I was, of course, overwhelmed by the beauty of the Taj Mahal. There, you understand how the proportions of certain monuments, the purity of their lines, the materials used in their construction, can become food for the soul. By looking at certain works of art, you can feel something within beginning to resonate with them, making their beauty and harmony your own. This can be the beginning of a whole inner work. There are so many monuments that can give us the taste and the impetus for this work! There are even some that were conceived with precisely this goal in mind by initiates, who infused them with their radiance and energy. All those who contemplate these works of art feel this beauty as food for the spiritual life.

But, surrounded by all these wonders and splendours, I continued to suffer seeing millions of people living in poverty and filth. And also, amongst all the so-called yogis and *sadhus* I met, I was most disappointed to see that very few had any real spiritual qualities. Many of them confuse inaction, laziness and spirituality. And even those who frequented the ashrams, what exactly were they looking for? I was aware that I needed to be very careful around some of them. As it is the custom to take off your shoes, I, too, took off mine, and one day I could not find them again. It was not a serious problem, and I thought of it as a sort of tithe that needed to be paid. Maybe my shoes had pleased someone, because they were different from the general run of shoes. I walked barefoot for a long time until those who were with me were so disturbed by the situation that they found me some sandals. And that was not the only time I had something stolen in an ashram.

I also became a little impatient when I saw the listlessness of Indians, their fatalistic acceptance of things, and I found it very hard to bear their complete disregard for punctuality, as if, for them, time did not exist. But I have to recognize that, for the most part, those I met showed me much respect and kindness: they were always ready to help me; it was just that I had to be a little patient. Some of them even asked if I would accept them as disciples. Yes, educated people, doctors and lawyers, wanted to become my disciples. My reply was, 'No, you have plenty of yogis and wise men here. I am not the one you should take as your Master.' They would insist, 'But with you, it is different; please accept us.' 'No, I cannot do that.' Sometimes I had to be very firm with them.

And how many magnificent people I met on the roads! Unknown ascetics clad in rags would walk along the roads far from all public notice and human affairs. Some of them were so very old that it was impossible to guess their age! Sometimes they would stop in front of me and look at me saying, 'O, you are Mahatma.' Taken aback, I would reply, 'No, I am not', and they would continue on their way. I met others sitting by the side of the road, all covered in dust. I sat beside them and I spoke with them. Even though they did not always understand English and I did not know their language, I felt that they gave me treasures from their souls.

You wonder perhaps why I did not stay longer in India when I had been so welcomed there. Quite simply, my work was not there. In a sense, it would even have been too easy. Yes, too easy... My work is here with you. That is why you should not expect any staggering revelations from me, and you should not be surprised that I return to the same topics over and over again. I will continue to stress the essential truths, as I have always done, until you make up your minds to go into them more deeply. If you do not understand my pedagogical techniques, that's too bad for me. Did you notice that I did not say that's too bad for you?

I spent a truly unusual year in India, during which I lived in unique circumstances, did unique work, had unique experiences, met unique people and learned unique things. I thank the divine Mother and all those who guided and helped me during this time. I drank water from springs and

I breathed the pure air of mountains! But I had to adapt to other customs, to speak a different language, and I never thought that, when I got back, I would have so much difficulty re-adapting to life here. When I was there I was constantly in touch with you in my thoughts, and I sent you messages. But I lost the rhythm of life here and also the desire to talk. It will take me a little while to adapt to life here once again.

On my return I learned of the catastrophe that hit Fréjus when the dam at Malpasset* broke, and so I made a brief trip to the Bonfin. I wanted to go to the places where it all happened: they were still pervaded by so much suffering and terror. So many men, women and children had perished hideously there. When I came back I was ill, not just because I had seen the scene of such desolation, but because I had felt all those souls who were still wandering around the ruins of their homes and looking for someone to help them. Who was aware of their distress? These souls hurled themselves at me, and I exhausted all my energies to help them. I succeeded, I assisted them, I calmed them, and before long I was myself again.

Now I am going to leave you for a few days, but before I go I am going to give you a talisman that will keep you inspired and supported in your work. This talisman is a name I was given, and the one who gave it to me was greater than Babaji. This new name is Omraam, and from now on my name is Omraam Mikhaël. *Om* is a sound which disintegrates all that is harmful and shadowy (it corresponds

* The dam on the River Reyran, above Fréjus, in the Var broke during the night of 2 December 1959, causing the death of more than 400 people.

to the word *solve* in the alchemical tradition), as it sends everything back to the source by transforming it into light. *Raam,* on the other hand, has the power through its vibrations to condense, to materialize, all that is subtle, and it corresponds to the *coagula* of the alchemists. So, in my name, the two alchemical processes are found united: *solve* and *coagula.*

These two syllables of my new name act on the two highest chakras, the *ajna* and the *sahasrara.* By pronouncing them, you can disintegrate all that limits and burdens you, and you can materialize all that you long for that is good and luminous. It is a magical word, and you should say it whenever you need to. Never use it in service of your own selfish interests or to harm someone, because not only will you receive nothing, but you run the risk of being severely called to order. Names act mysteriously on people, and the use of names is a branch of science very close to that of numbers, for name and number represent the same reality.

This gift I have given you today is intangible, but you will be able to feel it. Until now, when you needed enlightenment and support, you called on me, but I have my limits. From now on, by saying my name, you will be calling on another 'me', who is rich, strong and inexhaustible. Heaven, in its desire to help me, has given me this name, Omraam, and you and I will both be helped. It is up to you to learn how to use this name.

Notes

1. and 2. See *Man's Subtle Bodies and Centres – the aura, the solar plexus, the hara centre, the chakras,* Izvor Coll. n° 219 and chap. 5: 'Kundalini force', chap. 6: 'The chakras: The chakra system I, The chakra system II, Ajna and sahasrara'.

3. See *The Mysteries of Yesod,* Foundations of the Spiritual Life, Complete Works, vol. 7, part II: 'Purity'.
4. See *The Book of Divine Magic,* Izvor Coll. n° 226, chap. 12: 'The hand' and chap. 13: 'The power of a glance'.
5. See *Marchez tant que vous avez la lumière,* Izvor Coll. n° 244, chap. 12: 'Au service du Principe divin' and chap. 13: 'Monter à l'autel du Seigneur'.
6. See *Hope for the World: Spiritual Galvanoplasty,* Izvor Coll. n° 214, chap. 2: 'Reflections of the two principles' and *Cosmic Balance –The Secret of Polarity,* Izvor Coll. n° 237, chap. 15: 'Union of the ego with the physical body', chap. 17: 'The androgynes of myth' and chap. 18: 'Union with the universal Soul and the cosmic Spirit'.
7. See *The Path of Silence,* Izvor Coll. n° 229, chap. 6: 'The inhabitants of silence' and *The Mysteries of Fire and Water,* Izvor Coll. n° 232, chap. 7: 'Water is born of mountains'.

12

I am a child of the sun

'Why do you conceal your identity? Why won't you tell us who you really are?' One day someone asked me these questions, and I answered, 'And what would you like to know?' 'We want to know if you really are an initiate.' 'Aha, I see what you are after. But, if I answered you, how would you be able to test if what I told you was, in fact, true? If I told you that I was an initiate, what difference would that make? Would the title of initiate add extra value to who and what I am? Would it make my work more worthwhile? It is not up to me to say what I am when I appear in public, and I am not even interested in knowing. Do you want some sort of label that would give you information? Would you like to see "I am an initiate" (or some such thing) written on my forehead, so that then you would be able to sleep more peacefully? But I have nothing to say to you on this topic.' I have no idea whether my questioner understood what I was saying.

One day, two madmen met by chance on a train. They introduced themselves. One of them said, 'I am the Christ,' and the other one said, 'I see. Well, if you are the Christ,

I am the Antichrist!' You see, you can boast of being the Christ, and you can boast of being the Antichrist... You could also boast of being an initiate, but what good would that do? So you see, I will not do it. Do you think, perhaps, that would give me more credit? That is not certain, but, on the other hand, what is sure is that I would lose my freedom. By saying nothing at all on this subject, I remain free. Then, know that when you start to want to categorize people, you end up leaving them on library shelves. Moreover, you do not need a list of initiates ranked by order of merit, but you do need a living being to stimulate you and sweep you along with them.

I do not know if I am an initiate, and it would be good if you paid as little attention to that as I do. It would be much better for you if you were to see me as a child carrying some hidden treasures. By claiming to be an initiate, I would lay a heavy burden on myself, and carrying burdens leads to rapid ageing. I do not worry about that; old age comes along quite quickly by itself, so why give it a boost? We must take time to be children. Young people, and spiritual seekers too, are in too much of a hurry. Children want to grow into being adults too quickly, and spiritual seekers want to clothe themselves with airs of authority far too quickly. This attitude does not interest me, even though some of you wish me to adopt it, so then you could boast that you follow a great Master. I do not want you to wear me like some sort of decoration.

Honestly, I do not claim to be an initiate. It would add nothing to what I am and would only bury me in complications for the future. Therefore, I will say only that love dwells in my heart and that I long to help people, to support them and to see them happy. As for my knowledge, I have gained it after years and years of study and work, not only in this life but in previous ones. The name that is given to this knowledge is absolutely unimportant; for me, only the results count. When you come to listen to me, do you receive light and joy? Does your soul expand? Yes? Well, what more do you want? If I told you that I am an initiate yet nothing changes in you, what is the point? What counts is what you yourself are living. What matters is that you learn to think correctly, that you know yourself better and become aware of truths that you did not know before.

And just as I do not present myself to you with the title of initiate or any other such thing, I will not grant you degrees or grades in the way that some spiritual or religious orders do. I speak to you, and I will always speak to you all, in the same way. I know that many of you are waiting for me to form a special class for the most advanced brothers and sisters, in which I will unveil mysteries. You have no idea of the complications that would follow such a decision. It is much better that you are all here together and that the same truths are taught to everyone, with words that reach each level of understanding. If necessary, I have methods for doing special work on certain individuals, and that does not necessarily take place on the physical plane. I can speak to each one of you by addressing your soul. Wherever you are, I know how to be face to face with your soul, and I can reveal what I think is good for it.

Believe me, instead of asking questions about me, put all your energies into studying and testing the Teaching I have given you. Do not waste your time comparing it with what you know already from the various books you have read. If, in what I say, you recognize your own desires, your hopes, your secret ideals, then follow me. If not, well, of course, you are free, and I hold no one against his or her wishes. You are the sole judge. If you want to know whether a dish is salty or sweet, you taste it; you do not go and look in a book. When you were children, your mother would test your soup so that you would not get burned, but now that you have grown up, it is up to you to taste for yourselves.

I am well aware that, whatever I say, there will still be some among you who will go on asking questions about me, even about my previous incarnations. Why? In order to know how far they can make use of me. Consciously or unconsciously, they are making calculations; if I were to mention the knowledge and powers I had from my past, they would be able to benefit from them. To do what? Would it be to work on themselves? Would it be to become true sons and daughters of God? I do not think so! For some it is because they feel that being close to me they will be protected, while others hope I will reveal certain secrets that will allow them to satisfy their ambitions and their greed. How can I make them understand that what I have given them is infinitely more precious than all that?

Those who are waiting for me to give easy ways of obtaining what can only be gained by intelligence, work, and patience are wasting their time; even I myself do not have such methods. Why? Because I have never sought them. I could have found them, as many occultists have done, if that was what I really wanted. However, that never interested me; on the contrary, I put up with poverty, with being despised, mocked and hated, so that I could concentrate on what I thought was essential: working on myself so that one day I would be able to enlighten and help others. With what aim? With the aim of contributing to the realization of the kingdom of God and his righteousness, as Jesus asked us when he said, *'Seek first the kingdom of God and his righteousness, and all these things will be given to you as well.'*[1]

Truly, all those who come to me hoping that I will give them talismans, magical secrets or magical powers have very little intuition. I have told you that, when I was very young, I was able to do such things. But I have also told you that one day I had a vision of two beings standing before me; one of them was power incarnate, the other, love incarnate. I chose the path of love, not that of power, and above all not the power that brings in money and material success.

Obviously, I will never be able to stop some people from concerning themselves with my past lives. How many so-called clairvoyants have come to tell me that in other lives I was this wise man, that magus, this alchemist, that cabbalist, this king, that prophet, high priest or hierophant and goodness knows who. That is the past, and the past does not interest me. What is important for me is to know who I am and what I do now, and who I will be and what I will do in the future. You, too, should tell yourselves the same thing. Do not go and consult clairvoyants to learn about your past lives. To tell the truth, your past is not difficult to know. According to who you are now, according to what qualities, what weaknesses, what strengths and deficiencies you have now, you can know – without going into the details, of course – what you have been; what you are in this incarnation has not come to you by chance. So, concentrate more on the present in order to create the future.[2]

Finally, think whatever you want, but for myself I am not interested in my past lives. I only know that I have thousands of years of experience. Where and when I gained this experience does not matter much, but I can simply tell you that all I have learned is present here in the teaching about the sun which I bring you. How many things I speak to you about that I never read in any book! Nor did I hear them from the mouth of Master Peter Deunov. So, where did I find them? The sun revealed them to me.

For me, the sun is above all other Masters. The sun is my Master; it is the sun that lights my mental universe, and the sun is not only my Master but also my father. So, if you really want to know who I am, this is what I am: a child of the sun. I feel that I am the son of the sun. You will say: 'Son of the sun; that's the title of the emperor of Japan.' I know. What I do not know is what meaning that title holds for him, or whether he even still has it. But, for myself, I know what it means to be a son of the sun.

Jesus said, *'Be perfect as your heavenly Father is perfect.'*[3] But how can we have any knowledge of the perfection of our heavenly Father? We have never seen him! The sun tells us; by looking at it, we discover that the heavenly Father is infinite light, warmth and life. And when Jesus said, *'I am the light of the world'*, what is the light of the world, if not the sun? Obviously, the sun with which Jesus identified himself was not the one we see in the sky; it is the Christ, the cosmic sun, of which our sun is merely a representative. But even if it is no more than a representative, by contemplating it we come closer to the perfection of our heavenly Father, closer to his life, his love and his wisdom.

Through the sun, the Christ, emanation of the Father, never stops pouring out his blessings; each day, his life, his blood, flows toward the earth. The earth is never abandoned. Christians seek Christ, they wait for his coming, but he is already here, present before them, blessing and bringing life to all creatures. At one and the same time, he is present throughout the universe, in all the stars of heaven, and for us humans he manifests in particular through the sun. Blessed are those who raise and expand their understanding of Christ, for their soul is raised and expanded. Yes, indeed, Christ manifests in the smallest things, in the tiniest gestures of love, but he is also present in the immensity of the universe, and those who refuse to recognize him in the sun, which enlightens, warms and brings life to all creatures, will never know Christ.

'I am the light of the world,' said Jesus, and the light of the world is the sun. But Jesus also said, *'You are the light of the world.'*[4] And I tell you too, 'I am a son of the sun'. And since I am a son of the sun, you too are sons and daughters of the sun, even if you do not yet know it. Yes, you are sons and daughters of the sun, and in order to lead you closer to it, one morning on the Rock of Prayer I consecrated the Brotherhood to the sun. What I did then with you is something you will understand later. Even those who were not present at the time, and those who are to come in the future, were dedicated to the sun. An immense being was present there on that occasion and received my words.

Some of you will say, 'But do you have the right to dedicate us to the sun? You never asked us if we agreed with this.' Do not worry, you have free will, and if you do not want to be children of the sun, you will not be compelled. I cannot force you, and I have no intention of doing so. Inwardly, you have the right to choose whose sons and daughters you wish to be. I dedicated you to the sun, but this dedication is effective only for those who desire it, and I know they are many. The others can choose another father; the sun (and all the entities that inhabit it) has no desire to impose itself on them.

It is a law of the spiritual world that luminous entities can enter only where the door is opened for them. Even if you are caught in the snares of creatures of darkness, angels who look down on human beings say, 'We have no right to impose our presence on these creatures; they have not asked for our help.' They respect the freedom of all, and they will not enter rooms if entry has been forbidden to them. Only evil spirits allow themselves to go in without permission. This is precisely the difference between luminous spirits and the spirits of darkness. The spirits of darkness show respect for no one, whereas a luminous spirit will always wait for the door to be opened and to be invited in.

I dedicated the Brotherhood to the sun, but it is up to each one of you to decide if you want to be inhabited by solar beings. If you accept, they will be overjoyed! They will see an awakened being in you, and they will sing, 'At last, we, the powers of heaven, can enter into these souls and work with them. Now these souls are born into the light, we can manifest our light through them,' and they will inspire your actions, your words, your looks and your smile. Never forget, however, that you are living beings, not mere objects, and so nothing at all within you remains immovable. Life exposes you to all sorts of currents; it will jostle you about, and you may lose your direction. I have dedicated you to the sun. God himself heard and received my words; the spirits that surround him and serve him also heard and replied, but it is you who must renew this consecration, each day, through your thoughts and your wishes, so that you maintain your solar orientation.

Perhaps you are wondering what the sun has taught me. First, it has taught me the difference between false and true riches, the difference between vanity and divine glory. I have been so solicited throughout my life! Some people certainly had no bad intentions, but if I had allowed myself to be persuaded by them, I would have been led down paths where I would have lost my way.

Even if you come from a very modest background, as I did, it is really not so difficult to achieve a certain social standing. What is more difficult is to give up this social standing when you realize that, to maintain it, you are required to accept all sorts of compromises that would lead you to betray your ideal. I do not know how I came to be mentioned in some circles, but one day a prince of royal blood asked me to look at his astrological chart to see whether he would ascend the throne to which he had a claim. A very distinguished gentleman was sent by the prince to ask me this. I accepted the request and, after I had studied his chart closely, I had to reply that nothing there indicated that he would ascend the throne. Of course, as usual, I had read this horoscope without charging anything for the work. Do you think I was even thanked for this? Not at all, I never heard from him again. On another occasion, I had dealings with a countess, who thought I could perform some magic trick that would ensure that she would get an inheritance, which was being contested in court, and as I was leaving her drawing room, I encountered the Empress Soraya. I am well aware that kings and rulers of the world often have astrologers, magi and alchemists around them, but these roles are not for me, and so, even when people beg me, I prefer to keep my distance.

I am not saying that, among the aristocrats, the rich and the famous, there are not some who feel the need for a spiritual life. In fact, just because they have all they want on the material or social plane, they feel a need within which neither their titles, wealth nor fame can fill. So sometimes they show an interest in spirituality. But spirituality is not limited to reading a few books, listening to a few lectures or having some conversations with a wise man: it demands real effort, exercises, renunciations and a perseverance of which they are rarely capable, and they soon go back to their frivolous existence. For me, when I have sat for a long time in the coolness and purity of the morning contemplating the sunrise, when I have drunk in that light and bathed in the colours of the dawn, I have felt that my whole life was there. I had no need to go to the drawing rooms of the famous; I would in the end have lost my soul.

Freemasons belonging to many lodges have invited me to become a part of their order. This is a great honour, but I did not accept. Being a member of the Universal White Brotherhood is enough for me. And then all those temples, ceremonies, rituals, vestments and degrees... I sensed that none of that was for me. What is for me is to go to the dawn, simply dressed, in the temple of nature, where the officiating high priest is the sun.

I have even been nominated for the Order of Malta. A couple of exiled monarchs, who are members of this order, wanted to induct me into it. This is a most prestigious society, and, once again, I was most honoured to have been considered, but I refused it for the same reasons. If I had accepted, how would all these distinguished people have reacted when I told them that, for me, the one true religion is the solar religion?

But what most surprised me was that before the Second Vatican Council, a French bishop who was going to attend sent me an invitation to go with him. He had read my books over the years; he appreciated them, and he thought it might be interesting for me to take part in all the discussions. Good God, what on earth could I have done there? I would have been excommunicated ten times, a hundred times, for my ideas! Yes, I could have been excommunicated, even though I have never felt myself to be outside the Church. All I have wanted is for the Church to explain more clearly the truths that it has been charged to teach, and it would do that so much better if it went to learn from the sun. Do you remember what I told you about the 'mystery' of the Holy Spirit? The sun is the only answer to this mystery, its only explanation.[5]

So I did not take part in the council, and when I saw the reports of it given on television I saw that I had been right not to go with the bishop who had invited me. One way or another, I would not have been able to stop myself from giving my opinion. What would have been the point of disturbing these fine fellows, who were already so very old? They needed peace and quiet. They wore the most magnificent robes, it is true, absolutely dazzling! But I was also expecting to see some light in their faces, something radiating from them. But no; they were all there, grave, serious, deep… tired. Doubtless, too much work. I looked at them, and all I could do was to send them good thoughts to support and encourage them in their heavy task.

Some mornings, I cannot drag myself away from contemplating the rising sun, this sun that is the source of all life. It is odd that this practice is met with so much misunderstanding, whereas people are not at all surprised to see thousands of people lighting candles before pictures or statues of wood and stone, or wearing medallions of the

Virgin, or kissing fragments of 'the true cross'! A whole forest must have been felled to make all these fragments of 'the true cross', but nobody seems to be surprised by that. Are we the mad ones when we link ourselves to the Creator by dwelling on the purest symbol of light, love and eternal life?

Each morning I nourish myself with the rays of the rising sun, for light is the best nourishment. But the air, the earth, the surrounding trees, they too bring elements to my kitchen. Yes, I am learning to cook. With my thoughts, with my love, I create delicious dishes out of all these elements. How many times have I told you that the spiritual life is nutrition? But all these elements must be cooked, so that they are transformed into wisdom, goodness, strength and peace. We contribute to this transformation by bringing all our attention to the sun as it rises. And then, in returning to our daily activities, each time we feel satisfied and stronger, richer. Yes, richer, because this light from the sun that we have received is gold, etheric gold, and this gold is worth more than all the ingots stacked in bank vaults. One day I was given the opportunity to learn a secret that would attract gold, but I do not want to use it. Once, and just once, I tried it out to see whether it really worked. A short while later, I found a box outside my door containing several gold coins from different countries. I never knew who had brought them there... But as I have no use for gold coins, I gave them to certain people as keepsakes.

Since I know how to attract gold, you may well ask why I will not use it, as it would be most useful for the Brotherhood! We could buy land and put up buildings. No, not only would it not be desirable, it could even be dangerous. Material abundance, even being comfortable, is a barrier to the life of the spirit. It is not my job to bring riches to the Brotherhood, to increase its possessions and to improve the physical conditions. My work is to bring you light. If you feel that this light is worth something, then you can do something for it; it is up to you to contribute according to your means. It is not land and buildings I want to leave one day as a legacy, only light. Never forget that!

Are you beginning to understand why I tell you that I am instructed by the sun? The sun taught me that light is the real gold, which we should seek each morning at dawn. At that moment, the sun shoots showers of golden spangles out into space, and these grains of gold can fill not only our physical pockets but all the 'pockets' of our spirit, our soul, our mind, our heart and our physical body. Yes, our whole organism can benefit from this gold, from head to toe.

There are many kinds of light. The one our nervous system and our entire organism needs the most is the light of the sun before it rises. It is the subtlest, the most spiritual light, and it acts on our psychic bodies. That is why, if we know how to contemplate the sun, something begins to open in our solar plexus, and we begin to drink light. It is like a reservoir filled with a precious quintessence, and when the reservoir overflows, the only thing you want to do is to distribute this elixir to all living beings, and there is no greater joy than to give what you have received from the sun. That is why, after I have contemplated the morning sun for a long time, I endeavour to give you something from the sun in the words I say, in the looks I give and also through my hand each time I greet you.

Ah, yes, the joy of giving is another thing the sun has taught me. It even told me, 'The day you are able to give as I do, you will become immortal.' So I asked, 'But you have been giving out your warmth and your light for thousands of years, so how is it that you have never exhausted your supply?' It replied, 'The secret lies in being able to both give and receive at the same time, to be able to inhale and exhale.' And it is possible; I once gave you a demonstration of it. I brought along a straw and a candle. I lit the candle, and through the straw I blew on the flame (we noticed that it always remained leaning in one direction), and at the same time I was breathing through my nose so that I could go on blowing through the straw. It is difficult, but it is possible, and it is what glass blowers do. It is also what the sun does; it gives and receives endlessly at the same time. In order to be able to give, you have to learn to receive, and what you have received you have to learn to give.[6] That is why, after a meditation, after a spiritual exercise of any kind, we have the power to bring something good to other people through the way we look at them, with a light in our face, a light that bears witness to the fact that we have been in contact with the spirit. But I was astonished to see that in India and also in Japan the faces of many people who had prayed and meditated remained closed and inexpressive.

In Japan I was welcomed into a monastery along with the person who accompanied me. In order to accommodate me, where I would not be disturbed by noise, they gave me a little temple. So there I was in the company of all the Shinto divinities, which was a new experience for me. Throughout the night in particular I felt their presence and I spoke with them. We had some very different and unusual conversations. In this monastery there were about a dozen very nice and likeable monks who were Zen Buddhist practitioners. Each day began with meditation, and then, when everyone in the monastery was gathered together, they would honour the two visitors who had come from France by playing the Marseillaise and raising the French flag! Yes, every morning this little ceremony would take place with the playing of a record of the Marseillaise, followed by the Japanese national anthem and the raising of flags of both countries. Many people who had come to the monastery from the town heard the Marseillaise and saw the French flag. Obviously, it was unexpected, and it was then that I understood that I was French, even though I had not yet become a naturalized citizen.

But let us return to the practice of Zen meditation, or *zazen*. It was done in a room with completely bare walls. Each person, sitting on a cushion in the lotus position, would face the wall. I will not give you all the details of how they were made to sit, how they had to hold their head, shoulders, hands and so on, as that will be of no use to you. What was interesting was the presence of a monk who held a stick in his hand. His job was to deliver a blow on the shoulder of anyone who was not holding a good posture or who had started to fall asleep. Apparently we have an important nerve centre in the shoulder, and when the staff hits this spot, it harmonizes the energies. The person who is falling asleep wakes up, and the person who is inwardly too disturbed to concentrate is calmed. I wanted to experience the effect of this staff, and I asked the monk to give me a blow before the meditation started. To start with, the monk refused, as he said I did not need it. I insisted, and he finally agreed to do it: I did not feel anything out of the ordinary – and perhaps it was because I did not need it – but, all the same, I gained something from the experience.

Now, I must say that I was very struck by the fact that monks of this monastery and also most of the monks I met who were Zen practitioners were lacking any expression on their faces after meditation. No light radiated from them; no life animated their features, and some of them even had very harsh features. Of course, I am not going to pass judgment on a discipline that I do not know well, but from the point of view of true Initiatic Science, a meditation which is not a contact with the light, a meditation that does not leave any traces of light and love on the face, that does not communicate something that is alive and vibrant, is not very useful. I will be told that the goal of *zazen* is to stop thought by stepping into emptiness. I understand that, but I find that in some cases this emptiness is a little too much. What good can we be to others when we have so little expression? We can only do good by bringing life, warmth and light.

Give like the sun; love like the sun. I do not know whether I will ever achieve this goal, but I live with this desire. And when I am irritated or discouraged by the behaviour of people, I turn towards the sun on high, which keeps on shining unwearied, unperturbed, and once again I am filled with courage. You will say, 'But it is so easy for the sun to stay unruffled; nothing can touch it as it is so far away.' Yes, but we, too, have something within us that is always out of reach – our higher self, for our higher self dwells in the sun. By contemplating the sun, we will one day be able to be reunited with our higher self and live as it does in a peace that nothing can disturb.[7]

Our higher self lives in the sun where it takes part in divine work. When we know how to harmonize our earthly self with our higher self, we will discover the treasures the Creator has placed in us. We are the heirs of these treasures, but we do not yet possess them. They will not become ours until the day when, through meditation, prayer and contemplation, we are able to re-establish the link between our two 'selves'. Little by little we will feel that we are receiving portions of this wonderful inheritance that our father, the sun, is holding in reserve for us – this inheritance of love, wisdom, and power, which are the attributes of God.

My greatest wish is to lead people to the sun, but for the moment, it is true, I am not understood. Some people become angry, others mock me, and there are those who, having no idea how to present things, say anything they please. And what do the journalists (who are supposed to be objective in their statement of facts) say? Someone came to see me at the Bonfin, because he had heard that we were called 'sunstruck sun worshippers': he wanted to see what was going on. I answered his questions, and off he went, satisfied. But what did I read in his article? He had a few unimportant accounts of our conversation, but what had most impressed him, if you can believe it, was that the lampposts in my garden had electric light. What on earth was he thinking? That I had no need to see in the dark? That the sun itself chose to bring me light in the middle of the night? He wrote that he was amazed that new fangled things like electricity had come to my house. Well, it was I who was more astonished by his amazement.

The year I went to Yugoslavia, I received on my return newspaper clippings that described me as 'the king of the sun', *kral na slănçéto*. How on earth did these journalists come up with such a statement? I stayed only a very short time in the country, and I never spoke to anyone about the sun. Somebody sent me an Italian magazine, which described me as 'the reincarnated sun god'. What do such outrageous myths mean? I have no need to become some sort of celebrity because of the sun. I have no need to be spoken about at all, because notoriety always brings more disadvantages than advantages. All I wish is that my ideas become known, because I know that they can do a lot of good. But these articles that portray me as a king or sun god are truly grotesque.

I can understand that some sensitive people feel that I have a very powerful link with the sun. This has happened occasionally with people who know nothing about my activities or me. One day, an English writer whom I had met briefly in India came with his wife to see me at Izgrev. He had hardly come into my house when he said, 'It is an extraordinary thing, Mr. Aïvanhov, but I have just seen the sun behind you.' Yes, that is possible, because I live constantly with the image of the sun, with the thought of the sun, with the presence of the sun, and each day the sun brings me something new. Believe me, the sun is the one and only being that is truly new each and every day. You may argue, 'Astronomers say that the sun is billions and billions of years old!' Yes, that is possible, but it is also forever young and new.

I was invited once to see an exhibition dedicated to the most recent archaeological discoveries that had been made in the area around Fréjus. I knew what to expect, but I agreed to go so as not to disappoint the person who had invited me. What was there to see? There were some rocks that had been part of houses built two thousand years ago by the Romans, and a few broken pots. For the people who had mounted the exhibition, these were valuable objects, and so they had all sorts of things to say about these rocks and pottery shards. In fact, there was nothing of interest, but it was Roman, and so, apparently, it was important to feed ourselves on all the history of this dusty debris. Why do people pay so much attention to all these bits and pieces from the past? They take no delight in the light and the pure air that God gives them every day, but look at what a song and dance they make over two thousand-year-old potsherds! And they present it, all decked out with Latin and Greek words to show their academic expertise! It is so hard not to smile when you see these scholars gathering together, patting each other on the back and being so proud of having assembled this heap of old rubbish.

When will people understand that life needs to be constantly springing forth, constantly new, as the sun itself is always new? The life of yesterday is already past; the sun of today is not the same as it was yesterday, and it renews its riches too. Each day it brings us something which did not exist the day before. Each morning at its rising the sun invites us to receive a new life, to enter into a different rhythm, to harmonize ourselves with the light, with eternity, and this is the true fountain of youth. Everywhere we hear, 'Life must change.' And yet they keep on wallowing in the old life. People go and dig up buried civilizations and are amazed at everything they discover in sarcophagi; they are more interested in secret catacombs, mummies or the remains of a mammoth frozen in polar ice than they are in the dazzling sun, which each morning sends us new, fresh life.

How many people walk among ruins without suspecting that just by looking at them they will begin to resemble them! It is very good to study them, but why do they not lift their heads up to look at the sun? A very learned scholar came to see me recently, and she told me that she had specialized in Egyptian archaeology, because she had been the wife of a pharaoh in a previous incarnation. Fine, I didn't object if that is what she wanted to believe. But what was she like now? I saw her as someone who was so dark, so sombre and lacklustre! As I am well bred and polite, I did not tell her that if her former pharaoh husband were to meet her once again he might not choose to marry her this time! When will all these scholars understand that they have to do their research in heaven's libraries, find their food in an eternal restaurant and their drink from that unique source, the sun? And that is what you should do too.

In the *book of Isaiah,* God says, *'I am about to create new heavens and a new earth.'*[8] How should we understand these words? Will God destroy the heaven and earth that he created in the beginning? No. This new heaven and new earth are symbols to express that life is always in the process of renewing itself. It is always in motion, and we should follow this movement without seeking to go back. That is why we should not try to bring back old religions and forgotten initiations, as some people try to do. I agree that they should be studied but without trying to bring them back to life. If they have faded away, it is for a reason. What are you going to find now in the Egyptian religion or that of ancient Greece? What will you find with the Druids, the Incas, the Aztecs or even the Cathars? There is a certain amount of truth to be found in these religions, these initiations, because they are linked to eternal verities. But we really should not go rummaging around the vestiges of ancient cults in order to bring them back to life.[9] You can be interested in them, and I myself am interested in them, too. On my trips to Egypt, Lebanon and Greece, I have visited many ancient sanctuaries. I have meditated at the Pyramids, at Baalbek, at Eleusis, at Delphi and at other places. But I go to the sun for my nourishment. Each day it reveals many things to me, because I believe in the sun, I love it, and when I have a difficult problem to solve I turn to the sun, and it answers me.

When the sun rises, do you not feel that something deep within you rises too? Don't you feel that, for a moment, your whole soul becomes just like the sun? Learn how to use the wonderful law of imitation that nature has put at our disposal, this possibility of identifying with what we are looking at. In order to help you, I am going to give you some formulas which you can say while you are watching the sun rise. Wait for the first ray of sun light, and then silently say these words with love:

'*As the sun rises over the world, so may the sun of freedom, immortality, eternity and truth rise in my spirit.*

'*As the sun rises over the world, so may the sun of love and immensity rise in my soul.*

'*As the sun rises over the world, so may the sun of intelligence, light and wisdom rise in my intellect.*

'*As the sun rises over the world, so may the sun of joy, happiness and purity rise in my heart.*

'*As this luminous, radiant sun rises over the world, so may the sun of strength, power, energy, dynamism and activity rise in my will.*

'*And as this luminous, radiant, living sun rises over the world, so may the sun of health, vitality and vigour rise throughout my entire body.*

'*Amen. So be it, for the kingdom of God and his right-eousness.*

'*Amen. So be it, for the glory of God.*'

This is a powerful and magical formula.

When humans finally succeed in identifying with the sun, they will live in such light and emanate such radiance that no one will be able to tell whether they are clothed or naked. We will no longer see their clothes; we will not see their nakedness; we will not even see their faces. As in the very distant past, in an earthly Paradise, light will clothe them better than any garments.

Of course, some of you will say, 'But in the summer we have to get up so early, to go up to the Rock of Prayer for the sunrise! We're still sleepy, so when we get there we fall asleep.' So, sleep! Since we have been going to the Rock of Prayer for so many years, it has become a sort of sanctuary, and it does you more good to come and sleep there than it would to stay asleep in your bed. On the Rock of Prayer you will at least gain a few good things from the nature spirits that come from all sides to work as the sun is rising.

In Greece, in ancient times, there were temples dedicated to Aesculapius, to Apollo, and so on. People who wanted to get a message from the god would come to sleep there in the hope that they would have prophetic dreams: the god would tell them what the future would be, would show them the ways to regain their health, and so on. So why, in the mornings, should not the Rock of Prayer be a temple for you? Of course, it is better to stay awake, so that you can be conscious of the work you are doing and so that you can receive all the blessings of the nature spirits as they travel down the sun's rays, but even if you are asleep they will give you something.

A new philosophy is coming now in the world, that of the rising sun. One day, everybody will go out at the beginning of the day to greet the sun, and it will bring a new viewpoint that will bring change in all areas: psychological, familial, social, political and economic. Everyone will leave behind the geocentric point of view in order to adopt the heliocentric point of view, the viewpoint of the sun. Do you not see how dishonest it is that human beings never recognize how much they owe the sun? They are the first to demand that they should be recognized, respected, thanked, congratulated, and yet they neglect the sun and pay it no attention, when it has given them everything – except when they want to know what the weather is going to be like. Then, yes, it is important for their fields or their gardens, or because they want to go for a walk, or sunbathe on the beach, and so on. But the sun, always silent, always generous, never demands anything from us. It thinks, 'I will continue to enlighten and warm these ungrateful beings. They are bitter, sour fruit, but I will make them ripe and sweet as honey, until they realize that they are my sons and daughters.'

It is said that, one day, human beings will surpass angels and archangels in their splendour, but for now they are still green fruit, hard, obstinate and stubborn. But this fruit is growing on the cosmic Tree of Life, and the sun watches it and sends its light and heat to ripen it, so that, one day, the fruit will be served as a delicious morsel on the divine table. As spiritual essence, it will enter the mind of the Creator, and its thoughts will be those of the Creator, the mighty Sun. The destiny of humanity is to be absorbed one day into the mighty Sun.

Generations come and go, empires crumble, but the sun continues, always present, steady, unshakeable and faithful, which is why I chose the sun as father, and seeing my steadfastness he adopted me; like father, like son. I may well be a very young member of his family. To someone who has lived so many billions of years, I may be only one month old in solar terms, or maybe just a day old, but even so, I am his son.

And because I am a son of the sun, I want to be a voice to declare this new life, this new light. Imagine, if you will, that I have a transmitter, and with the help of many other beings on the earth, and even from distant planets, I am able to saturate the atmosphere with thoughts of the new life. These waves travel through space and inscribe themselves in the subconscious of people everywhere. My transmitter works every day, and it says, over and over again, 'Open yourselves up to the rays of the rising sun! Rejoice in this abundance of light and life!'

One day, I was in the Pyrenees, as the sun was rising, and once again I sent out these messages, when some eagles came and circled above me. I was so happy! Eagles are the only ones that can soar to dizzying heights in the sky and look at the sun without burning their eyes. It was as if they were saying to me, 'We are your friends, and we support you.'

You wonder if my messages are heard? Yes, even if it is not as much as I would wish. Otherwise, why do you think that 23 June 1979 was declared 'the day of the sun'? Throughout the whole world, astronomers, physicists, writers, artists, all spoke of the sun and celebrated the sun. And above all, many people gathered to watch the sunrise on that day! As energy waves travel, as light and sound travel and multiply, so do thoughts. Clearly it takes a long time for them to be captured, but I am confident.

Sometimes I receive letters from brothers and sisters saying, 'Oh Master, we would so like to be like you. You are an example for us.' But I say that you should take the sun as your example, as I do. I look to the sun, and I point toward it to encourage you to go in that direction. Do not stop at me; go right past me to the sun, immerse yourself in its life, its warmth and its light, so that you can become like it. As for me, think of me as being a signpost that shows you the path you should take. So, do not stop at the signpost. When you travel along a road, and you see a sign that says Paris or Fréjus, you do not stop there and hug it saying, 'How I love you, dear signpost. How I love your beautiful lettering, and how well you point out the direction I should take!' No, you keep travelling until you reach Paris or Fréjus.

What did John the Baptist say to his disciples, when they questioned him about Jesus? *'I baptize you with water…, but one who is more powerful than I is coming after me; I am not worthy to carry his sandals. He will baptize you with the Holy Spirit and fire.'* Then one day, when he saw Jesus coming toward him, he said, *'Here is the lamb of God who takes away the sin of the world! This is he of whom I said, "After me comes a man who ranks ahead of me because he was before me."'* And I say to you, 'Here is the sun; go to the sun, for it is so much greater than I am.' All I can do is show you the way to it by giving you these methods and exercises, showing you how to regard the sun, how to love it, how to let it penetrate you, how to identify with it, so that one day you, too, may become like it.

Set out each morning to meet the sun with an awakened consciousness; otherwise, when you come down from the Rock of Prayer, all you will be able to say is that the sky was blue, there were some trees and some mountains in the distance. But that is not what you came for. You climb up to the Rock of Prayer in order to feel the sun reveal all the splendours of creation, the power of God and his love. Without an awakened consciousness, it is impossible to become a citizen of the spiritual world; you can be no more than a passing tourist.

Each morning I climb up to the sun, and I want to lead you, too, to the sun that is the homeland of our soul, the land of the living. That is why I have dedicated you to it. In dedicating you, I have committed myself to certain obligations. This dedication has opened a door for you, and it is up to you to decide whether you want to go through it.

Notes
1. See *The True Meaning of Christ's Teaching*, Izvor Coll. n° 215, chap. 4: 'Seek first the kingdom of God and his righteousness'.
2. See *Marchez tant que vous avez la lumière*, Izvor Coll. n° 244, chap. 5: 'Seul le présent nous appartient' and chap. 6: 'Avant que le soleil se couche'.
3. See *The True Meaning of Christ's Teaching*, Izvor Coll. n° 215, chap. 3: 'Be perfect as your heavenly Father is perfect'.
4. See *The Philosopher's Stone – In the Gospels and in Alchemy*, Izvor Coll. n° 241, chap. 6: 'You are the light of the world'.
5. See *The Splendour of Tiphareth – The Yoga of the Sun*, Complete Works, vol. 10, chap. 4: 'The Creator sows seeds in us and the sun makes them grow – The sun reflects the blessed Trinity' and chap. 15: 'The sun is in the image and likeness of God – 'In spirit and in truth'.
6. See *The Key to the Problems of Existence*, Complete Works, vol. 11, chap. 3: 'Giving and taking'.
7. See *The Splendour of Tiphareth – The Yoga of the Sun*, Complete Works, vol. 10, chap. 3: 'Our higher self dwells in the sun'.
8. See *The Book of Revelations: A Commentary*, Izvor Coll. n° 230, chap. 16: 'The new heaven and the new earth'.
9. See *'In Spirit and in Truth'*, Izvor Coll. n° 235, chap. 13: 'The Spirit is not held captive in relics' and chap. 14: 'Speak to the spirit of those you love'.

13

Between speech and silence

How many times have I thought, 'Ah, here's an important topic to talk about in my next lecture', and I turn over, in my mind, the way I should present it. But when the time comes, I have forgotten everything. This has happened so often that I made a decision not to prepare anything beforehand, because it never turns out as I hoped, and I am disappointed. In order to talk to you, I need the topic to come to me in a flash, as an inspiration, a suggestion that comes from elsewhere. When that happens, despite the fact that some things are left out or there are mistakes in my French and a scholar might criticize the format, everything works.

I have told you that when I first came from Bulgaria, even though I knew a little French because of the books I had read, I could not speak it. I learned it alone by listening to people or the radio, or by going to the cinema. Basically, I learned as children do, learning to talk by listening to what is said around them, but not as a child who would ever have gone to school! The day I learned to say, 'What's going on?' 'What's the matter?' I was so happy! To be able to say,

'What's going on?' was such progress for me. Added to that, I never really studied grammar or correct phrasing, but I have always loved learning new words. Here's an example...

One morning, at Sevres, I went to the market to buy some fruit. There were two elegant young women, of refined appearance, standing beside me at the fruit stand. Without wishing to listen in, I heard what they were saying. One said to the other, 'I've got no grub at all.' At that time, I had not sufficiently explored the French vocabulary to recognize this word 'grub', but as the word was accompanied with an eloquent gesture I understood it. I said to myself, 'Aha, here's a new word', and as these young girls looked so refined, I thought that the word 'grub' was equally elegant. Then, one day in a lecture, believing that I was going to stun my audience of brothers and sisters with my progress in language, I used the word. My goodness, when I saw how their eyes stared at me, I felt like a child repeating a word it has heard without understanding what it means and is told, 'No, no, you must never use that word; it's not a good one!'

A few months after my arrival in Paris, I started to give public lectures and I needed to prepare them beforehand. But it felt to me as if I was reading from a text, and the life that comes from improvisation was missing, and I found it boring! Even I, listening to myself, was bored... I need what I am going to say to come down naturally from on high. That is why, before I speak, I have a moment of concentration, so that when the moment comes, the spring within me can bubble forth. This approach obviously requires a different kind of preparation.

A lecturer who turns up to lecture with their text all written out is relaxed; they only have to take it out of their pocket or their briefcase. Before addressing their audience they can chat, laugh or argue with someone, and this will not affect what they are going to say. It is different for me. As it is impossible for me to prepare anything in advance, I have to prepare myself before I arrive, so that I will be able to sense what you need. What concerns me is what I can bring to you, what I can give, what you will leave with, and whether you will feel enlightened, strengthened, and enriched... that is what preoccupies me.

When I am at home I prepare myself. I bless this day that once again has given us the chance to meet together. I thank the Lord, and I say to him, 'My God, you know everything that is going on in the souls of my brothers and sisters. You know everything they need. Put into my mouth the words they need!' Since I do not prepare what I am going to say to you, I have to capture the currents in the atmosphere that will inform me of all your preoccupations, all your expectations. You have often told me that when you come to hear me you find I answer the questions you are asking yourselves. This is because my only concern is to be useful to you. I link myself to heaven, and I become like an antenna; I receive indications on the topics that I need to talk to you about today... not another day, today.

When I leave home I have a hundred metres to walk to the lecture hall, and I never allow anyone to stop me for a conversation when I am on this path. Why? Because, at this moment, I am still preparing myself to meet you. When I am on this path, it is my custom to murmur certain formulas and prayers to myself, so that I can give you the best in my heart and soul. If you have something to say to me or to ask of me, find another time to do so; at that particular moment, I do not wish to be disturbed. If someone comes to speak to me, they should not be surprised if I keep on walking without replying. This is not the moment to distract me from my work by speaking about personal problems.

Some people say that all they want to do is to walk beside me. That is very nice, and I know that I must take their wish as a mark of affection, but I have no need to be accompanied. On this path I want to be alone. In my thoughts and by the words I say, I am getting ready to bring something pure and luminous, some seeds of heaven, to all the Brotherhood. Perhaps you are not yet aware of that, perhaps you think I just turn up at the hall without thinking of anything in particular. It does not really matter what you believe, but I know for myself that I must stay concentrated, and so I avoid everything that could block any one of you from receiving all that I want to bring.

Even the richest of languages has a finite number of words, but what can be conveyed by those words is infinite. The important thing for me, as I speak to you, is not just to use the most accurate words to convey what I want to say; what is essential is that I should fill those words with a subtle quintessence that will act on your soul and make it light up. That is what I am working on as I walk down the path. And even then, when I reach the lecture hall, my mind is not really at rest, because I say to myself, 'I am going into the presence of living beings, each of whom carries burdens; they are sending me their thoughts, and they are waiting for me to bring them something. Provided that I am helped by heavenly beings, I will know how to respond to their needs!'

Then, when I come into the hall, I do not speak straight away. We begin by meditating so as to create the best conditions for me to speak to you and for you to hear me. For, depending on where you have been and what you have been doing, each one of you comes here with your own preoccupations, and the hall is filled with a variety of thoughts and feelings. I feel all this, because the psychic work I have done over the years has made me very sensitive to atmospheres. Without doubt this is a precious faculty. But what efforts I must make sometimes in order to change this atmosphere and to harmonize you, so that you can vibrate with these spiritual truths that I want you to be aware of and so be able to return home with clearer thoughts and better feelings!

In order to talk to you, I need to feel a harmonious atmosphere in the hall. I cannot behave like some lecturers, who do not pay much attention to the state of their audience. Before I come to speak to you, I have to prepare myself, but are you as careful of the state you are in when you come to hear me? That is why it is important to begin our meetings with songs, so that each one of you can establish harmony inside yourselves, then with everyone else and with me. It is in this harmony that I find the nourishment your soul and spirit need most for this particular day. Singing, of course, requires technique, and there are certain rules to be respected, but song has powers beyond the mere production of pleasant sounds to the ear. If we know how to sing with all our soul, waves will form, forces will circulate, and these waves, these energies, will attract luminous beings.[1] It is these presences which inspire me.

Harmony can create a sort of intoxication, not the intoxication that disturbs the spirit, but the kind which makes us more aware, clearer. This harmony is not just of voices, but also of souls and spirits. It is this harmony I seek, in order to imbue my words with a quintessence that comes from very far away and that is true spiritual nourishment. So many other beings from the invisible world are ready, together with me, to bring you their light, so that you, too, may finally experience abundant and unlimited life.

We sing together to establish communication with heaven, which then sends us currents of pure energies. If, after each song, we spend a brief moment in silence, it is so that we can bathe as long as possible in these energies and use them for our work.[2] But often, at that moment, instead of meditating, some of you look at me wondering what I am doing. What am I doing? I am thinking of you, I am trying to bring our souls together, I am praying that heaven will open your windows, so that the new life can enter you. So, instead of disturbing me in my work by staring at me, link to my thoughts and my prayers; you won't get any closer to understanding who I am and what I do by fixing your eyes on me. Think too of these friends on high who, thanks to the harmony we have created, seek to reveal things to you. What is the point of you coming here, if not to benefit from these sacred moments when you can meet the spirits of love, wisdom and beauty?

When you have learned how to participate in my work by making these moments of silence we have created to-gether more and more alive, more and more vibrant, we will succeed in building a pyramid of light, which will reach right up to the throne of God. In these silences I experience such states as you cannot possibly imagine. For this reason, be patient, and realize that you too can already benefit from them; since you are present here and close to me, these states are imprinted on you, and one day you, too, will live them.

If we pray, if we meditate and sing before I speak, again it is because I need vivid, expressive faces before me, not stiff and frozen ones. Then I look at you, and I am happy. You will say, 'But why? What do you see?' I see all sorts of things that you could not possibly guess. I see that you are sons and daughters of God, and that is the only thing which interests me. When I feel that I am among sons and daughters of God, how could I not be happy?

Now, of course, if I wished, I could see all sorts of other things, less joyful things, but, actually, I do not want to see them. It is enough for me to know that they exist, but I do not look at them, as I want to see only what is divine in people. The divine spark in each being – that is what we should look for. Sometimes we must dig very deeply to find it, but that spark is there, buried in everyone, and that is what I talk to when I speak.

If I were not on a platform, nobody beyond the third or fourth row would be able to see me, but I do not like being up on a platform. So I look at you and pray, 'Show me, my God, a way that I can become closer to my friends!' I look for little pathways that will allow me to come closer to you, and very often it is just as I am looking at you that I discover what it is I should say. You are the ones who provide my topics, but as you are not aware of this it makes my task more difficult. So you must help me find the topics I have to talk to you about.

If I speak, it is so that I can be understood, but, first of all, I want to understand what is right in front of me. That is why, when someone asks for a meeting with me, before the conversation begins I close my eyes and spend a few moments in silence. I am aware that this is not the usual way things are done, but I need this moment of concentration. I prepare myself to listen to this person, to feel, even before they speak, what they need, their difficulties and sufferings, so that I can help. You will say, 'But you have the person right there to tell you all about it!' Yes, but it is not always the case that people know how to express themselves clearly. In fact, it is very rare to find people who know how to state precisely what preoccupies them or what makes them suffer. That is why I take a few moments to fathom what is going on in their soul, and it is desirable if those who come to see me would take the time to think out, as clearly as possible, exactly what they want to say. These few moments of silence allow us to become harmonized, as this will help our understanding. You, too, should think about this, when you have any conversations. I understand that you cannot always close your eyes and concentrate, but it is very important that you should do that inner preparation before you start speaking to someone or listening to what they have to say.

Some of you do not have a clear idea of my philosophy and the way I think, because I often touch on many different topics without going deeply into any of them. I am well aware of this, for my goal is not to give you an authoritative lecture in an orderly format. I am more like a painter standing in front of a huge canvas: one day they paint a person, the next a tree, or an animal, or a column, or a mountain, and, for a long time, it is not easy to make out what the actual subject of the painting is. My canvas is still in the process of creation, but, little by little, if you are patient, persistent and attentive, one day you will be able to see clearly where I am taking you. I speak to you in a way that may seem illogical and disconnected, but each one of you receives the answer you were seeking, a moment of enlightenment, and so you are able to leave feeling strengthened. If I were to give you a well prepared lecture with an introduction, followed by a first part, second part, third part and conclusion, no doubt you would feel much more satisfied intellectually. But you must not come here to be taught; you must come to live, to be inspired, to feel a joy in your spirit. When you have life, you learn ten times more and so much better.

Each day I tell you the things that are right for today, for your worries today, for your problems and your sufferings today, and it is my love that senses your need when I see you sitting there before me – because my work is all about you, how you need to be oriented, purified and vivified. That is what interests me, not just feeding your brains, then leaving you to flounder; I want to give you methods to overcome all the difficulties that you meet in your daily lives. So when you come to listen to me, at least try to remember why you have come. My words are food for you, they are pieces of my heart and soul; I give you my life, my blood, and I cannot do anything else. When I talk to you, you are breathing my life; you are touching my life.

There are times, I know, when I wish I had a greater, richer vocabulary. I could always find some more by opening a dictionary; that's not a very difficult thing to do, and there are so many words in the book that are not used very often or whose meaning is unknown. However, the most important thing is not to find different words, but to maintain the life within them. If we allow that life to escape, the words remain useless, like empty receptacles. That is why I will only speak to you about what I live, so that you will be able to live it yourself one day. Stop thinking that this possibility is unachievable and irrelevant! It is a long-term project, but not an impossible one: it depends on you whether you enter into a new world whose beauty surpasses everything you have experienced up to now. Sometimes, while I am speaking, I see that some faces light up all of a sudden as if a little light has been switched on inside, and that gives me such joy!

Your spirit asks only to soar into the realms of light. Try to become aware of your spirit's longing. I do not speak to you about subjects that are foreign to you; I just speak of what is in you, in fact, the only thing which is truly you: your spirit, your divine spark. But you let it go out, and then I am continually obliged to tell you how to nourish it so that it can be rekindled once again...

Some of you say to me, 'O Master, we admire your knowledge, your goodness, your patience, your self control... If we could only have just a little of these qualities!' What are they hoping for? Do they expect me to wave a magic wand so that these qualities become part of them? I give you the most effective method here: this method is the atmosphere, the conditions that I have created around myself and around you when I speak, but it is only through your own work that you will obtain them. I can be a transmitter of the divine world for you, but it is up to you to put yourself in that inner state which will open you to its currents. Do not let them pass by without doing anything; seize them, take them deep inside, and your inner eyes will discover a whole new world!

Sometimes, instead of coming to speak to you, I prefer to walk in the forest. You cannot imagine how much effort it takes for me to be always talking, explaining, repeating things over and over to you. It is truly painful... When I am in silence, I live beyond time, in bliss, with all the eternal truths which nourish me. When I have to talk, I fall back into time. Yes, speaking for me is a descent into time, and that makes me feel so limited. Even if I talk to you for hours trying to make my explanations complete and clear, I still feel that I have not got my point across. I do it, of course, hoping it is useful to you all the same, but it is rare for me to feel satisfied.

I would like to be able to speak to you always in silence, so that I could speak to your soul, and I wait impatiently for the day when I can speak in this way. At the moment, it is impossible. You accept silence well for a few minutes before, during, or after the lecture, but if our meetings were to take place without my uttering a single word, I know that very few of you would be able to bear it. Maybe this will happen one day. And while we wait for that time, during these brief moments of silence try to move beyond the place of just not making a noise, and create silence also in yourselves, so that you can hear what I say to your soul which cannot be expressed in words. In these silences I am trying to open your consciousness, to awaken it to the spiritual world and its laws.[3]

I speak because I believe that this can help you. Is this vanity? But then, thanks to my vanity, you receive many things, and I have also understood that by preparing honey for you, I am able to taste it as well. You think I am trying to find a way to justify my actions? That is possible, but when we have weaknesses we need to harness them, to put them to work, so that they can be useful to others. Let's say, if you wish, that I am vain, but would you prefer it if I was proud? If I was proud, I would keep my distance, be very sparing with my words. I would be like those initiates who guarded their knowledge jealously, because they thought others were unworthy of sharing it with them. I speak because I am impatient, because I am eager to share my knowledge with you. Sometimes I have allowed myself to say things when it would have been much wiser to have remained silent. Afterwards heaven chastises me: 'Why aren't you more sensible? Why do you reveal truths to them that they are not yet capable of understanding or using? If they use them to no good purpose, it will be your fault.'

This is why when I am with you I often tell you things in silence that I cannot reveal with words; I am forbidden to tell you truths that you are not yet ready to understand fully, as I would cause more harm than good. There are truths I can only whisper to you, hoping that, one day, you will be able to discover them yourselves. Thought is an inaudible voice, it is true, but the person who has worked on developing subtler instruments will be able to pick up this voice and decipher what it says.

During these moments of silence, I have greater possibilities to speak to your souls rather than to your ears. I have no need to look for words, words which often do not exist, to reveal the realities of the invisible world to you. Even when the words exist, you would not necessarily accept what I tell you; inwardly you would protest. In that case, not only would these words which were intended to help you not help you, but they would arouse all sorts of negative reactions in you, and they would be profaned. I already tell you many things which you struggle to accept! They get lost somewhere in your head, or you just erase them.

Even when I use words everyone knows, it is sometimes difficult for me to make myself understood. You have spoken French since you were infants, and you spontaneously associate certain words with experiences you have had. Words for each of you, therefore, do not have the meaning found in the dictionary, but when you hear or speak them you add something of your feelings, your desires, your fears, your suffering and your joys. I say, for example, the word 'life' or the word 'love', and consciously or unconsciously each one of you associates them with what you know of life and love. If I were to say these words, giving them their divine dimensions, would I be understood? If, however, I speak to you in silence, I know that even if you do not hear me for the moment, what I have told you is imprinted on you, and one day my words will surface in your consciousness, and you will feel them not only as clarification but also as beneficial energies

Is it possible to measure the effects of a spoken word? The spiritual world is criss-crossed with mighty currents of energy that require us to have certain capacities if we are to be able to bear them. When I speak to you about certain topics, I have to be very careful indeed, because speech is never without consequences. Speaking is not just pronouncing words and making sounds; it also attracts powerful currents of energy in space, energy powerful enough to flatten a person to the ground. What would happen if I collapsed in front of you? So, when I speak to you, I have to be most attentive. Sometimes, when I'm speaking, I pause for a moment and close my eyes, so that I can control and handle the energies that could carry me away. Of course, this would not lead to my death, but they could make me lose an instant of consciousness. Doubtless you are not aware of this, and it is much better that it should be this way, as I do not want to cause you any anxiety

A spiritual Master tries, through his words, to take his disciples as far as he can, but then he must remain silent. It is impossible for him to reveal all that he lives in his soul and in his spirit. Do words exist that can truly convey what an ecstasy is, that moment when a person is torn from their body and projected to dizzying heights? A master can only affirm the reality of such unimaginable experiences to his disciples. As these experiences permeate every cell of his being, they also permeate every word when he speaks about them afterwards. Whatever the topic may be, it will be touched with something that has come from far away, from most high. In this way the Master can convey to others the desire to live what he has lived, and then with his explanations and the methods he gives them, he prepares the conditions and indicates the path to them.

Do not just rely on the things I say to you on the physical level, because, quite frankly, that is very little. Get rid of the conviction that all that matters are the words you hear with your ears, and begin, when we are all together, to work on the idea that you can hear and understand me on other levels. Instead of becoming impatient when the silences become longer, learn to develop your antennae, feel that your teacher is thinking of you, thinking of your future, and try to divine what he is preparing for you and where he wants to lead you. And when the meeting is over, try also to leave the hall in silence. I have been waiting for years to see if after the lectures you are capable of not immediately descending into noise and chatter. Do you do it because, having spent two or three hours in silence and harmony, you feel repressed and unhappy? You behave like children let out of school, who throw their books and notebooks in the air. Long live freedom!

When you are here, you are given essential truths for your lives, but it seems that you cannot hold on to something profound for very long. That is why you do not make much progress; all that you have heard is quickly forgotten or erased. Learn, from now on, to let these great truths do their work in you. When I speak to you, I put all my heart, all my soul, all my energy into these words so that they can work on you, but you do not feel it. Tomorrow, you will come back to hear another lecture, and all your life will pass by with you waiting for the next lecture. But in the next lecture I will have to repeat the same elementary truths. If you do not want to hear me always outlining these basic truths, try to start applying them, so that I will not need to keep repeating them and will, instead, be able to tackle new topics.

Whatever topics I deal with, I never swerve from the essential subject, which is you and your progress to perfection. I say it, I emphasize it, and you should not expect anything else from me. In the world, the whole of literature, science and technological progress is laid out before you, and you can treat yourself to whatever you want, but when you come here, know that you will always hear variations on the same topic: how to become perfect. Besides, if you have really understood what the spiritual life is, you would never be weary of hearing the same truths, because each time you would hear them in a different way. The truths of spiritual science are never understood once and for all. You have to come back to them, again and again, in order to discover more and more aspects, each one new and different. If I did not return to these truths, over and over again, to remind you of them, and if I did not try to find different arguments and new images each time, you would forget them. You say that you are curious to know other things, and, yes, I am well aware of that. Your curiosity, your desire to skip lightly and superficially from one topic to another, however, is no way for you to make inner progress.

Which of you ever tires of hearing your beloved say, 'I love you'? Even if it happens every day, and several times a day, these words resonate as if for the very first time, and each time there is always a different nuance to them. Spiritual truths, which are amongst the most precious that exist, should be heard in just the same way as when you hear someone say, 'I love you'. Try to feel that the life I transmit through my words is never the same, it is like flowing water, and that each day I put new life into them. If you are sensitive, you will be able to feel that this water, this life, never comes from the same realms. I, too, do not really know where it comes from, but I do know that it comes from a very high place.

Think of a river. Its name is always the same, but the water that flows in its bed is never the same, and no one knows where it comes from. For example, snow melts on the slopes of the Himalayas. Where did the water come from that fell in the form of snow? Then the snow melts and goes to feed, let's say, the Ganges. In time, sooner or later, the water will evaporate, condense into clouds and then fall to earth once again, who knows where, as rain, hail or snow. The same thing is true with what we receive from other human beings; we do not know where their thoughts and feelings have come from, or what regions they have passed through. Even though I repeat the same truths, the life and the love that I put into my words are never the same. Try to understand, try to feel, that this water, this life, this love, comes from heavenly regions, and then you will benefit from them so much more

Have you really had enough of hearing me repeat certain truths? Just tell yourselves that I do it for myself too, because I like it and it does me good. Yes, I love to recall these truths;

that is why I repeat them, because they nourish me. You do not need to listen to me, but nature listens to me: the earth, the grass, the trees, the flowers, the birds, all of heaven… And the sun, too, is happy each time I speak about it.

I feel like a river, ready to fill you up. But you come before me with your tiny little receptacles: little saucepans and tiny mugs. Do you think they are big enough to hold all that I have to give you? It is a shame that I have to pour myself out into such small containers. Try to come with bigger ones! In fact, I do not need your physical presence here in front of me to be able to talk to you. Even over great distances, I can speak to you. After our meetings, when I go back to my house, I still go on giving you explanations and advice. I am free, I have no family to take care of, I have no personal worries. So, when I get home, I go on thinking of you and talking to you. Yes, indeed, I talk to you day and night.

Some nights I do not sleep at all, because I feel that this is the right moment to do some work. On these nights I do not sleep; I pray, I meditate, and I send thoughts of love and light to all my brothers and sisters, and to the whole world. When morning comes, I do not feel any tiredness. It is as if my energies have been replaced by new energy from the divine world. So, yes, I think about you and work for you, even during the night. You may tell me that you have not felt anything at all, but that is because you have developed such thick skins that even the Lord could not penetrate to make himself heard…

The more you refine your spiritual perceptions, the more you will be able to feel that I am with you, and that I speak to you. Some people can feel it when they are far away or even in another country. When they wake, they have only the vaguest memory, but they write to me saying that they have dreamed of me, that I was speaking to them, even though they cannot remember the words I said. Obviously, they would have liked to remember them. But in order to do that you have to realize that the life of the spirit is not independent of the physical body. The life you have lived the day before, with all its different activities, will affect your spirit when you sleep. You must watch over yourself, accept a certain discipline in those activities, and then you will find that during sleep you will be taught by spiritual beings or by your master.[4] And, providing you do this, you will one day be able to help other beings.

On the physical plane, I do not have much time to spend with each one of you. When I meet you I can only give you a nut, a pistachio, a candy or a smile... let's put it like that. But when you climb higher into the realms of thought and spirit, you will feel that I talk to you and that I work with you ceaselessly: every day, at every moment of the day and night, you are receiving something from me. You may ask how that could be possible. I tell you it is possible, because those who have learned to work with their thoughts and their love are capable of creating energy currents on the subtle planes: they project themselves into space, and they penetrate all living beings with their quintessence, as far as the stars. Love gives the gift of ubiquity – it can be everywhere, it can address thousands of souls at the same time, and live within them. It is through his love that a spiritual Master becomes a collective being. On the physical plane he is limited, but through his love he exists everywhere in the universe, even on other planets, and he is helped in his work by the thousands of spirits which accompany him.

Some will say, 'But all that is absurd!' Let them say what they will! How is it that, when someone speaks on the radio, this voice can be heard in millions of towns throughout the world? How has this voice multiplied? It happens because people have installed receivers in their homes. In just the same way, a spiritual Master can speak to millions of souls in the invisible world, as long as they have developed and installed 'receivers' in themselves. I can be everywhere on earth and, at the same time, in your home; it all depends on your ability to receive me.

If you are able to seek me out in realms other than the physical, you will discover that I never stop talking to you. How? That is my business, but I tell you that this is the only thing that interests me: taking care of you and many others whom you do not know. I tell you in all simplicity and humility that, whether I am at home or travelling, I always find opportunities to talk to you, to advise you or to tell you about my discoveries. You have no idea of all the work I do. I have told you so very little up till now. It is possible that one day I will tell you more. For now, however, it would be pointless, as you would not understand me.

You believe that you come to me to be instructed, but in fact you come to me to be fed. I think of myself as a cook. In my restaurant, I prepare different dishes every day, and the food I make for you is always fresh; you can see it steaming as it comes straight from the cooker. I do not prepare it a long time in advance. I make it at the very moment I give it to you.

I also feed millions of beings in the world. If I had to have an audience in front of me in order to give something out, what would I do with everything that flows from my head and my heart? Even if you are not present here, know that whole trainloads of nourishment are leaving my heart and my head. You see, in some ways, all I do is cook. Perhaps you have never thought of me as a cook, yet every day I make dishes of the finest quality that I send out in little trucks to all corners of the earth, and even beyond.

And you too, if you decide to expand your activity, the activity of your thoughts and feelings, one day you will be able to send nourishment, heavenly food, throughout the world. You may wonder how this can be done. Here is an example. Suppose you meet a man or a woman who fills you with love and admiration. Tell yourself that, as your thoughts and feelings travel through the invisible world, they will touch not only this man or woman but many other people who find themselves on this route, who, without knowing how or why, will suddenly find themselves full of love, joy and hope.[5] So many waves of energy circulate in space, sent out and received by people who are totally unaware of their presence. Try, from now on, to take this truth seriously, so that you, too, are able to give everyone the best nourishment from your heart and soul.

You hear my words, and not only you but millions of other people are receiving them too. Neither you nor they are yet aware of it, but one day something will happen and these truths will surface once again in your consciousness and in theirs. That is why I never become discouraged, even if I labour under no illusions. I am well aware that a few moments after I have spoken you have already forgotten what I just told you. Maybe you were thinking of something else when I was speaking, but, even so, these words have been engraved in you. You may not be aware of them, but they are still working away within you, and they will not leave you in peace. Some time or another, when you are least expecting it, they will pop up and speak to you.

You will say, 'If that is so, we will never have any peace!' That depends on what you mean by peace. If peace for you is the chance to give free rein, without discernment, to all your thoughts, feelings, desires and whims, do not be surprised if some of the truths you have heard from me surface to warn you that you are letting yourself be led astray. And these truths will sting a little, will gnaw at you, will pull your hair. It is true that they will not leave you in peace. But if you pay attention to them and go in the right direction, on the contrary, what peace you will experience!

When I talk to you, my efforts all go in the same direction. I do everything I can so that when I open my mouth the divine world speaks to you, so that you can hear the greatest truths, which will feed your hunger and quench your thirst. If you do not believe me, it does not worry me, because, once again, when I make these efforts, I am the one who benefits. I know the laws. I know that words are powerful, that thoughts influence and that they produce results, whether in this world or in another.

So there you are. This is my work. I have no other work. Everything I do is based on the physical law of wave transmission. These vibrations, these waves, begin by stirring something in your subconscious, and one day they will surface in your consciousness. You will open yourself to new truths as if they were your very own discoveries. You will have a moment of enlightenment, and it will steer you in a good direction. You will not know where this impulse came from, but that does not matter, as that is the way my work goes. If I had wanted to be recognized for all that I do, I would have chosen a completely different job.

I also know that, sometimes when I speak to you, my words resonate so well in you that you think, 'But I know all this… I knew this before… I have already learned it somewhere… How could I have forgotten it?' You forgot it because you went wandering off the path, and these truths became covered in dust. They are still there but lie buried, asleep inside you, so you need someone to come and awaken them. That is what I do when I speak to you. That is why I must recognize that, fundamentally, I have nothing, or very little, to teach you. We could say that what I do is to give a few gentle taps on your door, shine a few rays of light through the window, and age-old memories rise up to the surface. For some people, this process happens very quickly; for others it will take much, much longer.

So then, why should you come and listen to me? You come so that you can discover, once again, what you already know. Yes, I only speak to you about what you already know, and one day or another this knowledge will come back into your memory. This is why I never get discouraged. If the truths I present help you, I know that I cannot take all the praise, because it was not I who put these truths in you; they were placed there by Cosmic Intelligence, by the Creator. My words only awaken an echo within you.

Never forget that I speak to you only about your life, the realities and possibilities lying within you. Even if you have not yet become aware of them, even if you do not quite understand what I am saying, I know that, with my words, I touch a being within you whose only longing is to emerge into the light. You can compare this being to the lotus flower, which begins to grow under water before it comes into bloom above the surface. Things are born, take shape and begin to grow in the darkness of the unconscious.

When they appear in consciousness, they are not at their beginning, but almost at their completion, because they have been in this process of realization for a long time. In the same way, my words stir a life, a spiritual entity, in the depths of your being, which, one day, just like the lotus flower, will emerge to bloom above the water.

Notes

1. See *The Wellsprings of Eternal Joy,* Izvor Coll. n° 242, chap. 18: 'Visits from angelic beings'.
2. See *The Path of Silence,* Izvor Coll. n° 229, chap. 5: 'Silence, a reservoir of energies'.
3. See above, chap. 11: 'A Master speaks in silence'.
4. See *Looking into the Invisible – Intuition, Clairvoyance, Dreams,* Izvor Coll. n° 228, chap. 15: 'Protect yourself while you are asleep'.
5. See *The Powers of Thought,* Izvor Coll. n° 224, chap. 4: 'Thoughts are living beings'.

14

I just write my own book

I could never list all the topics you bring to me for my opinion, my advice, or my intervention; you ask about your physical and psychic health, your studies, your choice of career, marriage or divorce, the education of children, the purchase of land or a house and relationships with neighbours or colleagues at work. And, at the same time, some of you have this completely unreal picture of me and my life; you think that I am never hungry, thirsty or sleepy, that I am never sick or tired, that I meditate for days on end, that I am free from emotion, grief or vexation, that I have never been subject to temptation, that I do not need to study if I wish to learn anything, that I am clairvoyant and have all powers. You need to stop and think about this! How on earth would I be able to be attentive to your needs and sufferings, how could I help anybody if my life was so unlike your own, if I was totally different from you? And besides, if I had to be as some of you imagine me to be, it would quite simply be death for me. I want to be a vibrant man, not a corpse.

When you come to me, I would like you to forget what you have read in some of those books written about the life of spiritual Masters. In order to write them, these authors have lumped together, without any discernment, some authentic facts with a collection of anecdotes, and sometimes they have completely invented stories. In any case, do not imagine that I amuse myself by spending my time appearing and disappearing, walking on water, flying through space, making banquets appear, materializing precious stones or pieces of gold, walking through walls of flame or making palaces rise up out of the ground. Even if I were capable of doing such things, I would not do them, because performing such spectacular acts for people does not help them to become better. The life of a spiritual Master is not a display for idle bumpkins!

A spiritual Master is just like any other human being: he has exactly the same organs which provoke the same needs and desires as other people. If you cut his flesh you will see that his blood flows, and it is red. He can be tired and become ill. Where he is different is in his consciousness, in his ideal, in his point of view, in the mastery he has over himself and, above all, in the conviction that, whatever else is going on, there is always work to be done.

During the course of a day, just like everyone else, I can become tired. So, here is an exercise I do, and which I suggest as being helpful for you. Sit down and concentrate on the centre between your eyes, which the Hindus call the ajna chakra.[1] Try not to think of anything, just breathe and let yourself float on an ocean of light. Little by little, in this passive state, (which is really another form of activity), you will feel peace and harmony spreading throughout your body. Thanks to this peace and harmony, you will attract energy and very subtle fluids from the atmosphere, and you will feel re-energized once again, ready to fulfil your obligations. Doing nothing is not the way to be rested

Even so, I am also well aware that I cannot be truly active during the period of the waxing moon, if I have not been in some way passive and receptive during the waning moon so as to receive energies. During the period of the waning moon, particularly the last two days, it is difficult for me to make physical efforts, to leave my home, to come out of myself and even to talk. But being limited on the physical plane does not mean that I am doing nothing. I repeat that to be passive in order to be receptive is another sort of action. There are so many activities possible on the psychic and spiritual planes! And these activities have a beneficial influence on the physical body, making it stronger and much more resistant.[2]

So, to be clear: when you come to see me, you will not find yourself in the presence of some phenomenal, wonderful creature, but you will be with a human being who, just like you, is subject to the laws of nature. Every day this man works, trains himself and encourages you, too, to do the same things.[3] The exercises are simple, they relate to everyday living, though some of you who have read some so-called Tibetan stories may find them disappointing, as you imagine I am going to put you through some ordeals which you think are more 'initiatic.' For example, there was a Master who gave a bag of coarse salt to his disciple, telling him, 'You must crush this into powder, but while you are crushing it make sure that you do not think of the word 'rhinoceros'!' Obviously, the poor boy, who had never had the slightest reason to think of the word 'rhinoceros' before, was quite unable to get the word out of his head. The Master ordered another disciple to withdraw to a cave and, while there, to meditate on identifying with a buffalo. Some time later, the Master came to the cave and called to the disciple to come out and speak with him. 'I cannot do that,' replied the disciple, 'the mouth of the cave is too narrow, and my horns make it impossible for me to cross the threshold.' He had identified so well with the buffalo that he imagined he had really grown mighty horns on his head! There are certainly many much more useful exercises to do for those seeking the light.

A spiritual Master is characterized by the qualities of wisdom, love, will power and self-mastery.[4] He was not able to acquire these qualities in a single lifetime; he has had to work for centuries, even millennia. The qualities acquired by a person's own efforts do not disappear at the time of death; he comes back each time with these qualities and continues to work on them. So, from incarnation to incarnation, he adds new spiritual elements, until the day he becomes a true conductor of light and divine virtues.

You will say, 'But Hindu philosophy teaches that we reincarnate because we have a karma to pay, to rectify mistakes.' Yes, that is the case for most people, but amongst those who have finished their evolution, you could say that there are some who have had enough of the joy and blessedness they have experienced in the bosom of the Eternal. They cannot totally wipe out the memory of their journey on earth. From time to time, they find themselves longing to revisit poor humanity among whom they once lived, and even though there is such a vast distance separating them, they still feel linked to them. After centuries and millennia, they still remember and, out of the abundance and richness of their hearts, they decide to come down and share their treasures with humanity.

Some time after my meeting with my Master, Peter Deunov, and whilst I was still very young, he said, 'Mikhaël, you need to know that before you came down to earth, you signed a contract. You pledged before heavenly beings that you would do a certain work down here. And so, whatever happens, you have to honour that contract.' That was all he said; he did not add anything else. I wished that he had given me some details, but I did not dare ask him any questions. I am sure that he thought these words would have more weight if he let me discover by myself what this agreement was that I had made. Little by little, the nature of the work I had to do has become evident to me.

So I kept these words of the Master close to my heart and they gave me much to reflect on. If you are to sign a contract, you have to be free; those who are not free find that their opinion is not taken into consideration and that, whether they wish to or not, they are bound to return once more. If I had signed a contract, it was because I was free. But from the moment I had agreed to return to earth, I had to submit, once again, to the terror of matter, this physical matter which limits us, imprisons us, which hinders us from hearing, seeing and understanding. Why should this be so? It is to oblige us to work with it, and I know now that all the trials I had to undergo were just the price I had to pay in order to fulfil my mission. You have to pay very heavily for the privilege of fulfilling a divine mission.[5]

Even if a spiritual Master does not have to reincarnate to pay karmic debts, once he is back on earth he is exposed to the same difficulties, to the same ordeals, that other people undergo, and he cannot shrink from them. The higher beings, with whom he signed the contract, watch over him to see that he is fulfilling it. So he has to work to recall what his soul promised and then do it without wondering what it will cost him in effort, exhaustion and suffering. Nothing must stop him. Do not be surprised if I tell you that his very first test is to enter a physical body. In order to form a body, all those who incarnate inevitably receive particles that have lost much of their resistance, vitality and purity. You need to understand that this material has passed from generation to generation throughout the centuries. How could it remain pure and intact? Even if he is born of the most exceptional parents, an initiate has much work to do on the material of his body, to purify it, enliven it, harmonize it, so that it becomes the perfect instrument for his spirit.

It is time to stop telling fantastic stories about initiates and spiritual Masters. The greatest spirits, when they come down to the physical plane, have to form their bodies through physical parents. Even the most remarkable of families always carry imperfections, which they hand down to their descendants. And what do we know of our distant ancestors? But it is also true that those who are born with a body of totally pure matter do not achieve very much. One who is predestined to become a true spiritual Master finds that the lords of destiny give him crude, raw material saying, 'Right then, now let's see you do something with that!' And if he is able to transform this tough, rebellious matter into refined matter that is no longer an obstacle for the spirit's activity, then he becomes even greater. Most people throughout their lives drag their defects about with them, the blemishes they cannot get rid of, and then bequeath them to their descendants. With initiates however we see the spirit at work: thanks to their patience and persistence, they succeed in conquering the physical and psychic weaknesses that have been handed down by heredity.

So you could say that when an initiate incarnates he receives a body that is foreign to him. But he knows that this body must be the material he works on, and so, over the years, he makes efforts, he becomes disciplined, and gradually he purifies and enlightens each particle of his being as he brings it to life with new vibrations. Then, one day, he feels that this body, which was foreign to him, really becomes his body, which means it is the home of his spirit, and he rediscovers inwardly the freedom he possessed on high before he came down to earth. Christians will say, 'But that is not the case for Jesus, who was the son of God, who was conceived by the work of the Holy Spirit, who was born of a virgin untouched by original sin...' I hope Christians will forgive me if I say that even Jesus was not born perfect; he, too, had to learn and do a mighty work of purification before he received the Holy Spirit when he was thirty years old. I have already given you plenty of explanations on this topic.[6]

No human beings, even among the greatest, have ever emerged from their mother's womb haloed in divine light. They have to pass through so many trials and tribulations in order to find their path, and once they have found it they must never stray! They, too, must weep and pray for help. Injustice, outrage and betrayal do not affect them deeply; they weep and plead only to receive and keep the light, until they can shape their physical and psychic being with this light and become permeated with it. But, my God, what a long and difficult road it is! At one moment their physical being is pliable and open to being shaped by the light, and then, suddenly, it resists, revolts and gets the upper hand.

Then, everything has to begin again. But we must not become discouraged for, little by little, this material will eventually give way.

I, too, have had to work for years and years on this material. The soul and spirit are divine in essence, and they know themselves and manifest as such on high, in their own world, but they must also learn to know themselves and manifest through the matter of the physical body. This is the greatest mystery of life. Initiates represented it by the symbol of the serpent that swallows its tail; the head, the higher self, the spirit, has to manifest itself through the tail, through the lower self, through matter. Spirit, which is on high, all knowing and all powerful, must be able to see itself in matter as in a mirror. That is the goal of initiation: to succeed in transforming matter so that it can reflect back to spirit its own image.

Since humanity has come to earth for this task of working on matter, we must not be surprised at all the difficulties the greatest Masters meet on their path. I will tell you also that since they have the means to do this work on matter, both inside themselves and outside themselves, and since they have the will power to do it, they are the ones who are given the heaviest tasks. It is they who must undergo the greatest ordeals, and they emerge nobler and stronger after each one.

So what differentiates a Master from other human beings is that, firstly, he is capable of mobilizing all the faculties given him by the Creator, and then he uses them in all the situations he encounters to take one step further on the path of light. He is never satisfied with who he is. Day and night, he works with mind, heart and will to eliminate that which is still dark and inharmonious in himself and attract the purest particles. This is how, little by little, his whole being vibrates differently, his etheric structure is changed, new possibilities are given him, and he experiences the subtlest joys, to the point that one day he scarcely recognizes himself.

To reach the point where he makes the decision to consecrate his life to this divine work, a spiritual Master must have already been prepared over a long time in previous incarnations. Otherwise, it is quite impossible. Even the person who longs to do so cannot, as his being does not yet resonate with this idea; it does not inspire him. On the contrary, in some way, it makes him fearful because he still has other needs, other desires to satisfy. Only someone who has taken on this work in previous lifetimes instinctively feels the need to continue it. From that moment, he receives the protection of heaven, he receives the light to direct him, he is guided, and no matter what happens, even in the greatest trials, he is always protected, always saved. These trials are sent only to strengthen him, to help him reach the greatest heights and to achieve victory. Heaven watches over him but does not hand him an easy life; rather, he is exposed to difficulties which allow him to develop, to blossom and to awaken all sorts of possibilities, faculties and powers that would never have awakened if he had been spared.

I imagine that you must be thinking, 'If you tell us that spiritual work is so very difficult, what on earth can we do?' Let me tell you the story that I once told two young brothers who came to see me.

I was still a student in Sofia. One afternoon, when I was reading in my room, I heard a tune from a violin in the street outside. The sound of this violin was so extraordinary that I went out to see who was playing in this way. What did I see? A gipsy, an old man in rags, and he was playing on an incredible violin! It was a box of some unusual wood, shaped in the strangest way with a few strings stretched over it, and it was from this box that he drew such heavenly sounds. I had never heard anything like it before and I was completely astounded. People were coming out of their houses or standing on their balconies to listen to him. When he had finished playing, I went up to him and asked, 'Where did this violin come from?' 'I made it myself.' 'Would you let me look at it?' 'Certainly.' When I looked at it, it was truly no more than a simple piece of hollowed out wood, all twisted, with a few strings across it. 'Would you sell it?' 'No, I would never sell it!'

This encounter remained in my mind for a long time afterwards. I could not understand how this man could draw such pure sounds from such a coarse instrument. Stradivarius would have been amazed! It was as if these sounds were drawn from his very soul. I thought about it and I ended by telling myself that I, too, with my very rudimentary violin – by which I mean myself – I, too, could work on producing some beautiful sounds. Of course, I did not have very good conditions, true, the wood of my violin was not the most valuable, and the strings did not vibrate very harmoniously, but my will power, my desire, my love of beauty, could triumph. And so I went back to work even more intensely.

Then I added for these young brothers, 'Whatever you do, never blame conditions. Even if you think that they are not very good, tell yourselves that perhaps your opinion is not absolutely correct. We all have our ideas of what is good or bad for us, but heaven has completely different ideas. So the wisest approach is to think that the conditions we are given are the very best ones. That is how I strive to behave, as I know that conditions are what we make of them. If we do not know how to make good use of them, then even the most favourable conditions produce nothing but catastrophes, whereas if we know how to use them, even the worst conditions can become the most beneficial. In this way, we work on our own material.'

I tell you how I think, how I assess the events I meet every day, and I can only tell you what I tell myself. Do you want to hear me say that you are quite right to complain and be weak in the face of difficulties?

For me, the essential question is the way we live. Yes, how we live, and I want you to understand what that really means. When you begin each day, for example, you expect that it will unfold, more or less, as you hope. However, this is not always the case, because all sorts of unexpected encounters or events can happen which upset or disturb you, and then you give in to your bad temper, anger or disappointment. In some way, this is normal, but this is not the way you will find a solution for dealing with the situation. What I have understood for myself is that, instead of waiting for life to fit in with my wishes, whatever the events and encounters I am faced with, I must discover the best way to consider them and then to take action in a way that ensures they are beneficial not only for me but for others. I cannot say that I am always successful, but I never give up hope.

We have not come here to earth to see events fit our particular desires (particularly as it is rare that the desires of one person match the desires of others), but we are here to learn how to draw lessons from everything, how to think, analyze and discover the laws that are behind them. We must accept the fact that we are sitting at the desks of the university of life, a university that offers us its libraries, laboratories, botanical gardens, zoos and everything we need to learn, if we are capable of observing closely and taking good notes. At regular intervals, life makes us take examinations, to see what level we have reached. We all have to pass through tests in heaven's schools, just as we do in the schools on earth, and that is why we must never neglect any of the preparatory exercises. Worries, grief and disappointments are the coarse, raw material that we have to work on, if we are to become strong and powerful.

All civilization is nothing other than a work on matter, but it is also a psychic work, not only on the people and things outside us, but also on the material inside us. All our instincts, all our impulses, thoughts, feelings, longings make up the material on which we must work. From a certain point of view, you could say that it is a work of creation similar to that of artistic creation.

When I was young, I was very drawn to artistic activities. To be able to express one's aspirations through painting, poetry, music, dance or architecture seemed marvellous to me. I did not have the right conditions, and without question I also did not have enough talent to become an artist. I regretted that until the day I discovered true Initiatic Science; it was then I understood that the laws of spiritual creation were identical to those of artistic creation.[7] So, by working on myself, according to the principles of Initiatic Science, I knew that not only could I live in beauty, in the harmony of sounds, colours, shapes and movements, but that I could also draw others along this path.

Artists use material outside themselves to create works of art which are external to themselves; they put all their effort into this external material, and they produce marvels. But if you were to meet some of them, you could be disappointed, because you would have to note that they, themselves, are bereft of all the beauty of their creations. They are talented; they have studied hard; they have acquired a technique which allows them to produce these works that the public comes to admire. I love and admire artists, but I will say that, for me, true artists are those who are capable of taking themselves as their creative matter. All the methods of the spiritual life are there at their disposal to help and inspire them in this task.

One day, at Izgrev, I was visited by a young sculptor. He was so proud to introduce himself as a sculptor! He stood there arrogantly, hands in his pockets, giving a definitive opinion on everything. I thought that, considering his age, he would benefit from a lesson, and so I said to him, 'You are a sculptor?' 'Yes.' 'Aha! And you know all the basic principles of sculpture?' 'Of course!' 'Well, I don't believe you.' 'What do you mean? I have created masterpieces!' 'That may well be so, but when I look at your… (I didn't say his 'ugly face') your face and your attitude, I cannot help observing that you do not know the laws of true sculpture, for if you were aware of them, you would have begun by applying them to yourself. You cannot make me believe that you are a sculptor. Nothing about you and nothing that emanates from you demonstrates it.

Of course, he was taken aback; he stood there, crestfallen, but he did take his hands out of his pockets as I explained to him that the day he began to work on himself would be the day he would become a true sculptor.

When I tell you things like this, I would not want you to go away with the impression that I undervalue artists.

On the contrary, everything they are capable of doing in their masterpieces inspires me with the longing to achieve that in myself. I tell you that I am filled with admiration when I see the performances of acrobats in the circus. What artists they are too! Before such men and women, who may not have a spiritual teaching, but who work with such concentration, endurance and tenacity to achieve such mastery in their gestures, I am dazzled. When I see how they risk their lives each and every evening to put on a show, I say to myself, 'Well, old boy, you have a task that is so much more important than entertaining the public, and do you have the same perseverance, the same mastery, the same courage? Back to work!'

Artists are those who are able to conceive and express realities that elude most people, and for this they should be admired. Even if their works are still imperfect, they are undeniable proof to me that the world of beauty exists. And perhaps even the word 'beauty' is inadequate, unless we understand that beauty and truth are synonymous. Yes, there are truths that artists relate better than scholars, philosophers and theologians. How can we not be grateful to them for these revelations?

However, many artists do not know what true creation is! What are they within themselves? What state are they in? When you approach them, you do not feel that anything has been built or developed. The true work of creation is spiritual work, because it involves the whole of our being: we reach as high as possible to discover this order, this structure, so that we can capture the purest and most luminous particles, which will become the material of our various bodies: our spiritual, psychic and physical bodies. It requires effort every day, every moment. Each day we add a pure colour, a harmonious shape, a crystalline sound.

From the point of view of Initiatic Science, true artists are those who seek to allow the beauty and harmony of creation to pass through them, to be reflected through them. You will say that no one can see or hear these creations. It all depends on what you mean by 'seeing' and 'hearing'. In fact, nothing we achieve within ourselves is without effect, and we ourselves are the first to feel it. If, through our thoughts, feelings and desires, we try to create paradise within, we will be the first to live there. And then, little by little, all who come near us will begin to sense springs of living water bubbling up within us, birds singing, flowers that scent the atmosphere, and they will say to one another, 'Do you know this garden? What beauty, what peace, what purity, what blessings!'[8]

May all those who have been given artistic gifts cultivate them, but those who do not have such gifts should not despair: inwardly, all possibilities are open to them to become the material for their creation. So, you too should work on preparing yourselves. Do not come up with the excuse that you are poor and miserable and therefore cannot produce anything from yourselves. Something can always be created, no matter what the material is, just like that gypsy who drew those heavenly sounds from a crude piece of wood. What matters most is having the will to succeed, to envision the goal, so that true beauty can be created. This idea of creation is the essence of our Teaching.

In the psychic world we can be musicians, poets, architects, sculptors, and so on. All the arts are contained in the work of a disciple of Initiatic Science. Even dance, for dancing does not necessarily mean doing pirouettes, leaps or holding certain poses. Even simple, plain steps and gestures, when we give them our attention and accompany them with a thought, become imbued with a suppleness and grace which resemble dance, and we feel light and in harmony with all the beings in space.

What a discovery it was for me the day I realized that I could work with material that was not foreign to me, but was my very own material, which heaven had given me and which belonged to me. I can sum up everything that I have just been explaining to you by saying that I just write my own book, that is to say, I have written nothing other than this book that I am. You will say, 'What about those books of yours that we read?' I have not written them; I have entrusted that work to other people, because if I were to write I would not have the time to live. I am concerned only with writing my own book, and it does not matter how much time it takes me. Are you wondering how I am writing this book? I am writing it by living. That is why I am a book for you. Of course, you, too, are books for me, but that is another matter all together...[9]

When I begin talking to you about myself, I notice that your curiosity is immediately aroused. If I talk about myself, it is not so that you should find my life fascinating, unique, or goodness knows what. It is so that I can give you what my life has taught me, so that you can benefit from it. What would be the point otherwise? We do not know people just by learning of the events they have lived through, but by understanding how they lived them and what wisdom they drew from these experiences. This wisdom is like a quintessence of their lives, something which is them but at the same time is much greater than them, and it is with this quintessence that they enlighten and nurture all who approach them.

A book is valuable only when the personal life of the author corresponds with what is being presented to the public, and then the author's worth becomes even greater. A creator should always strive to be of greater value than his or her creations. Humans are attached to masterpieces, but heaven does not have the same point of view. It says, 'Yes, the work is fine, but we want to see what the author is like.' So, I live, that is all, and I am happy to talk, since I know that to talk is also to write. Yes, I talk while striving to imprint heavenly words on your souls. It may well be that I have not succeeded completely, but I go on practising so that one day all these truths will be inscribed in you in indelible letters, and that is the exercise which gives me the greatest joy. You will say, 'So, you need us in order to write?' Need? No. Whether you are there or not, I write, I write everywhere, on all beings, throughout the entire universe. With you or without you, I continue, but you need to be here, to benefit from my writings.

One day, in the little Macedonian village where I was born, I had followed my mother as she went to hang out the washing. A gipsy stopped to speak to her (at that time gypsies often passed through villages looking for kettles and saucepans for tin plating). She came up to me, grasped my hand, looked at it and then said to my mother, 'Oh you have no idea what the future holds for your son. I see him sitting at a table busy writing... He will become a famous person.' I must have been about seven at the time, and when I heard this I imagined that sitting at a table and writing was something glorious, unique! Imagine my disappointment when some time later I arrived in Varna, and everywhere I looked, in offices and elsewhere, I saw people sitting at tables busy writing! For many years I did not have a table.

I sat on the ground with a piece of cardboard on my knees, which acted as my desk. But now, here I am sitting at a table in front of you all, and while I talk I am writing on your souls. So, the gipsy's prophecy has come true.

Only those who have had experiences, who have struggled, who have striven to surpass themselves, no matter what the difficulties, become interesting books for others. Even heavenly spirits come and consult them. You are surprised: 'Really, do highly evolved beings come to read us?' Why not? Don't zoologists, botanists and geologists study animals, plants, rocks and crystals, which belong to the so-called lower kingdoms? They study them, they dissect them, they categorize them, and then they write books about all they have discovered, and in this way they can inform us about events that happened in prehistoric times. Even though humanity belongs to a much higher hierarchy than those of rocks, plants and animals, they do not hesitate to dedicate years of study to them, and then they communicate to us the results of their observations.

All living creatures can be the most fascinating books, so think how much more interesting human beings are! Each one of us is a book, a book we are each writing; all our thoughts and feelings trace letters which will be engraved on the substance of our subtle bodies. Those who have never tried to do anything great, strong and noble give us almost nothing to read, except for a few scribbles. The spirits on high will not pay much attention to them, because they prefer to read ones written by those who have worked, thought, loved and suffered in order to go beyond themselves, to surpass themselves; the spirits gather around these to give them support and encouragement. People who work on themselves, who work to write their own books, who work to create themselves, these are the people who are seen by the spirits as benefactors of all humanity, because they are living books.

And now, perhaps one day books will be written about me. All very good, if good things are said about me; this will make readers want to read my books, where they will find light, advice and methods that will help them find their path. As for me, the most important thing is this book that I am, which I am constantly writing each and every day, to make it more luminous, warmer and even more vibrant.

Notes

1. See *Man's Subtle Bodies and Centres – the Aura, the Solar Plexus, the Chakras*, Izvor Coll. n° 219, chap. 6: 'The chakra system: 2, Ajna and sahasrara.'
2. See *Harmony and Health*, Izvor Coll. n° 225, chap. 8: 'How to become tireless'.
3. See *A New Earth – Methods, exercises, formulas, prayers*, Complete Works, Vol. 13, and *Golden Rules for Everyday Life*, Izvor Coll. n° 227.
4. See *What is a Spiritual Master?* Izvor Coll. n° 207, chap. 1: 'How to recognize a true spiritual Master'.
5. See *The Wellsprings of Eternal Joy*, Izvor Coll. n° 242, chap. 7: 'A commitment to heaven'.
6. See *Sons and Daughters of God*, Izvor Coll. n° 240, chap. 6: 'Jesus, priest of the most high according to the order of Melchizedek' and chap. 7: 'The man, Jesus, and the cosmic principle of the Christ'.
7. See *Creation: Artistic and Spiritual*, Izvor Coll. n° 223.
8. See *The Seeds of Happiness*, Izvor Coll. n° 231, chap. 19: 'The garden of souls and spirits'.
9. See *La pédagogie initiatique*, Œuvres complètes, t. 28, chap. 4: 'Lire et écrire'.

15

All creation speaks to me, and I speak to it

On the east wall of our meeting hall at the Bonfin, you can see a stained glass window in the shape of a pentagram. Actually there are two pentagrams, one big one with a smaller one drawn inside it. What do these two pentagrams mean, and why did I want these symbols placed there? The large pentagram represents the universe, in whose image the human being, the small pentagram, was created. Human beings have their place in the universe, like the small pentagram within the big one. The five psychic principles which make up the human being are: the will, the heart, the intellect, the soul and the spirit, making them a living pentagram, and it is through these five principles that they are given all possibilities to communicate with the great pentagram, the universe, and to vibrate in harmony with it. When you look at the small pentagram inside the large one, it seems like a child nestled in the bosom of its mother where it is fed and protected. In the same way, we, too, should feel we are in the bosom of nature.

If we should decide that, one day, we will sever our links with the physical world, we will not live long. The same thing applies to those who cut the link with the spiritual world. The small pentagram demonstrates that our faculties allow us to have exchanges, not only with the whole cosmos but with the universal Soul that inhabits it. If we do not vibrate in harmony with this great Soul, if we work against it, it is we who will suffer, not the universal Soul.

We are the small pentagram which must surrender spontaneously, with all its heart, to the cosmic order, the large pentagram. Even though nowadays not many people accept this philosophy, you, at least, must try to accept this order, try to harmonize with it and vibrate in unison with it. Heavenly beings will then think of you as sons and daughters of Cosmic Intelligence, and they will give you all their riches. They will, of course, give them a little at a time, for if the sluice gates of heaven opened for you all at once you would be drowned and swept away. You are not yet ready to bear the power of this heavenly current. As soon as this small pentagram that is you adjusts its lines and angles to those of the large pentagram, it receives light, love, joy, hope and strength. All these blessings can be summed up in one word: life. For life, true life, contains everything.

One of the most important things I have learned in my life is the need to harmonize with the cosmic order. That is why I never stop repeating, both to you and to myself, that to become great we have to begin by agreeing to become small. By this, I mean that we have to conform to the cosmic order by becoming subservient to the will of God. When we do that we then become great, because we embody the Almighty, the One and Only, and one day all beings, both visible and invisible, will recognize us as authentically powerful. They will feel the power of the large pentagram shining through us, the small pentagram. Keep returning in your mind to this symbol, and remember what it is saying to you.

Faced with the immensity of the universe, we do not represent very much, but that is no reason for us to feel lost and alone. Between this universe and us, there are comparisons that we should reflect on more deeply. This law of correspondence is the key to self-knowledge and self-mastery. Because initiates have this key, they are able to vibrate in harmony with innumerable beings throughout space and are able to receive their messages in return. This is how they keep learning; each day they open new windows on the universe, in order to receive messages from even more distant regions.

Exchanges are the basis of life. Thanks to the exchanges we make not only with other people but also with nature and the beings of the invisible world, we are able to dwell in different realms – the physical, the psychic and the spiritual. That is why each morning when I open my window, I greet the whole of nature with my hand; I send a blessing to the trees, to the sky, to the sun, to all living beings, to the four elements and to all the beings who dwell there. I say, 'I give you my love. I long to be in harmony with you!' I feel them rejoicing because, at last, someone has thought of them and greeted them. If you do this, you, too, will sense that nature is inhabited by friendly beings. Your greeting will give them light, love and strength, and in return you will receive light, love and strength. Wherever I go, I am always sending out greetings, at least with my thoughts, for to give a greeting is to open oneself, and when we open ourselves we receive life.

The Danish writer, J. Anker Larsen, in his novel *The Philosopher's Stone,* speaks of the contacts that humans can have with nature. He speaks of the 'open world' and the 'closed world', explaining how nature opens to sensitive, innocent people, particularly to children, whereas it stays closed to the majority, who have not learned to receive the vibratory energies of the subtle worlds: trees, lakes, rivers and mountains are nothing more than lifeless landscapes, and they have no communication with them. Those, however, who live in the open world feel not only that they are part of nature but that all of nature is a part of them. So, when they touch a rock, a tree, an animal or any other creature, they are aware that they live in this rock, this tree, this animal, this creature, that they are part of the soul and being of everything.

Nature speaks to us, all of creation speaks to us, but because it does not use words people do not hear it. However, when the sun rises how can they not feel that its light, its warmth and its beauty are telling them so many things? They pick a fruit: its form, its colour and its scent are a language, and there is such language in its taste, when they begin to eat it! Sound and movement are also languages, some of which are very easy to interpret. When someone coughs or sneezes, we understand immediately what that means, and similarly for those who walk slowly or drag themselves along. When a car makes an odd rumbling or jerks forward, we know that it is time to take it to the garage. These are just a few examples of how all animate or inanimate objects speak to us, but they can also hear and understand us.

In order to speak to animals, plants and stones and be understood by them, we must know where to find the entity governing the realm they belong to. The entity which rules over the animal kingdom is found on the astral plane of the universe; the one ruling the plant kingdom is found on the mental plane; the one in charge of the mineral kingdom is on the causal plane, which is so far away that stones to us appear lifeless. However, stones are alive; they are alive and conscious. How do I know this? In the same way that you, too, can know it: by getting into the habit of communicating with them. Take a stone in your hand and listen to it: little by little you will feel that it can tell you the history of the earth, all the events it has taken part in and that are recorded in it, because everything is recorded. And you, too, can hear what a stone has to say. How? By speaking to it with love, for love is the universal language that all creation understands. Touch a stone with love and it will immediately vibrate differently, and it can reply with love. When you know how to speak to stones, you will be able to give them messages. You will take a stone and fill it with your love, you will ask it to bring peace and joy to the person who is going to receive it. Every time I have done this, I sensed that the stone was happy that I gave it such a mission.

Get into the habit too of speaking to the plants and seeds you plant in the ground. Say a few words to encourage them to grow and blossom. Do you know that there are plants that you can ask to protect you? Cacti, for example. Some of them have large, sharp prickles, and if you have them near you, ask them to protect you from the toxic, unhealthy energies in the atmosphere: the cactus prickles will disintegrate these energies before they reach you.

As for animals, even if we do not pay much attention to them, they are part of our life, and we can learn much from those that live close to us. But how do most people view animals, and how do they behave towards them? The way certain species are exploited is truly vile. In order to have their flesh, fur, leather, horns or any other part of their bodies, some people do not shrink from using any kind of cruelty. I have already told you that humans will be condemned and will have to pay dearly for such cruelty to animals.

Even if it seems that the causes of war are only political and economic, the reality is that they are also the consequence of all the animal slaughter of which humans are guilty. The implacable law of justice will force people to pay, with their own blood, for all that has been shed in the killing of animals. How many litres of blood shed on earth are crying out to heaven for revenge! The evaporation of this blood attracts a host of larvae and lower entities from the astral world, and they poison the earth's atmosphere and maintain conflicts. People say they want peace, but as long as they continue to kill animals they will have war. This truth is unknown and perhaps will not be accepted, but whether it is accepted or not, I have to tell you. Humans will be treated in the same way that they treat animals.[1]

It is said that in ancient times the first people lived in harmony with animals; the animals had nothing to fear from them and did not flee at their approach. But now, even if there are a few exceptions, that link is broken, and what animals think about humans is rarely to their credit. When they talk together, you should hear what they say about people, how they judge and criticize them! People think they are so superior, but the animals watch them and say to each other, 'They think we are stupid and understand nothing. Let's not put them right; let's carry on watching them.'

When you speak to an animal, it may look as if it does not understand you, but in reality it can understand very well when it suits it! We do not know what goes on in an animal's head, but it may well understand better than we do what goes on in our heads. We may not understand them, but they understand us, or more precisely they feel us. Many of those who love dogs, cats and horses have had proof of that.

Sometimes, when trying to attract the attention of some animals, we get the impression that they are hiding something from us. Where does this impression come from? It happens because sometimes they are inhabited by astral entities which are watching us through their eyes. Yes, other living intelligent creatures can look at us through the eyes of a dog, a cat or a horse. That is what gives us this strange feeling that they are more than just a mere animal. I hardly dare speak on this subject for fear that people will think I am crazy, yet the truth is that sometimes entities come into the body of an animal, and we meet the gaze of these entities in its eyes.

This relationship that animals have with the invisible world explains why some religions have given animal forms to their gods. For example, in the Egyptian religion, Horus is represented by a falcon, Hathor by a cow, Toth by an ibis, Sekmet by a lion and Bastet by a cat. Bastet was seen as a feminine god, because cats, which are linked to the night and to the moon, have receptive and mediumistic qualities. Egyptian priests used cats as a kind of antenna which could detect energies in the surrounding atmosphere, but they also used them as intermediaries, as ways of communication. They knew how to release the astral bodies of these animals and send them into space to carry certain messages to their destination.

Since cats are receptive animals, they can pick up both good and bad influences. They have been, and still are, used to attract, absorb and deflect harmful influences. In Paris, I knew certain occultists who kept several cats around them in order to protect themselves from attacks directed at them by those they thought of as enemies. It is certainly an effective method but not one I would use. I have told of you of better ways I know, such as working to purify and strengthen our auras. The most effective protection is the aura.

Cats possess other very interesting characteristics. Even if they swallow mice with their skin and guts, they are clean; they wash themselves constantly and they bury their excrement. They can also see in the dark and have developed extremely acute hearing. They are very patient and have great powers of concentration (watch them lie in wait for a mouse!). Lastly, when a cat plays with its tail, it is reproducing the great mystery of cosmic Man.

A cat playing with its tail does not realize at first that its tail is part of its own body. But when it catches and bites it, it realizes that the tail is connected to it, because it feels the bite. This leads to a flash of an awakening consciousness – cat consciousness! I have told you several times of the symbolism of the snake biting its tail.[2] But how many of you have ever seen a snake biting its tail even just once? I doubt it, whereas I know you have seen a cat do so. Disciples on the path of initiation, who long to become identified with cosmic Man, are like the cat that tries to catch its tail; they have a head and a tail, which are situated at opposite ends of the universe, and as long as these are not joined together, they cannot know themselves.

Cosmic Man is made in the image of God, who lives through all beings. For the time being, we are only his tail, but the One who is the head wants to know himself through us. Yes, indeed. God wants to know himself through each and every human being. Once he knows himself in us, then we will be perfect, and we will no longer be separated from him. So, Indian yogis who repeat the formula, 'I am He' are striving to unite with their higher self, which lives in God. They are below and their higher self is on high. The meeting of the two can be represented by a circle. Why? Because the lower self cannot join the higher until the yogi has understood, embraced and, in some fashion, squeezed the universe into a circle, of which the zodiac is a representation.

It matters little whether you resort to a snake or a cat to understand this reality. What is essential to understand is that animals are not just creatures you can choose to ignore or use in whatever way you like, but that they are symbols of psychic and spiritual processes.

There are so many things to tell you about the different ways animals can participate in our lives, and even in our spiritual life. Once, in Switzerland, I was having a meeting with some brothers and sisters at Villeneuve, beside Lake Geneva. In the neighbourhood there was a wood of oak trees, but I had chosen to sit in the shade of a cherry tree in a nearby orchard. We had meditated for a long time in the deepest silence when a small cat arrived. It was very pretty and graceful, and it climbed up the tree trunk of the cherry tree and then jumped onto my shoulders, where it snuggled down for a long time. From this position it looked at the brothers and sisters in the sweetest of ways. After a while it climbed down and took up another position nearby, where it remained motionless.

What was the meaning of this small cat's visit? We were a long way from any houses, and so why did it come to us? I will tell you the answer that the invisible world gave me. Even if I know that perhaps you will find this hard to believe, I must tell you because it is the truth. You are here at an initiatic school, and you need to become acquainted with certain realities in the kingdom of living nature.

So, here's the answer. Thanks to the silence, the peace, the harmony that we had been able to create, we had drawn heavenly friends to us. At that particular moment, the mineral kingdom, the plant kingdom, the human kingdom and that of the luminous spirits of the invisible world were all present; only animals were absent from this chain of beings taking part in our gathering, and this cat was sent by the elemental spirits; they asked it to act as a conductor, to transmit this message of brotherly harmony for the benefit of the animal kingdom. You need not believe me, but that this little cat was our messenger to all the animal kingdom is the reality. In other exceptional circumstances, a dog has come to take part in a meeting. We do not know what entities enter into animals either to help us or for us to help them. In any case, nothing happens by chance.

Some years ago, at the Bonfin, we had a cat that behaved in the most surprising way with me. Each morning, it came to my door and waited for me. When I came out, it would follow me and accompany me right up to the Rock of Prayer for the sunrise. I would sit down, and then it would jump up onto my knees and would stay there motionless for as long as I was meditating. Then it would come down the hill with me. One day, it disappeared. I waited for it and people looked for it. Someone told me that a neighbouring countryman, who was very poor, used to trap cats for food; it was surely this man who had caught the cat. I was sad about this, and even now I find myself thinking about this cat, which truly had something extraordinary about it. I am sorry that I do not have a photograph of it, curled up on my lap, as I meditated on the Rock of Prayer.

What a mystery animals are! Perhaps they seem to be indifferent; perhaps they are more present and shrewder than we believe them to be, but they do not want us to know it. People have told me stories about dogs and cats which have disappeared after their owners had spoken about getting rid of them. How did they guess this? Were they able to interpret certain looks, or was there something in the tone of voice informing them of their owners' feelings for them?

One day, at Izgrev, we were given the gift of a dog to guard our property. We had to give him a name, and so I called him Jafar. I had to explain more than once to those who did not know, or who had forgotten, that Jafar was a notable character in the *'The Arabian Nights'*. He was the grand vizier of the caliph Haroun-al-Raschid. Then, our Jafar began to take on a different bearing, as if he thought he really was someone important. He became vain and capricious, and we could no longer talk to him. Had he understood me when I explained where his name came from? Who knows?

Tradition states that Solomon understood the language of animals, and in certain books on magic you can read about ways to develop such a gift. I have never tried out such methods, but they must be possible to a certain extent. Even though I speak about animals as if I were able to interpret their actions, I have to say that I, too, find that they remain a mystery, though there are times when I try to see if I can communicate with them.

One day when I was meditating under a tree, three birds came to sit on the branch overhead. As they were silent, I asked them to sing, and they sang. When they stopped, I asked them to continue, and they did so. Once again they stopped, and for the third time I asked them to sing. This time, when they stopped, I made no further demands on them, but they had responded three times to my desire to hear them sing.

Sometimes, in spring, I would find a nest with several eggs in our garden at Izgrev. I would keep a close watch, and when they were hatched I would go each day to bring a few crumbs of food to the little newborns. My God, they were so touching! In the beginning, the parents went mad when they saw me coming towards them, but they quickly sensed that I wished them no harm, and then when I talked to their little ones they watched me quite peacefully from a nearby branch. It was absolutely delightful!

There are doves in my garden at the Bonfin. They live in a big aviary where they can come and go freely, and they are used to coming up to me so that I can give them seeds. When I put out the seeds, five or six doves fly to the table. I sit down and I talk to them, saying, 'Oh, you are so pretty! I love you so much, and I would love to stroke you.' I pick one up, stroke it, and it does not struggle to get free. Sometimes they are on the grass, and when I pass by them, they show no fear and do not fly away.

Whether we are aware of it or not, animals, and particularly birds, are involved with our lives. They come and go without anyone paying much attention to them, and yet sometimes they are message bearers. They can bring us good news, but they can also bring news of the death of a parent or a friend. At first we do not know how to interpret what they come to tell us; it is later on that we understand. Even in towns, there are birds perched on trees, balconies, the roofs of houses. There could be times when you are in your room, full of grief and worry. You beg the Lord to help you, and you think you are alone. Yet there, on the sill of your open window, is a little bird which has heard your cry for help in your suffering, and it carries your prayer to heaven.

Do not wait for this to happen by chance, but get into the habit of confiding your wishes to birds. Do you see a bird passing near you? Formulate in your mind a request that is beautiful and pure. Then, tell the bird to carry it away, and it will do it. Even if you have nothing special to request, when you see a bird, always think of it as a messenger that can carry your good thoughts throughout the world. Take it as an opportunity to enter into contact with all winged beings. Where could you find a more poetic task? The bird is an intermediary between heaven and earth. It would take much too long to explain why this is so. Just accept that I am not going to say anything more about it.

It's a shame that so many animals are not friendlier towards us and are afraid when we get close. Obviously the best way to attract them and tame them is to give them food. That is what I did when I was in the Arizona desert. In this desert there is a type of grey squirrel. I loved watching them run and jump, but when I came closer, they fled. Each day I brought them a little food, and little by little they allowed themselves to be tamed. The evening before I left, I went to say good-bye to them; they had become used to me and I wanted to warn them that I would not be there the next day to feed them.

I had a very unusual experience with snakes. It was in the Luchon region, near Bagnères-de-Bigorre. When I went for a walk in the forest, I was amazed to come across so many snakes, particularly because they did not slither away, whereas normally snakes escape as fast as possible at the slightest hint of people approaching. Sometimes I would sit at the foot of a tree to meditate, and when I opened my eyes I was surrounded by lots of them, and some were even quite big. I was told they were harmless because of the sulphuric vapours which came out of the ground, which was the reason why there were thermal spas in this area to treat people with respiratory troubles. I also learned that the sulphur vapours could render the snakes' venom harmless, and I had some very interesting conversations with some of the snakes which gathered in a circle around me. Snakes are loaded with so much symbolism, whether they are seen as beneficial or as evil!

I have quite different conversations with insects – for example, ants. In the summer at the Bonfin, ants come into my chalet. It is always possible to get rid of them with insecticide, but as I prefer not to kill them I pick up one ant, like this, between my thumb and index finger and I say to it, 'Listen, my friend, do this for me… Go to your boss (yes, you must always address the boss) and tell him that if, within one hour (you see, I make sure I give him a time limit), you have not all cleared off, you will all be exterminated.' Then I carefully put him back on the ground and get on with my business. One hour later, when I come back, all the ants have gone. The message has been delivered, most effectively.

Here's a story for you about a cricket. In Paris I had a Bulgarian friend who invited me, when I arrived in France, to come and live for a time with him. He lived in a small apartment in the north of the town, and when we saw each other again this is what he told me. Hiding somewhere behind his kitchen sink was a cricket, and every evening this cricket would begin to sing. One evening, when he came home tired from work, he found this ceaseless loud noise unbearable, and he shouted, 'Oh that's enough now!' He took a little stick and tried to chase the cricket from the hole where he thought it was hidden. From that moment on, the cricket stopped singing. The next day and for days after, he heard nothing more, and he thought that the cricket had either left or had died. Some time later, an evening when he felt alone and sad, he began to sigh, 'Oh, if I had not said such harsh words to that little cricket, perhaps he would sing again, and I would at least have his company.' A few moments later, to his great amazement, the cricket began to sing once again. You may say that this was just coincidence. Yes, perhaps it was, but that is always the way we explain the things we do not understand.

All the time, wherever we are, we can be in contact with all living beings. The language does not matter, because thoughts (and even more so, words) produce waves of energy which influence all creation. Those who have worked for a long time at controlling their inner lives will be able to possess the power of the Word.[3] Their purified and illumined lives release a power which permits them to take the etheric double of a tree, a flower, a rock or a spring and use it to serve the world. Yes, for example, they can speak to a rock and ask it to go to the aid of a fragile person, to make that person stronger and more stable. They can also go to a spring and ask it to purify and bring new life to their friends. One day, at the Bonfin, I burned some incense on the Rock of Prayer and asked it to go to the brothers and sisters who lived in and around Paris. Several of them told me that they had sensed it. You wonder why I do not do that every day?

I do it when it is the right time to do it. You have very little idea of all that I do.

Wherever I go, I am aware that nature and its inhabitants are speaking to me and I speak to them. On my travels I have often stayed close to oceans and seas: in Hawaii, California, Israel, Lebanon, Thailand and many other places. I have often spoken to the water spirits. I asked them to bless all those who live and work beside the water, all who bathe in it, all who cross it in boats. I am busy all the time, and that is why I am never bored, because I always find something to do. All of creation is so vast and so populated! Why not think about talking to its inhabitants?

Obviously, in order to be heard by the nature spirits, it is essential to be in a state of harmony, purity and light. These are the conditions we have each morning when we go to watch the sun rise. So, on your way, spare a loving, grateful thought to the sky, the trees, the flowers, the pebbles, the earth. Think too of all the invisible beings that surround us. Thanks to them nature is alive and able to offer us all its gifts. Speak to them; say, 'O you, gentle children of earth, water, air and fire, you, gnomes, undines, sylphs and salamanders, I love you. May you be blessed and thanked for all your work.'

People bustle about looking as if they are awake, but in truth they are asleep. They pass through life with their eyes shut as they trample through the sanctuary of nature. They do not feel the invisible presence of living, intelligent beings near them or the other forces which surround them; they just limit themselves to what is accessible to their five senses. To be awake means to be consciously aware of all the beings that surround us and to remain in contact with them. Are there still those in the world who have not lost this contact? Undoubtedly there are, and so they offer the invisible beings flowers and food, because they feel that they participate in their lives. They speak to them; they invite them into their homes, give them a place near the hearth and ask them to keep an eye on all members of the family, but especially on the children. They see them as their friends. Sometimes I have asked you to listen to the flute and harp melody from Berlioz's oratorio, *The Childhood of Christ.* Music like this marvellously evokes the presence of airy, diaphanous beings. We can feel them, and almost see them, dancing amongst us.

Nature spirits are waiting for you to ask for their help and protection. If you are unaware of them, what can they do? I am sure that some of you are thinking, as you listen to me, 'What on earth is he telling us? We are living in a scientific and technological century, and he wants us to believe that we can be in touch with elemental spirits, and that they will come to help us! We are never going to believe such a thing.' Well, well, well, let me tell you that I believe it.[4] One day, I read a very interesting book on the subject of the spirits of the four elements, of their nature, their customs and their relationship with people. It was called *The Count of Gabalis, Conversations on the Secret Knowledge* of the Abbot Montfaucon de Villars. Some parts of this are difficult to understand and interpret, but it is well worth the effort to read it. Why was the author assassinated on the road to Lyon, right after this book was published? It is said that it was because he had revealed things that should have stayed hidden from the uninitiated.

Earth, water, air and fire… Most of the time people see them only as impersonal brute forces that get noticed when they cause disaster. As for me, I say that the four elements are inhabited by living and intelligent beings, which can help us in our spiritual work and which can respond to the requests of those who know how to compel them solely by the power and radiance of their spirit. I know that the four elements in nature have their work, their programme of activity which we need to respect, and that is why I do not like to disturb them. From time to time, however, I do make a request of them. We always have the right to ask, but they have the right not to grant our request. So it is never exactly clear what their reply will be.

Some years ago I was returning from Paris; it was summer, and night had fallen hours before. The metro only went as far as the bridge at Sèvres. It was pouring with rain, and there were no buses or taxis. I did not have an umbrella with me, and it would take nearly an hour to walk to our house on rue Jeanne d'Arc in Sèvres. I was used to doing this... but on such a night as this, with so much rain! So I spoke to the spirits of the air and said, 'Look at my situation. If it is at all possible, could you please abate the rain a little until I get home?' As I told you, you can always ask, but your prayer is not always granted, so I had no idea what the response would be. To my great astonishment, the rain stopped abruptly. I left very quickly, running almost all the way until I reached the garden gate. I went in, and no sooner had I set foot in the house than the rain began falling once again, with the most tremendous force! A brother who was there making bread saw me, and he was amazed to see that I was not soaking wet. I said, 'Yes, that's how it is!'

Some mornings at the Bonfin, when big clouds hide the sunrise, I say to the angel of the air, 'We are here on the Rock of Prayer for the sun, and not for the clouds. I beg you, can you please move them just a little? There is so much space in the sky!' I do not insist; I concentrate instead on some other topic. Often, a moment later, when I open my eyes, I find that the sun is shining. But the angel of air does not always answer my request, for it has its work to do: so I understand, I accept it. One year, on Michaelmas eve at the end of September, I asked the angel to give us fine weather for the next day, and it just poured all day, a real downpour!

When I was in India a clairvoyant predicted that one day I would have all power to command the spirits of the air. I do not claim to have this power, and the truth is that I have more important things to do than to command the elements. If there are forest fires, as there often are in the summer on the Côte D'Azur, it is not my job to ask the nature spirits to put out these fires lit by the careless, the unaware or criminals, but let me tell you what happened on one occasion

It was again at the Bonfin, at the beginning of autumn. Night had fallen. Some brothers knocked on my door to tell me that a fire had started a few kilometres away, near Cannes, and that the wind was blowing the fire in our direction. I asked them to accompany me to the Rock of Prayer, and from there we could see the flames. I asked them to leave me alone and I began to speak to the angel of the air, 'O, angel of air, years ago my village in Macedonia was burned to the ground, and my mother and all of us barely escaped to safety... Now it is the Bonfin and the village of Capitou next to it which is in danger of being burned. I beg you, do something so that this fire will be extinguished.' I concentrated for a moment longer, and then imagine my surprise and delight when, less than five minutes later, enormous drops of rain began to fall. Doubtless, the firemen were also doing their work, but the rain helped them tremendously, and I spent a long time thanking the angel of air.

In all my travels, I have, of course, been to many towns, but I particularly like to spend time in forests. When I can see beautiful trees, something happens within me, and I come back happy. What riches, what blessings, dwell in trees! Walking amongst them, I consider how all trees are condensed light. Yes, these trunks, branches and leaves nourish themselves with light, they are just condensed solar light, and I am amazed at the thought that the sun's love is found here in such abundance. By purifying the atmosphere with the oxygen they release, trees are our benefactors, and those who live near a forest are truly privileged.

I have seen magnificent forests in India, Ceylon, Lebanon, England, Sweden, Norway, Switzerland, France; in Canada and the United States too, of course. I went to the famous sequoia forest in California's Yosemite Park. These trees, four thousand years old, have become world famous because some of them have trunks so enormous that you can drive a car through a tunnel carved in the trunk. I too have gone through in a car, and it was indeed impressive, but it is a pity that the forest does not feel very alive. You could say that the nature spirits have abandoned it.

A forest, of its very nature, is a place which is lived in, and as soon as I start to walk amongst trees I feel presences. That is why I speak to them. I know how to address them, how to commune with their souls, and they understand me. I have had a link with trees for such a long time that it is natural for me to say that they are my brothers. I go up to one of them and, as I hug it, I whisper, 'I am giving you a message for all the trees in this forest. Tell them that I love them and that I want to hug them all.' It passes on my message, and all the other trees are happy, practically dancing as I go on my way.

A brother surprised me one day in my garden as I was hugging a cypress tree, and he told me afterwards how astonished he had been. Why? There was nothing very surprising in my action. I talk to trees and sometimes I hug them. They sense that I love them, and they respond to me. Humans would be a lot happier if they knew how to have real relationships with trees. What is a cypress tree? What is a fir tree? What is a eucalyptus tree? You have to spend hours with them to discover their souls and to commune with them. I do this often, and it is impossible for me to express all that I feel and the revelations I am given. At that same moment, something changes in the tree's vibrations and in its colours.

There are forests which have lost their inhabitants, because the humans visiting the forests were so noisy, so disrespectful and coarse that they drove them away. In all countries, however, there are still some places that have not been desecrated, so when you go into these forests, be aware that you are entering a territory which belongs to the nature spirits; put yourself in harmony with them, and you, too, will feel their presence. What I am telling you is not make believe; fairies exist and Merlin the wizard is not the only one to have kept company with them in the forest of Broceliande. Once I was invited to Brittany, and I, too, visited this forest…

The whole of creation speaks to me, and I speak to it. That is why when I see the prosaic world some want us to live in, I think about the writers who gave us fairy tales for children: the brothers Grimm, Andersen, Perrault and many others, and also the films of Walt Disney. You will say, 'Really, are you still looking at Walt Disney films and reading fairy tales?' No, I have not read them for a long time, and I have no need of them to live with the fairies. I live with them without looking at films and reading storybooks. But what I have said to you obviously needs a little clarification. For if some of you were to take this as an invitation to abandon all your responsibilities and duties and dive into fairy stories, you would find it ends badly for you! I walk in the world of fairies, but I keep my feet well and truly on the ground. Ever since I was a child, I knew that beyond what we see there lives a world which is invisible yet which is just as real. So I live with the awareness of these two realities, the visible and the invisible, which merge into each other.

The world of invisible beings is as real to me as the world of human beings. Even if I do not see them, I sense that space is inhabited with those beings we call fairies, nature spirits or the spirits of the four elements. From time to time they come and alight on my shoulders or on my head – yes, just like birds, but you do not see them, and they can also alight on you. Children will often see these beings.

In their first years on earth, children live in contact with invisible beings – they smile at them, they have conversations with them, listening to and answering them. However, when they speak to adults about them, in particular to their parents, they are ignored or they are told to be quiet with these fantasies. So, since nobody believes them, the children say no more and even start to doubt what they have experienced, until the day when they forget all about it. This forgetfulness sets in when the child is about seven years old. If adults would just take the time to listen to the stories of their children and ask them questions, they would receive the most astonishing revelations. As it is, they deprive themselves of something very precious.[5] So many adults behave no better with children than they do with animals!

Children have a link with the invisible world; the moment you meet a child, or take care of one, think about this. Be aware, too, that this child has been sent by heaven to awaken something delicate, poetic and spiritual within you. Close to each child is a guardian angel, which has been given the special task of watching over it, and if it sees that you, too, are caring for the child, it will give you its blessing.

What do you think I do when parents bring their children to me? Of course, I speak with the parents, but I also speak to the children. I may stroke their cheeks or give them a hug, but that is only the external side of things. In fact, even if I say nothing, I entrust these children into the care of invisible beings, and I ask their guardian angels to watch over them. I know that heaven did not put these children into the sole care of their parents. In the angelic hierarchy there is one particular group whose task is to look after children; this order is that of the *Elohim,* which dwell in the sephirah, *Netzach,*[6] and children feel safe with them. Sometimes they talk to them, and they do not understand why adults do not do the same. Children feel these companions as part of the family, and they are not frightened, or even surprised, when they see them appear.

Children carry with them memories of distant epochs, when human beings thought nature was a living organism with which they were in constant relationship. This memory remains in some children, but it gets stamped out of them as they grow, because of their education and the language and attitude of adults, so that, one day, they will even laugh as they remember their childish way of thinking. Yet these things were traces of a distant past written on their souls, and it is a pity that they end up erasing them.

When parents, psychologists and teachers grasp certain initiatic truths, they will truly be able to study the life of children. They will read in the book of their souls all that is reflected there up to a certain age. They will discover that what children know in their unconscious is unimaginably profound. There may be some mothers who have a vague feeling that the whole life of the universe is being revealed to them by their baby, and in this way, you could say that they are the students of their child. Other mothers, who take on the role of teachers to their children, do not learn much. A mother who is full of love, attentiveness and wisdom receives a real initiation throughout those first years of her child's life.

Once I had a most surprising experience with a baby who was just a few months old. It was at Izgrev, and after my lecture I had had appointments with many brothers and sisters who had asked to meet me. I had talked and talked and was utterly drained. I needed at least ten minutes alone, in silence, to recharge myself. But at that moment a little angel was brought to me. Yes, her parents wanted me to bless their little girl. I thought, 'What blessing could I bring to this child? I am absolutely exhausted.' I was going to ask them to come back a little later when the little girl, who was carried by her father, began to look at me, smile and make all sorts of gestures, as she held out her arms to me. When her parents came closer, she grabbed hold of my beard and whiskers with her little hands and would not let go. She pulled and pulled. The parents, of course, were a little embarrassed, but they were also happy to see how their child was giving me such a warm welcome.

It was then that something extraordinary happened. All of a sudden, I did not feel any weariness, as if, by pulling on my beard, this little being had filled me with energy. I had known for a long time that hair acts as antennae picking up currents of energy. But there, in that way, it was so unexpected, especially coming from a baby who was only a few months old. My fatigue flew away instantly. You could say that this child had been sent by heaven at that very moment, and that she knew instinctively what she had to do to help me carry on with my work until the end of the day. What had she seen and felt that led her to behave in that way?

We must pay great loving attention to all that little children manifest, even in those who seem the least awakened, because their spirits, which have not yet completely incarnated, live partially outside their bodies, and so they can see and feel what the adults do not see or feel. Apparently, when I was a child, I would say things no one quite knew how to interpret. A child does not fully incarnate into its physical body until it is seven years old. Up to then, it lives part of the time out of its physical body, and that is why it is in contact with the beings of the invisible world. For the good of their children, but also for their own good, parents need to look into this question. They should observe their children during their early years in order to read the true secrets of the life written on the book of their souls.

Children are still a great mystery. As much as possible they must be protected and kept in an atmosphere of peace, harmony and purity, even while asleep, because they are receptive to all the currents circulating around them. Their astral body sleeps, and their mental body is still far away, but their etheric body is very active and absorbs all the currents and elements in the psychic atmosphere. If parents are attentive to the atmosphere they create around their infant, later in life their child will be well equipped for meeting all the shocks and hardships of life.[7]

When a child comes to earth, the parents do not know what spirit inhabits it. They should tell themselves that this child does not belong to them, that it is a son or daughter of God, to whom they have only given a body, a house, for the spirit to live in. And all those who come close to the child must also treat it with great attention and respect, in order to protect it. Above all, they must avoid abusing its trust, setting it bad examples or giving harmful advice. What a child sees, what it hears, what it experiences, will be stamped on it forever. That is why I can never repeat enough that the responsibility parents and other adults have for their children is immense. They should tremble at the thought that they are capable of harsh words or negative actions that will scar their children forever. Adults who do not respect children will, one day or another, be punished by heaven, and that punishment will be terrible.*

What is also remarkable about very young children is their perception of the physical world, to the point of

---

* On 28 September, 1985, Michaelmas eve, at the Bonfin, the Master spoke for the last time to the Brotherhood gathered around a big fire. After he had talked for about half an hour, he ended by saying, 'I am giving you light. Look after this light most carefully. And if you have children, never forget the obligations you have to them. These children are souls whom you have invited into your home. Each and every day, through your words, but more by your example, you are leaving your imprints stamped on them. Make sure that these impressions are good and beautiful. Yes, you need to take this very seriously. And now, good evening and good night. Even if am no longer with you physically, I am with you more than I have ever been.'

believing that everything is alive – even inanimate objects. In Maeterlinck's *Blue Bird,* the children feel that all the objects surrounding them are like family members, some friendly, some hostile, and they find it perfectly normal to tell these objects what they are thinking and what they want from them. If they bump into a piece of furniture or hurt themselves on an object, they believe that the furniture or object wanted to hurt them, and so they talk crossly to the offender. Why do they think these things are alive? Is it because they are still young and a little naïve? Perhaps, but that is not all there is to it. They are capable of sensing that, to some extent, these objects are alive, with a life that is still veiled in mystery for us.

One day I had to leave Videlinata* to go to Lausanne to catch the train to Paris. I got into the car of the brother who was going to drive me to the station, but it just would not start. He tried everything he could, but the car refused to move. Time was passing and I began to be a little uneasy, because I really needed to leave, so I began to talk to the car as if it were able to understand me. I said, 'Dear car, you are such a nice car, I know, and I want you to listen carefully to me. I have to catch a train, and you know that there are no other cars to take me there. Please make an effort and drive us to the station. Once there, if you want, you can stop, and I will not reproach you.' I continued for a few moments more to encourage it with my thoughts and a few friendly pats, and then I said to the brother, 'Let's go now.' Lo and behold, the engine began to turn over and we were on our way…

An hour later we arrived in Lausanne, but we were scarcely within sight of the station when the car came to

* The centre of the Universal White Brotherhood in Switzerland.

a complete standstill; it was impossible to make it go any further. We were in the middle of the road and beginning to cause a traffic jam. Behind us all the cars were hooting. The only thing for me to do was to get out with my suitcase and hurry to catch the train, leaving the brother (with the aid of several passersby) to push the car to the side of the road!

What had happened there gave me food for thought. It is not unusual for a car not to start, and then to begin to move, but in this case, what was astonishing was the way in which it stopped. It could have done it earlier, or later, on its return from the station. However, I had asked it to go as far as the station, and as soon as it saw the station (through what eyes, I wonder!), it decided that since I would be able to catch my train it need not go any further. It had done all that was asked of it, and so that was that.

I could tell you other stories like that, but it is not necessary. I hope that this little tale will draw your attention to the fact that objects are a mystery to us, as are the relationships we can have with them.

What is essential is that we should be conscious that we are part of a whole, that this whole is alive, and since it is alive we are making exchanges with it all the time. We speak and it replies; it speaks to us and we reply.[8] Everything we do, say or ask receives answers: they may be confirmation or refutation, approval or condemnation. The invisible world is always present, here, all around us. It watches us, it listens to us, and it always gives us answers. The only problem is that its language is very different from our own and is not necessarily all that easy to understand.

One year, when I had been invited to Greece, I stayed for a while on the island of Patmos, where according to tradition the apostle John wrote the *Book of Revelation.* One day, in my hotel room, I burnt some incense and meditated, as I wished to ask the invisible world certain questions. Then I went out for a walk in the hills with some friends who had come with me. There, at the side of the road, was a woman whose outward appearance was very simple, even poor, but she had a magnificent face. She looked as if she was waiting for us, and when we came close to her she came up to me, kissed my hand with great respect and then said a few words in Greek. They were translated for me, and there in what she said was the answer to the question I had asked in my meditation. Heaven had used her to give me the answer. I was so happy! The words spoken to me by this stranger were prophetic; she had given me the answer I sought from heaven. You should know that it is very easy for heaven to send its replies through a human being or an animal, but also through natural phenomena.

Once again, when I was in Switzerland, I wanted to do a certain work, and I climbed up to the Rochers de Naye above Montreux, a splendid place, at an altitude of a little more than two thousand metres. Evening was drawing in; there were no walkers, and everything was silent. I let myself be guided by friends on high, who showed me where the mountain spirits gathered, in a strategic spot where there is a view of all the surrounding peaks.* And it was there that I began my work... As there was nobody around, I recited sacred formulas in a very loud voice. And then, suddenly, somewhere, three sheep began to bleat gently, very gently. Sheep are a symbol of Christ[9], and I understood that this

---

* These are the Savoy Alps, the Mont Blanc chain, the Valais Alps and the Bernese Alps.

was to encourage me to continue this work. So I went on for a long time, for a very long time.

Then, when I had finished and I was getting ready to go down the mountain, a huge explosion was heard, and the whole mountain shook. In all my life I have never heard such an explosion. I was most struck by it. I understood that the mountain spirits had given me a reply, and then that same evening, on the radio, they announced that on that very day there had been three very strong solar flares. Why this coincidence? The spirits had led me to do a certain work on the same day that these phenomena were occurring in the sun.

So, now, I say this to you. The day we understand universal life, which we are a part of, we will be able to speak the true word of life. At that moment, perhaps, God will say to us, as he said to the prophet Ezekiel, that we should speak to the multitudes of dry bones and bring the dead to life. And then, like Ezekiel, we will say, *'Come from the four winds, O spirit, and breathe upon these slain, that they may live!'* Obviously, this is symbolic, but what is symbolic is also real.

Notes

1. See *The Yoga of Nutrition*, Izvor Coll. no 204, chap. 5: 'Vegetarianism'.
2. See *Langage symbolique, langage de la nature*, Oeuvres complètes, t. 8, chap. IV: 'Le temps et l'éternité', partie 1.
3. See *The Path of Silence*, Izvor Coll. no 229, chap. 10: 'Speech and the Logos'.
4. See *The Fruits of the Tree of Life – The Cabbalistic Tradition*, Complete Works, vol. 32, chap 7: 'The four elements' and chap. 22: 'Nature spirits'. See also *The Book of Divine Magic*, Izvor Coll. no 226, chap. 8: 'Working with nature spirits'.

5. See *Education Begins Before Birth*, Izvor Coll. no 203, chap. 9: 'Protect your children's sense of wonder'.
6. See *Angels and Other Mysteries of the Tree of Life*, Izvor Coll. no 236, chap. 3: 'The angelic hierarchies'.
7. See *Education Begins Before Birth*, Izvor Coll. no 203, chap, 6: 'The magic word'.
8. See *The Wellsprings of Eternal Joy*, Izvor Coll. no 242, chap. 10: 'Our place on the cosmic Tree'.
9. See *The Book of Revelations – A Commentary*, Izvor Coll. no 230, chap. 8: 'The scroll and the lamb' and chap. 14: 'The wedding feast of the lamb'.

16

An ideal of fraternal life

Here's a letter someone wrote to me: 'Master, I love and admire your teaching, and that is why I want to go on meeting with you, but you alone, not your disciples. I find all these people who surround you ignorant nobodies. I have nothing in common with them, we do not come from the same background, we do not have the same education,' and so on and so forth. I have received letters which say this sort of thing several times, and the people who write in this way have no idea how they are disgracing themselves in my eyes. I cannot give them my friendship and I prefer to do without such people. I have no need of rich, learned or powerful people. For the work I envisage, knowledge, power, an elite education and money are not of much use.

When I meet a new person, I am not interested in their social position, degrees or fortune. Good looks and fine clothes are not important either; they may be important for the owner, but not for me. The important thing for me is the ideal people hold, the model they try to adhere to, and I look for this not only in their words but in their looks, their gestures and everything emanating from them, because it is by these signs, which are sometimes imperceptible, that they truly reveal themselves. These indicators are like diplomas that nature has inscribed on them, and they demonstrate the virtues that people have strived to develop.

Given the nature of the work we do here, I need to know on whom I may count, and I can rely only on those who have a deep need to become free and to conquer their weaknesses. I have no illusions about the others; they will soon leave me or they may even try to harm me. As they have come here, I accept them, I must give them a chance, I try to help them, because I know how difficult life is for each of them – they may not have had good examples or good conditions. But the reality is there and I know what awaits me. Obviously I keep these observations to myself; I say nothing, and I welcome all those who come here.

In my room I have a picture of the Virgin, full of love, bending over the infant Jesus, a tiny child whom she holds in her arms. I often look at this image, which is so pure. I could show it to you, and I would say, 'Look, this is the infant Brotherhood I am holding in my arms.' For this Brotherhood, which the Master Peter Deunov sent me to create in France, is in some way my child and I, too, am holding it in my arms.

The idea of brotherhood which we are working for is like a newborn child. In order for it to grow, we must give it food and clothing, and I go as far as the stars looking for this food and clothing. Each day, I ask them for something for this child, and the stars bend over it with love. I also talk to the trees: 'Will you give me something?' I speak to the whole universe about this child who wants to grow, learn to walk and be educated. I know all its needs, and my constant concern is to look after its basic needs and its growth; I have no other work and I must be so vigilant! I have a whole laboratory to analyze all the food it is given. I make sure that it is pure and healthy, and that it does not contain any seed of disruption. In fact, when this child has grown up, it will be able to overthrow the old world. So, I ask you too to take great care of this child. It needs so much love. Deprived of love, like all children, it could die.

This idea of brotherhood – that and that alone has the power to bring peace to the world. One day when I was walking in the forest, I was singing Master Peter Deunov's song, '*Ni smé slaveïčéta gorski:* We are the nightingales of the woods.'[1] Then a dove came from nowhere and alighted on my head, then on my hand. Nowadays, you can see this symbol of peace everywhere, but it is not enough to put it on a poster or to have endless meetings in which people discuss ways of ending wars. The dove which landed on me spoke of a peace that comes from the deepest part of the human being.[2]

I came to you so that here, in France, the ideal of fraternal life could be established, which would serve as an example for the future. Throughout the world, France is considered as the country of liberty and human rights; it has taught the whole world that each and every individual must be respected as a free, independent entity, whom nobody is allowed to dominate or enslave. But now, it has another mission to fulfil, that of creating a model of collective, fraternal life, where each individual will consciously accept a sort of magnificent servitude so as to attain another truer, deeper freedom, that of their higher self. Now is the time to live an experience that people have not attempted as yet, one that will free them from their illusions, their isolation and their powerlessness.

With the means technological progress and science have put at their disposal, if human beings do not decide to abandon their egotism and their own particular viewpoints and learn how to live together, the whole earth will soon be no more than a battlefield. So, all those of you who come here thinking that I am going to give them all sorts of revelations about esoteric science, know that you will be disappointed! Much more often you will hear me say over and over again that the essential thing is to work on your character and to improve your way of life. Of course, to do this, astrology, alchemy, magic, the Cabbalah and so on can be useful to a certain extent, but they are far from being the most important. For those who have no high ideal, for those who have not overcome their self-centredness, their need to dominate others, this initiatic knowledge not only will give them nothing, but may even be dangerous.

As for those who believe that I am going to give them ways to become clairvoyant, I must also warn them that I do not have this clairvoyance they are seeking. The clairvoyance I have is that of the heart. Yes, I have very special eyes, and they are in my heart: that is why I see things that others fail to see. I see what the Creator has deposited in people and what needs to be nourished and developed. This is the only clairvoyance that I can teach.[3]

For the work I am visualizing, I need people who are rich in their hearts and their souls. We can no longer be satisfied with talking about love, peace and brotherhood; we must live them by learning to meet each other and make exchanges in realms where the values extolled by society are of no great importance. You have everything here to live in joy, but on the condition that you understand first of all that your joy depends on *your* love, not on that of others.

The Brotherhood is like a choir. You have a voice, so do not refuse to join the others because you think they do not sing as well as you would like. How can we form a choir if all those who know how to sing decide that they are going to stand aside? It is easy to point out the weaknesses and inadequacies of others, but what good does that do you? I suggest instead that you come and support me in my work, lend your strength and set a good example of fraternal spirit. You say that you love your country, but what do you do so that everyone can live there in harmony? You do not yet realize how your example can become contagious.

I do not interfere in your private life, unless of course you yourself have come to confide in me. In our meeting hall, you are all sitting in front of me, and that is enough for me to know what you are living inwardly. On some faces I can see clarity, whereas, on others, I can see gloom and confusion. I have no idea what people have done or not done, and I do not need to know the details. I can even say that it does not interest me and that I ask no one to come and confess their faults to me. I give you all a teaching and methods so that you can walk on the path of good. I send encouraging thoughts to those I feel are making progress and freeing themselves so that they can continue, and to those I feel are losing their way I send my light so that they can find the path once again.

I know that some of you have a clear picture of yourselves and question my attitude. These people say, 'But he does not know how we are! He receives us, he smiles at us and gives us signs of friendship. If he only knew, he would speak to us differently.' They do not understand why I behave as I do. The truth is that I do not want to see, I do not want to know, certain things. I give credit to people, and by behaving this way I hope that they will follow my example, that they will stop dwelling on the faults of others. I see, but I turn my eyes away.[4]

I believe that I know all that it is necessary to know about human nature. There have been occasions when I have gone into bars, night-clubs and casinos to help my understanding. It is easy enough to have a theoretical knowledge of human beings, but it is quite different to see them as flesh and blood, to feel what goes on in their souls. To experience what someone feels as they leave the casino after having squandered every penny they possess, and even what they do not have, is terrifying. You are surprised; you did not imagine that I would set foot in such places? I was asked one day to go to a nudist camp, and I accepted, on the condition that I could keep my clothes on. Trust me, when you have spent two years of your life in prison, you can go anywhere. And if you had any idea of what I am told in confidence or what I read in the letters I receive! That is why, when I talk to you about human beings, I know what I am talking about. I try to see beyond what is in front of me, and I strive to see what they will become one day.

When you are sitting here, I try to see the divinities that you have not yet become. I am not interested in what you are now. Each time I meet you, I think of this divine spark buried inside you, which is waiting for the moment when you will at last allow it to show itself. This is the highest expression of love: to know how to connect to the divine spark in each and every one, in a way that feeds and strengthens it. What do you think a master does for his disciples, if not precisely that? And what do you think that I do with you? I work with this divine spark in you, which is the most precious possession you have. If you love me, and many of you tell me you do, it should be only for this: because you feel that I address what is the best and most precious part in you.

Human relationships would be so very different if everyone, when they met, thought that the man or woman standing before them had been entrusted with that spark of divine fire! Even if you meet a criminal, you should look for this spark, and try to bring it back to life. It is not always possible, but you must at least try. We often do not know why a person has allowed themselves to go down a slippery slope, nor do we know what could make them stand up again and re-ignite that spark. Victor Hugo developed this idea in *Les Misérables* when describing how Monseigneur Myriel acted with Jean Valjean.

The divine spark in so many beings in the world is just a little dark, or asleep! But with the methods in our Teaching, it is possible to revive that spark, and then miracles happen. Unlike most people who are always ready to condemn and punish, Providence knows very well that even if someone is capable of serious faults, it is not written in stone that they will persevere forever in their evil ways; all people can improve, and so they should be helped. We can only help them by concentrating on that divine spark they carry inside. When men and women meet, they should say to themselves, 'We are alike, because we all have that divine spark inside. So, we should treat everyone as if they were our brothers and sisters.'[5] But instead of that, they say that these people are 'the others', that they have nothing in common with them and can do nothing with them. That is when they do not consider them as enemies to be crushed one way or another!

Listening to me, some people will think, 'It is all very well for you; the life of the brotherhood is easy. Here, everyone listens to you, respects you and loves you.' Ah, is that what you believe? Certainly, when I come to the meeting hall, everyone gets up to greet me and everyone remains quiet to listen to me. But do you have any idea of the letters I receive? When brothers and sisters come to see me, do you have any idea what they expect from me? When they ask for advice, do you have any idea of how they deal with it, and of all the complications that ensue? Where do you think all the slander and injustices that I am subjected to come from?

In accepting the role of teacher, I am well aware of all the difficulties awaiting me, but I continue to trust. That is what I am like, and I cannot do anything about it. I have so often been told that I should be more cautious and not let just anyone come here. Maybe one day I will agree to do that, because I cannot risk the whole Brotherhood for a few people. I am, however, unhappy at the thought of shutting the door to someone; I tell myself that I must give them a chance as perhaps something good will awaken in them. Which is the better course for me to take? Should I be unhappy because I have turned someone away or because of all the complications caused by letting them in? You see, we must always choose between two inconveniences. Truly, I find myself in situations where others, in my position, would have 'shut up shop', as you say, but that is not the right solution.

And now, would you like me to make a confession to you? I feel that I am rich, very rich indeed. Yes, in meeting you, listening to you, and accepting all the difficulties you create for me, I enrich my understanding, my forbearance and my patience. Are those not true riches? Yes, my riches come from who I am with you and from taking an interest in you. If it was not for you, I don't think I would have gained so much. And don't you want to become as rich as me?

The truth is that we are not alone: invisible beings are with us and they are attentive to all our needs and our efforts. So, when they see all the efforts I make to enlighten you, to support you, they hurry to help me. I ask for their help so that I can meet all situations, and since they are most generous they give me a lot: thanks to you, whole packing cases and truckloads arrive here from all sides. And if you, too, agree to live as brothers and sisters with each other, these heavenly beings will see that you lack for nothing.

Whatever we long to do for others, heavenly beings will do the same for us. If we turn our attention to others, heaven will turn their attention to us. If we bear the difficulties created for us by imperfect people in our environment, if we become more patient, these beings will be patient with us, will support and uphold us. Try this out for yourselves, instead of coming to tell me that it is quite impossible for you to live in harmony with others for a few days or a few weeks. And don't flatter me, as some do, by saying, 'How have you managed to put up with us for such a long time? It is quite extraordinary, and you really are to be admired.' I would prefer it if you admired me less but, instead, tried to understand why I am so patient and what methods I use to achieve this patience.[6]

Those who have hearts full of love are happy with everybody. Yes, they see qualities and riches in everyone. They find inadequacies only in themselves. In general, what happens is the opposite, and instead of saying, 'If I find others so hard to bear, it must be because I am lacking in both love and wisdom,' they come and tell me what so-and-so said or did. What do they think that will teach me? I know perfectly well that I am not surrounded by perfect people, but I also know that the angels and archangels do not need me. What did Jesus say? *'Those who are well have no need of a physician, but those who are sick.'* What is essential for me is that those who are ill really want to be healthy, which means that all those here have decided to work on themselves, to improve. So, instead of watching other people and criticizing them, let each person begin by looking at themselves, for each one has something that needs improvement.

And now, suppose that I find you all totally disagreeable, or that one day I cannot tolerate you any longer, what should I do? Well, quite simply I should go on working with you, talking to you, smiling at you and looking at you with love. You say, 'But that would be hypocritical!' No, it is a teaching method that I impose upon myself, because reason tells me that this is best for me. Why? Because we should never let ourselves be ruled by either sympathy or antipathy or our moods. It is no good for others and even worse for ourselves.[7] So, why do you not embrace this same reasoning? If there are some faces in the Brotherhood that you do not like, behave as if you like them; that is how you will grow.

You will argue, 'But that's so difficult!' Yes indeed, it is difficult, but what do you think you will achieve if you are always looking for the easy way? The only way to conquer difficulties is not to stand there pondering them, but to understand how much you will gain by accepting them. Do you think that it is easy for me to be always among you?

Do you think I like hearing you always talking about the difficulties you have with each other? But I know that in this way I develop myself, and I can then help you. What do I do when I see a fault in someone? I become like a painter; I think of this fault as a mark on a canvas, and so I take a brush and I turn this mark into something which belongs in the picture's composition. People who see it say, 'My God, isn't that unusual! How did that detail fit so perfectly?' That is how it is; everything has been worked out. How can we put human peculiarities to good use? How can we neutralize their faults by helping them to fit into a larger picture? It is obviously an art, an art we practise in our school of the Universal White Brotherhood. All our imperfections must be modified. This modification of all these differing elements contributes to creating a new life, and that is what's marvellous. Otherwise, always criticizing, always finding fault, nothing is easier. In Bulgaria we say, 'My grandmother knows how to do that.'

If you want to understand what a spiritual Master really is, you must get rid of this idea of a hermit who has withdrawn from the world but who, from time to time, emerges from his solitude to offer a few pearls of wisdom to the waiting crowd. How can we help people if we do not understand them? How can we understand them if we do not live among them to know their difficulties and their suffering? Of course, it is both normal and even necessary that we withdraw from time to time to find ourselves, to recharge, so that we can be useful once again. But even then, it is necessary to remain aware that, even though we are alone, others exist, so that when we meet with them we can be attentive, vigilant and perceptive.

Contrary to what most people think, the wise do not look at people from afar. On the contrary, they know how to enter right into their situation, and that is why their observations are deep, their decisions measured and their actions well-balanced. You may ask, 'How far can one go in this way?' and my answer is, 'To infinity!' Those who try to put themselves in others' shoes begin intuitively, instinctively, to feel everything that goes on in their soul. Once warned by their intuition and instinct, they know how to act, in order to avoid certain obstacles or take advantage of certain initiatives, and their life becomes richer and richer and more beautiful.

I have often told you that animals can teach us many things. They have character traits and ways that give us food for thought. Take bats, for example. Do not be surprised if I talk to you about bats. Dozens of them can fly in the darkness of a cave without ever bumping into each other, because they have a sort of radar which permits them to miss obstacles. Bats are an example that human beings should think about. People do not know how to moderate their gestures, their words or their looks, and all they do is bump, jostle and knock into one another. You know something about that, don't you? Learning how to move gracefully among obstacles is quite an art, one that you can learn if you develop this radar called respect and attention... Yes, even if it is only attention to objects.

Every day you move about among many objects. But you are in a hurry or nervous, and you bump into a chair as you pass it. This irritates you as you see it as an obstacle in your path, and so you give it a kick. The kick perhaps is not of great importance, but what is important is what is going on inside you. Bumping into a chair shows that you do not know how to gauge your movements, and then giving it a kick because it has slowed you down shows not only a lack of intelligence, as it does not help the situation, but also a lack of love because you gave way to anger. Anyone who acts in this way to objects is behaving in a coarse, rough manner and will obviously behave in the same way with people. Worse than this, this person's aura will lose its clarity and something precious will be erased. So the kick you give is actually a kick to yourself; you are mistreating yourself.

All of us, myself included, can have moments of inattention, when we bump into things. But then, what do I do? I put it carefully back into the right place and give it a little friendly pat. Sometimes I even talk to it, but of course I don't do it out loud. I say, 'Forgive me. Look, I am putting you back in place.' Perhaps these objects are not much affected whether you deal with them carefully and gently or not, but it is you who will benefit, you who will feel good, as you harmonize all the energies within and around you. If you do not know how to behave with harmless objects, how will you deal with people when they come to you for help or when they have harmed you?

Life is one, everything is interconnected, and we need to be conscious of what we are doing each and every moment because no gesture remains isolated; everything, whether inner or outer, has repercussions. That is why I think it is tremendously important to encourage you to pay attention to the way you greet each other. Tell yourself that you have come here to create a brotherly life. So, each time you meet, think consciously about the way you greet each other so that your hands communicate life to one another, currents of energy and rays of colour. The most powerful and most beneficial exchanges are not necessarily those made when people are physically closer. So much love and light can be put into a hand gesture and into the look that goes with it. Also, let your soul and your spirit participate in this greeting! If you came here just to learn how to greet each other, that would be a lot. As for me, because I do not have time to receive each one of you – there are too many of you – I know that at least I can give you something of myself when I greet you.

And do not tell me, as some people have, that this salutation is reminiscent of Hitler's gesture, for they have truly not studied the difference between the way Hitler saluted and the way I greet you. Have you seen that, when a train begins to leave the station, people who have come to send off their parents or their friends, stand on the platform with their hands held high for the longest time? Does that make you think of Hitler? Let's leave Hitler where he is, and when you raise your hand in blessing, put life, strength and love into your hand so that each person can be aware that what they have felt goes right to their hearts and makes them better. It is so important to have harmonious psychic contacts first, before meeting to work or talk on the physical plane.

In our Brotherhood, we pray and meditate together, and before we eat together we sing. Throughout the day, each of us has been living our own life, meeting different people and working at different jobs. So, when we come to eat together, each one of us is preoccupied with our own thoughts and feelings which may not be in harmony with the others'. We sing so that we become unified and harmonized.

It sometimes happens that in this harmony you all form just one soul, a soul so radiant and vibrant that I get carried right out of my body. I know these moments of light and expansion, of course, when I participate in the life of the universal Soul, but in those moments, more often than not, I am alone. What joy it would be if I could live such moments with you, too! So, then, as I try to use more than just my thoughts to inscribe certain things within you, I take my pen, a sheet of paper, and I write. Yes, I write a few words and ask them to go, like seeds, and be planted deep within you, in both your subconscious and your superconscious, in the hope that one day these seeds will grow into your consciousness too.

After that we eat in silence.[8] For some of you, who are used to joking (or even quarrelling) during a meal, this silence is deadly, a desert. Yet, this silence is the indispensable condition for heavenly beings to come and help us in this most important moment, this moment when, through the intermediary of food, we are able to communicate with the flesh and blood of Christ.[9] To nourish oneself is the first letter of the holy alphabet, and so for me to eat in silence, harmony and a brotherly atmosphere is true communion.

I have been invited to dine with ambassadors, bankers, aristocrats, and truly I have found it a little difficult to bear. All that bustle of being served with all those different plates, which keep being taken away by servants, who sometimes come to your right, and sometimes to your left… Is this ritual really necessary? And not to mention the conversations that it is polite to take part in! You no longer even know what you are eating. One day, because I had known my hosts for some time, I ended up saying to them, 'Can't we simplify things? I understand that, when you are entertaining some people, you have to follow the conventions. But, please, at least make an exception for me. It really is no longer necessary to treat me with such formality.' The lady of the house smiled, and it seemed to me that she even gave a little sigh of relief. I must say that during this formal kind of meal I find myself missing the simplicity and the silence of our fraternal meals.

It is because the atmosphere at our meals is inhabited by all sorts of luminous beings attracted by our songs, our thoughts and prayers that it is alive, and you have no idea how much protection this can be for you. Yes, when we are in the habit of breathing clear, fresh, pure, luminous air, we cannot help noticing the contrast of a heavy, dark atmosphere and the dangers it signals. Often, the atmosphere is the main indicator we have by which to judge people and situations.

Some years ago I journeyed to Spain with a brother. We were near Granada. We had been told that there was a village of cave dwellers nearby, which was well worth a visit. We went there with a group of tourists, but we had hardly got in when I said to the brother, 'We are not staying here, let's get out at once!' The men and women who lived in these caves had a disturbing and troubled gleam in their eyes, but, above all, I felt something really terrible in the atmosphere: passions had been unleashed, crimes had been committed, and elementals, lower entities, were moving around feeding on the emanations from those present. You need to know that humans are never alone in the places they live. Other beings, attracted by their emanations, come and go, and live with them.

We were the only ones who left immediately, but the next day other tourists told us that they wished they had followed us; they said that they had experienced a horrible time there, and they had been swindled and cheated. I do not know what magical practices they wanted to show them, but they said, 'These people descended on us like vultures.' I wonder why they did not pick up immediately that there was something really disturbing in the atmosphere? I am not saying that it is a bad thing to be a little curious and to want to see what people are like, as they too are our brothers and sisters, but it is vital to be sensitive to atmospheres so that you can escape before becoming a victim.

This harmony we create all together is sometimes expressed in the form of colours: an immense rainbow forms overhead and it attracts heavenly beings and angels. Yes, it attracts angels, and this is not just a poetic phrase that I am using. Angels exist, and they come to visit us. You will say, 'So, you have seen angels, have you? Tell us about them!' It was such a splendid experience that my heart almost stopped beating, but there is nothing to tell you. I will just say that we must long for these angelic presences more than anything else.

It would certainly be a good thing if we could have a few more buildings here, but my goal is not to enrich the Brotherhood with some more buildings. Each society, each organism, that is born begins by being preoccupied with the buildings in which it will set itself up, and that is why we have churches, temples, parliaments; there is the headquarters of the United Nations, that of the Red Cross and so on. But wars continue, and injustice, poverty and crime. Having a few more buildings does not change much as long as people are not yet capable of raising buildings of light and love in the invisible realms by means of their thoughts, their feelings and their will power. These invisible buildings are just as real as ones made out of concrete or glass, and more effective.

It is such a monument that I want us to build together, something of such power that every consciousness in the world is turned upside down and captivated by it. Yes, suddenly, there will be such an upheaval in everyone's consciousness that each one will be carried along by an irresistible current. Without asking any questions, they will put their selfish interests to one side and will decided to work for the coming of brotherhood. I do not wonder whether I will be successful in building such a monument one day, but I am working towards it. This work gives meaning to my life, and I wish all of you who come here would make this goal yours, working for this understanding and this brotherly love for one another. Each person must come to add a stone to this building, and do not ask what your place will be, as God knows where to put this stone.

Wherever I have travelled, I have seen wonderful creations, beautiful buildings set in gardens and parks, the like of which the Brotherhood will never have. But often, they have reminded me of empty tombs, because the men and women who live there were not filled with the spirit, with love. Besides, what I long for is that you make Izgrev, the Bonfin and all our fraternal centres in France and other countries centres that are truly inhabited,[10] to the point where, already, on entering, you can sense something subtle, light and full of peace in the atmosphere.

I know that has begun to happen. People who come to the Bonfin for the first time tell me so, or they say it to the brothers and sisters. Sometimes even, the workers, who come from Fréjus, the truck drivers who bring food or building materials, have commented on it. They do not always know how to express it, but they say that there is something special here which does them good. Yes, because even the earth, the rocks, the trees are imbued with our prayers, our songs, our thoughts and brotherly feelings. Try to be still more conscious of all this, for it is you who will benefit from it, as will all those who come in the future.

You must all try to cultivate at least one quality – respect for others, good humour, perseverance, stability, gratitude, a sense of order, aesthetics (there are so many!) – knowing that, thanks to this quality, you purify and lighten the atmosphere, but you will also have a beneficial effect on others, and you will become a model for them. Obviously, I am not so naïve as to think that, in general, people are not naturally more inclined to envy the success, glory and riches of others, rather than their qualities of patience, kindness and devotion. They will do all they can to benefit from others' qualities; it is so much more advantageous to profit from others' qualities rather than working themselves to acquire them! Even so, just being in contact with them will have an influence.

I know how difficult it is to set an example for those around us, but it is worth the effort to try. Analyze yourselves and find which of your qualities can be built up, affirmed and strengthened. Choose just one of them and cultivate it with perseverance, and it will become a centre around which all your other qualities will converge. If you attempt to work on all your qualities at once, you will not be successful; you must give yourself a centre. If you decide that the axis of your being will be kindness, all sorts of other virtues will come and join it: patience, generosity, wisdom, and even clairvoyance. Yes, this clairvoyance will allow you to see into the hearts of others, to feel what they need and how to speak and behave with them.

Since you have decided to come here, try to take part in my work so that one day we will be able to touch many other consciousnesses in the world! In this way your life is filled with meaning and joy. What could be more terrible than to leave this earth one day without having done anything good for other people? Luckily, God has placed the desire to be useful in the human heart. It begins with the need to look after family, friends and country, but that alone is not enough. We need to think of the whole world and even of other planets, where beings exist whose evolution we can help. Even if you cannot manage, as yet, to envisage such work, you should at least know that it is possible, and, thanks to this, you will enter into communication with more evolved beings who will be able to draw you further along and to greater heights.

I know that some of you are thinking, 'What is the point of praying, meditating and making an effort to live in purity and light? It has no effect on anything and cannot even be seen by anyone.' Well, you are mistaken! From the moment that you make an effort towards living in harmony and light, your very presence brings something so precious that you cannot even begin to assess its influence.

One day I put on the television and, quite by chance, I came across a programme called 'Mireille's Little Academy.' There were boys and girls who took turns in singing a song, and their teacher, Mireille, was showing them how to conquer their shyness, how to pitch their voices and so on. It was very interesting. At one moment, my attention had been drawn to a young girl who sat very quietly in her seat. She radiated something so refined, so subtle, that I was amazed. Looking at her I said to myself, 'But what had she done to have this charm, this grace?' Her size, her gestures, her face, her hair, her forehead, her eyes, her nose, her mouth, her complexion, her smile… everything was so pretty and well-proportioned! Her friends did not pay her much attention, but it was clear to me that just her presence alone must influence them and that, wherever she went, this young girl aroused poetry and inspiration in everyone, particularly in girls, who would feel the secret longing to be like her. She had no need to say, 'Look at me, be like me!' No girl could fail to be touched by the desire to be like her.

Do not be surprised that I give you an example of the young girl I saw on television. For me, all examples can be used to help you understand the truths of the psychological world. I see that you have not yet measured the weight of influence. Yes, it's so simple! We see it everyday. A well-known actress changes her hairstyle… She does not go around saying that people should copy her, but her photograph goes into magazines, she appears on television, and all of a sudden lots of women begin to do their hair like hers and dress like her. A spiritual influence is, of course, much more subtle, but it is still an influence, and it works almost imperceptibly. That is why you must work on yourselves so that you, too, become living books who will inspire everyone you meet. Even without opening your mouth you are speaking, and that is what is magnificent. Words are not always the most persuasive. So, become living books; that is the work you must take seriously from now on, because you will have a beneficial influence on all those you meet. This is brotherly love, too.

There are undiscovered flowers and trees on earth in places where humans have never ventured and perhaps will never go. We might sometimes wonder about the point of such plants, which no one will benefit from, since no one will see them: some think this makes no sense, that nature is not intelligent. Some materialistic philosophers have even used this argument to demonstrate that creation has no purpose and that everything has only happened by chance. Perhaps you yourselves have been in fairly uninhabited regions and you have found really beautiful flowers and wondered, 'What use are these flowers no one knows about? Why are they here, unknown, useless and neglected?' But this is not so. No flower, no plant remains unknown in nature; not one is neglected and useless. If not human beings, the beings of the invisible world come to these most hidden flowers to gather their emanations.

Why would human beings be the only ones who know how to make use of plants, minerals and animals? There are a multitude of beings we do not see but which exist nonetheless: the spirits of the four elements, or the souls of the dead... Like chemists, they extract certain substances on which they feed or which they transport elsewhere to help other creatures. Nothing is useless in nature or in society, nothing and no one. Remember well what I have just said to you here. Yes, even if they remain unknown and hidden, the light and love which emanates from a person are received by invisible beings which feed on them, and these beings can also carry that light and love great distances to save beings who are calling for help.

When we pray, many spirits can come and take quintessences from us to help heal the evils of humanity. Think about this, and all at once your life will take on greater meaning. The Creator, in his infinite wisdom, has left nothing without use. I have verified this so many times, and this is why I can now say to you that you, too, can become a fount of blessing for all humankind.

Sometimes people say to me, 'Oh Master, how alone you must feel!' That all depends on what you mean by solitude. Of course, when I realize that I am neither understood nor supported in my work with you, I can feel alone. But I never feel alone in the invisible world. I have often spoken to you of the law of attraction, by which all beings who have the same ideal, the same thoughts, the same feelings, the same longing, are linked in the subtle world.[11] So, in the invisible, I know and feel that I am helped, supported by all beings past and present who are animated with the same wish as I have to bring peace and brotherhood in the world. When you find yourselves feeling alone, try to remember this law of affinity. In fact, we are never alone

On the last day of my trip to Turkey, I was in Istanbul. From my hotel room window, I looked onto the street, the houses, cars and people passing by... In the house next door, I saw an old man of shabby appearance come into the courtyard; his clothes were faded and torn in places. He was carrying a small mat with him, but it was so threadbare that I am sure you could see right through it. He laid his mat very carefully on the ground and then he got on his knees to say his prayers as Muslims do. That was when his attitude captured my total attention. He prayed with such fervour, such faith, such concentration, that I started praying too, with him, and I asked heaven that his prayers should be granted. His bearing and his gestures demonstrated all the adoration a creature has for his Creator, and even though he was poor it was quite clear that he was not asking for money. But he seemed so totally destitute that I wanted to do something for him. Unfortunately, by the time I got down to the courtyard, he had already left. I could not find him, and I was disappointed, because he had really touched me.

For a long time I continued to think about this old man, and I said to myself, 'Dear God, how could his prayers not be answered.' Never imagining that he was being observed, he prayed in the secret of his heart with such simplicity, such sincerity. And what I want you to understand in telling you this story is that, in the same way, when you pray with all your heart, someone is watching you, even if it is not from a hotel room window! There is always someone watching you from the invisible world, and if you touch that heart, that being can decide to add its thought and love to your prayer so that it may be granted. Yes indeed, you are never alone, there are always some 'prying eyes' watching you. And when they see that you are sincere and disinterested, they decide to support you.

There is so much suffering in the world we do not know about! Yes, we pick up a few scraps of information from the newspapers, the radio and television, but it is impossible to list and describe all the sorrows that strike humanity every day, because what happens is indescribable. The spirits of the invisible realm would like to alleviate all this suffering, but they cannot do so, because they do not have the ability to intervene directly here on earth. If they are to act, they must use human beings as their intermediaries. But where are those who, if they have the power, even think of doing something? So our task is to give these heavenly spirits what they need, and what they need is us. If there are devoted servants who place themselves at their service, the spirits can, through them, bring great improvements to the earth.

One day, in the middle of a lecture, I put on a serious face and with a solemn voice, I asked, 'My dear brothers and sisters, do you know who I am?' Everyone was most affected and thought that I was going to say that I was Pythagoras, or Orpheus, or Buddha, or Zoroaster… or, who knows, maybe Genghis Khan? Clearly, it had to be some famous person. So they all looked at me, waiting for my revelation, and after a few moments, still with the same serious face and the same solemn voice, I said, 'I am traitor number one.' And then, poor things, what a shock, what a disappointment! Some were certainly a little worried. A traitor, that's not too good!

So, I had to explain. 'The whole earth is like some unassailable fortress, where even the most powerful entities of the divine world cannot enter in order to bring harmony, justice, peace and love. Why not? Because these entities are not made of physical material. In order for them to intervene, human beings themselves must provide them with the possibility. On earth, humans are as powerful as all the heavenly armies, but if they are obstinate, nothing can be done. They can only penetrate this fortress if, inside, someone at least opens a door for them. Does that surprise you? How many books or films tell of besieged towns which the enemy could not take, until the moment a traitor, on the inside, let them in?

Well, the same thing applies to the earth. It will never be penetrated from the outside by the heavenly army. Traitors on the inside must open some breaches in the ramparts so that heaven can come in. That is why I decided to become a traitor… I know the word sounds a little odd, but that does not matter; at least, with this word and the pictures it evokes, you understand what I mean. So, I am a traitor who wants to create an opening so that the heavenly army can get in and save humanity by inspiring them to have greater fraternal feelings for one another. So, do you not want to help me a little and become traitors yourselves?

If humanity has not disappeared, if it survives still in spite of those who consciously or unconsciously have done everything to destroy it, it is thanks to a small number of beings who strive to neutralize the destructive currents. These beings work in secret; the majority are unknown, hidden we know not where, but they are so happy when they see men and women who have consciously decided to join them in this most vital work of saving humanity! I long to inspire you so that you will join me in this work.

Notes

1. A song from the Prosveta edition of 'Songs of the Universal White Brotherhood'. *Chants de la Fraternité Blanche Universelle*, CD 1510, CD 2, song n° 8.
2. See *The Egregor of the Dove or The Reign of Peace*, Izvor Coll. n° 208, chap. 1: 'Towards a better understanding of peace'.
3. See *Looking into the Invisible*, Izvor Coll. n° 228, chap. 6: 'Love and your eyes will be opened', chap. 10: 'The spiritual eye' and chap. 19: 'Sensation is preferable to vision'.
4. See *Love Greater Than Faith*, Izvor Coll. n° 239, chap. 10: 'Base your trust on vigilance'.
5. See *Sons and Daughters of God*, Izvor Coll. n° 240, chap. 13: 'Sons and daughters of God are brothers and sisters to all people'.
6. See *The Wellsprings of Eternal Joy*, Izvor Coll. n° 242, chap. 12: 'Patience: its unexpected treasures'.
7. See *On the Art of Teaching*, Complete Works, vol. 29, chap. 7: 'On participating in the work of the Universal White Brotherhood', part 2.

8. See *The Path of Silence,* Izvor Coll. n° 229, chap. 4: 'Make your meals an exercise in silence'.

9. See *The Yoga of Nutrition,* Izvor Coll. n° 204, chap. 3: 'Food: a love-letter from God', chap. 8: 'Communion' and chap. 9: 'The meaning of the blessing'.

10. See *A Philosophy of Universality,* Izvor Coll. n° 206, chap. 9: 'The annual conventions at the Bonfin'.

11. See *The Book of Divine Magic,* Izvor Coll. n° 226, chap. 11: 'The three great laws of magic: 2. 'The law of affinity'.

17

All I want is for you to be free

Those who have worked for a long time to acquire light, self-discipline and inner peace are often tempted to isolate themselves from the rest of humanity so as not to be disturbed: they can write books, run workshops, give lectures without others becoming involved in their private lives, for they already foresee all the difficulties that this will create. Make no mistake: just because people recognize the moral and spiritual worth of someone and decide to be taught by them does not mean they know how to behave toward them. They are still so dominated by their prejudices, their selfish desires that they expect their teacher to agree with their point of view, and then the complications begin. This is why, often, a wise man chooses to remain apart from all the chaos and passions of humanity.

A true spiritual Master is not guided by wisdom alone, but is inspired by love. He says to himself, 'I know that I am going to meet all sorts of difficulties which will slow me down in my work, but what is the point of going ahead by myself? I cannot abandon my brothers and sisters in the shadows of darkness, doubt and grief. I would be free, of course, but I would not be happy if I did not contribute to their freedom.'

In India, yogis strive to reach nirvana, but to reach nirvana while still here on earth you must remain isolated. And that is something I cannot do. When my Master said to me, 'Don't forget you have signed a contract', it was not so that I could seek bliss somewhere far from everything. Our earthly life is short; we will have plenty of time to taste bliss in the other world. For a long time I have known that I am a space traveller, that the earth is not my country, and that my true home is elsewhere. But, for the time being, I am on earth, and for as long as I am here I want to be useful to my human brothers and sisters whatever the difficulties.

You call me Master, but I have never asked you to do so. For many years I was called, 'brother Mikhaël' and that suited me just fine; I would have been quite happy if you had continued calling me that. Only those who are unaware of the reality of spiritual work need a title that gives them prestige and glory. I never wanted the title of Master; it was when I returned from India that the Brotherhood gave me this title, and I have never thought of it as an honour but rather as a heavy burden that I bear with patience. I still think of myself as your brother; I make great efforts to help you, but do you help me to help you?

The truth is that I never feel I am adequately prepared for my work. Even now, I still do not feel ready. What do I mean by being ready? I want to be an effective intermediary, a mediator between heaven and earth, between heavenly beings and human beings. This can be achieved only by someone who has purified all the elements that can either hold or block heavenly energy. And who can claim to have reached such a level of purity and transparency?

Of course, you will object, 'If you feel you are not yet ready, why do you keep on telling us that there is nothing greater than this teaching which you are giving us?' Ah well, that is something else. Sometimes, walking around Paris, I saw how the street pedlars tried to draw the attention of passers-by to the goods they wanted to sell. They would call out, 'Come over here, over here. Look at this miraculous liquid that gets rid of every type of stain. Nowhere will you find a more effective product!' And so on, and so forth. This type of advertising shocks no one; people stop, look, listen and then buy. So, I said to myself that this would be an example to copy, and I decided that I, too, would 'sell' my wares, my truths, which are of inestimable value. I act in this way to catch your attention. If I did not say, 'Here's the greatest truth', 'Here's an idea you won't find anywhere else', 'This is the first time such a thing has been revealed', would you have made the effort to listen to me? But, as far as I myself am concerned, I know, I feel that I am not yet ready for the work that I believe is the only one worthy of being undertaken.

On my return from India, some brothers and sisters were expecting me to behave from then on like one of those gurus about whom they had read all sorts of stories: I would wear a robe, I would remain immobile for hours on end like a statue before which they would come and prostrate themselves, and, from time to time, I would open my mouth to say a few words and give orders, which would be carried out immediately. But, they had to admit I was still just the same, except that now I had grown a beard. They were disappointed and told me so, because they really were expecting me to fit with their idea of a Master, according to the books they had read. As if a year in India was enough to make me different from what I am at my very core!

Really, would a crowd of obedient and submissive people make you happy? Personally, I do not think there would be any happiness in that. My own freedom is enough; I do not need to take yours. I find my happiness elsewhere, and my happiness is to see you intelligent, powerful and free. Yes, free. You will say, 'Then, everyone can do exactly what they want.' No, quite the contrary; everyone would be aware that what I advise is what is best for them. If I agree that you can consider me as your Master, it is so that I can help you blossom; it is not to impose my will on yours. What would I do with characterless, worn down human beings? On the contrary, for the work we have to do together I need independent, powerful people, and the rules we have here have no other goal than to strengthen you and free you… I mean to strengthen and liberate the divine principle in you. For the time being the divine principle is suffering, imprisoned like a king who has been dethroned and locked in a dungeon; you abuse it, you give it nothing to eat and nothing to drink, and all I want to do is to help you get it out of prison.[1]

And some of those who only read my books do not understand this either. People think I want to limit them. I often receive letters from people I do not know who, instead of benefiting from my knowledge, tell me that they do not agree with me. What do they want me to do? If my books disturb them, they can always stop reading them! I can only fulfil my role as a teacher to those who are capable of understanding that my only goal is to help them free themselves. As for the others…

I have told you before that when someone is introduced to me for the first time, I do not take into consideration their degrees, their titles or their wealth. I look at their words, their attitude, their gestures, and in particular I want to find out what their ideal is. Why? Because if people do not have a spiritual ideal, I know they will very quickly accuse me of trying to enslave them.

What concept of freedom do people have when they decide to become the disciples of a Master? That is a good question... On the slightest pretext they are ready to blame him for trying to limit them, and at the same time they never stop asking him to help them out of their difficulties. They do not see that this is a contradiction! They have not understood that freedom means they do not need someone to help them make progress. What idea do they have of their freedom when they never stop clamouring for support, for crutches and walking sticks... or they seek a Master imagining that he will change the course of their lives and shelter them from all ordeals?

Like all human beings, disciples of a Master have their destiny, karmic debts to pay, and the Master has no right to intervene and change the course of events. If he sometimes intervenes, it is because he feels the moment is right, because he is sure that he is not interrupting the unfolding of a necessary process. More frequently, he has to limit himself to explaining certain truths to his disciples, to giving them advice and recommending certain methods. So, do not expect me to intervene directly in your life. What you must understand first of all is how you got into this mess and how you can get out of it. I give you light; if you do not accept it or if you cannot see anything, what can I do? Suppose

I could lift you out of your difficulties… If you have not understood where they come from and have not made any effort to overcome them, you would just fall right back into them. And what will you do when I am no longer with you? So, my power is limited. But thanks to the explanations and methods I give you, you will not suffer so much in these ordeals, which are inevitable. And when you have overcome them, you will be clearer, stronger and richer.

So, let us be clear: I will not free you from your karma, but I teach you to transform these painful experiences that it imposes on you. I can show you how to seek freedom on the level of consciousness.[2] Each difficulty you meet is an opportunity to teach you something; if I intervene to take it away from you, all I have done is to hinder your progress. All I do is to give you light and some methods, so that you can undertake the work yourself. Do you think that my life is easy? By accepting this role of teacher, I attract all sorts of difficulties. But I look on these difficulties as a blessing, and I would not exchange them for all the treasures in the world. I tell myself that I, too, have to progress.

It is essential that you know what you may expect and not expect from me. But people are not rational. Some people, having only just met me or just read a few of my books, decide that I am the fountain of all knowledge and all worldly powers. They turn me into a statue, which they place on a pedestal, and they say, 'You are my Master.' Then, quite soon, when they find that I do not match this statue they have erected, they hurl it to the ground. What is the statue guilty of? What am I guilty of, if I am not what they had imagined, without my even knowing? Some people have said, 'You looked like a god to me, and now I see that you are not one.' They should have seen that straightaway! And how very pretentious to believe that a god would agree to teach them and live amongst them! What have they done to deserve heaven sending them a god? Then, they met me, because they certainly did not deserve better. If they cannot understand the humble teacher that I am, what would they do when faced with greater ones?

Let us say that it is not a bad idea to take an introductory course with me and that I am preparing you for those greater than me. Then, you will leave me, and that will be just fine. What did John the Baptist say to his disciples when he saw Jesus pass by? *'Behold, the lamb of God!'* And then his disciples followed Jesus. I would be very happy if you left me in order to follow the Christ. But I am sad to see that some leave me only to get bogged down in swamps.

I have never told you how to regard me; I have always left you to form your own opinion. I ask only that you reflect on the fact that if I have crossed your path it is not by chance, and therefore there is something to be understood. Why are we all together? I know why you are here before me and with me. It is you who often have no idea. In any case, I leave you free: free to come, free to go, free to remain. If you leave me, I will not be disconsolate, and if you stay I will not grieve either at the prospect of the difficulties you will undoubtedly create for me. You see, I am very nice; I accept everything. You wonder if I am being serious? Think what you like!

It seems that some people want to participate in our congresses but do not come, because once they were told that if they set foot in the Brotherhood I would force them to stay. What a silly idea! I would be really stupid to act in such a way. If people do not want to stay, I much prefer them to leave; otherwise they would disturb the work that we must do here, in good will and harmony. You see, people are not logical! And I would make this suggestion to you: if someone already belongs to another spiritual teaching, do not try to bring them to the Brotherhood. Since they can develop and blossom in that teaching, leave them there. Obviously, if someone wants to come to the Brotherhood, that is a completely different situation; but if they show no desire, I beg you, do nothing to draw them to us; that would not be honest.

Sometimes I get letters in which people write, 'You are both father and mother to me.' Do you think I am proud and happy to learn that I represent something so important to them? Well, not at all, because I can already see all the ensuing complications. For do you, yourselves, know many children who are satisfied with their parents? For a large part of their lives, they only complain about them. Later on, when they themselves become parents and see how difficult it is, or when their own parents are old or dead, they finally realize what good parents they had and regret having been so disagreeable and ungrateful. Yes, that is what will happen with me too; many will wait until I am dead to realize all the good that I could have done them. Until then, it is up to me to find the best way to help them, and that is often very difficult!

In my lectures I deal with general questions and speak to everyone, but sometimes, when I speak harshly, some brothers and sisters think that I am speaking directly to them. They pick up on a detail which concerns them in particular, and they are annoyed. If they feel upset, it is perfectly normal, isn't it? But if what I said was not relevant to anybody, what would be the point of speaking to you? So, as what I say concerns everyone here, it is inevitable that you will see yourselves in what I say. I look at each one of you as an open book; I read a page from each one of you, and from what I read I draw teaching material from which you will all benefit one day or another. Have you not noticed that everything I explain to you in my lectures I have read in you, in the books that you are? If you were not there, I would perhaps not have much to say to you... So, instead of becoming irritated, each one of you should try to take what is useful for you, correct and improve yourselves without wasting time tormenting yourselves on the pretext that you have recognised yourselves in my words

As soon as some people begin to come regularly to the Brotherhood, I know that I run the risk of being seen as responsible for all the discomfort they feel. Until now, they have lived a disorderly life and, faced with the truths they hear here, they become anxious and troubled. But because they have never thought about the link between the chaos of their previous lives and the anxiety they feel, they do not understand what could have caused it. And one day, at last, they discover – they have a magnificent brainwave, that I have asked these entities to pursue them and punish them for having lived so chaotically before! I am to blame, and they tell me so, whereas they themselves are absolutely blameless. To others, it seems, I send terrifying nightmares. As if I had nothing better to do than to disturb people's sleep! Fortunately, when they accept my explanations, the majority of them become aware that the source of their miseries is in themselves and they stop accusing me. But until that time...

So, what should I do when I have personal remarks to make? First of all, I have to decide to speak only when I feel that I will be understood. That is why I often give the impression that I see nothing! It would be so easy for me to summon a sister or brother to warn them that they are in danger of wandering off the path and to describe what awaits them if they continue in this way. But if they are not yet ready to understand, it would be a waste of time, as they could argue with me or even distance themselves to calmly continue elsewhere, and then I could not be of any more help. For the time being, I can only help by thought and prayer, nothing else. If I were to give the impression of meddling in anyone's affairs without having been asked to do so, I would raise a barrier between them and me; to continue working with them, I must maintain the link. And what often happens? After a time, this brother or sister, who has realized that he or she has taken a wrong turning, comes to confide in me and to ask my advice.

I am not saying that I never intervene. With brothers and sisters who have known me for a long time and who I know trust me, sometimes I can speak very harshly. First of all, of course, they are very unhappy to have been shaken in this way and they may also be a little angry and rebellious, but they accept what has been said, even if they do not understand it immediately. They know that I want to help them avoid making mistakes which it will take great effort to repair. After a little time has passed and they have come to understand what I was saying, they come and thank me. You can imagine my joy at having been able to help them.

There are, however, certain brothers and sisters who say, 'Oh, Master, I so long to become perfect, so please will you tell me what my weaknesses and failings are?' 'I would be glad to, but will you accept what I have to say? Are you sure it won't upset you?' 'No, no, not at all. I beg you to tell me as I long to know the truth.' Some people take what I say very stoically, but with others, I have hardly said three words when I see a distraught face before me, totally distraught, and if it is a sister she bursts into tears. Often they do not even have a handkerchief with them, and so I have to go and fetch one. Luckily, I have a lot of handkerchiefs! So you can understand why I sometimes wait years to tell someone what they need to hear. If they break down and burst into tears instead of understanding what I am saying, it is a waste of time.

Of course, there are still those who cannot accept the slightest comment I make. One day a brother wrote to me, 'I will never forgive you for what you said to me. I hate you.' And what had I said to him? That he was lazy. Poor chap, instead of hating me he would have done better to think about it, as that would have been much more useful for him. It was not a question of loving or hating me but just thinking about it, that is all. It seems a pity to me that people who live in difficulties and suffering cannot recognize what could help them. In any case, I am well-armoured against bad thoughts and bad feelings. Yes, I have to be armoured; I had to learn to protect myself from those who used black magic against me, so that they could not reach me. If you only knew what comes to me in the mail! I have also been forced to work on my photos so that there is no link between them and me, so that they cannot be used to harm me. But let's not dwell on that now...

Every day, brothers and sister ask for meetings with me because, they say, they have questions to ask me in order to solve their problems. Very good, but when I hear their questions, I often look at them in amazement. How many times have I already given the answers in my lectures! And the answers are also in my books. But have they read them? And if they have, why can they not find the answers they need? Of course, I know what some of them think when they ask me questions; they think that if I give them a personal reply, my words would act like magic to resolve their problems and smooth out all the difficulties in which they are entangled. No, my words have no magical power over their difficulties. They must understand the laws of the psychic and spiritual life that I give you, and then apply them by adapting them to their particular situation. They behave like passengers in a sinking boat: they struggle, they call for help, yet they do not notice that all the time I am throwing them lifelines that could bring them to safety. What more can I do?

The path of initiation is difficult, I know. I would like it if you found no obstacles along your path, but events are stronger than I am. If the heavenly beings would listen to my prayers, everything would take place gently, kindly and easily, but they think differently. I could say to them, 'These are my children and I do not want them to suffer', and they would reply, 'They need to face difficulties, to be shaken up, because these difficulties will make them think, study, analyze themselves and find solutions.' What I want for you all is love, peace and harmony, and I appear to be understanding and indulgent, but even so, beyond that, I realize what is necessary for your own good.

I receive a vast amount of mail. Some letters begin very reasonably saying, 'Dear Master, I will keep this short because I know how very precious your time is…' and then come a dozen pages written in the tiniest handwriting that I can only read with a magnifying glass. And what are these letters all about? They are stories of women, husbands, lovers, mistresses, mothers-in-law, neighbours, colleagues at work… Finally, you must understand that I cannot solve the problems that each of you meets in your family and your circle of friends. When will you learn to adapt all the explanations and methods I have given over the years to your particular situation so that you can resolve any difficulties?

Yes, sometimes, I do give personal advice, but there again, have I been understood?… and has my advice been taken?… Often people understand something which is quite different from what I said, or they apply the advice clumsily, without any psychological awareness, and then the result is even worse. And then who do they see as responsible for all these new problems? Who is guilty of casting a spell on them, driving them mad and destroying their families? Why, me, of course!

When I speak, I must always expect to be misunderstood, and sometimes I really have reason to be worried. At other times, it is true, the results can be very funny. Do you want an example?

At a time when the Brotherhood had not yet moved into the house in Sèvres, we would gather for the sunrise on a bank in the Saint-Cloud park.* It was a magnificent spot, and at the time (though I do not know what it is like now) you could hear no noise. So here, in the spring, I would see the sisters arrive every morning wearing hats of such dreary and miserable colours! Why did they wear brown, grey or black when they were coming to the sunrise?

One day, I decided to say a few words on the subject. So, I suggested that perhaps they could wear hats in lighter

---

* before 1947.

colours and maybe even add a flower or two. What did I see the next day? Some of them were wearing not hats but rather what looked like a garden; there were flowers, fruits, birds and ribbons in all colours of the rainbow. One of these hats, in particular, was a veritable fruit basket with cherries, grapes, apples and pears... I wondered, 'Where on earth could they have gone to find all that?' At the sight of all these flowers and fruits on their heads, I really had to struggle not to burst out laughing. And I also told myself, despite the early morning hour, they could not have passed unnoticed; they must have met a few people, those on their way to work... I imagined the remarks that must have been made at the sight of them.

That was when I discovered what a delicate matter it is to say anything to women about the way they dress. Once again, I had to intervene to ask for a little more simplicity. Some years later I saw, on television, the same kind of hats covered with ribbons, flowers and fruits, but it was for the Feast of St. Catherine.* You see how I was understood on something as simple as a matter of hats, so you can imagine what can happen with much more important matters!

'The school of life' is an expression that is often used, but for most people it remains only words. You can see that if they had really understood that life is a school, they would tackle each new difficulty as if it was a new exercise to do, and they would say, 'Here's another chance to evolve.' And when they had mastered that difficulty they would rejoice just as

---

* Originally young milliners who were still spinsters at 25 years old celebrated the feast of St. Catherine on 25 November by making and wearing such hats. This tradition was expanded to include all young unmarried women, but nowadays few remember the origin.

students do when they have passed an examination.[3] When some people come to tell me about their disappointments and their suffering, I cannot remain indifferent to their plight. But I have to note that their troubles come firstly from their ignorance of this basic truth: we are all here on earth to study and to exert ourselves. Most people seem convinced that they are here for a life of ease, comfort, riches and the love of others, as if they are entitled to it. Well, no, all that is not part of Cosmic Intelligence's plan.

You will say, 'But then, Cosmic Intelligence wants human beings to toil and suffer?' No, Cosmic Intelligence does not see things that way; it wants people to be happy, but it has arranged things in such a way that they can find happiness only by developing their higher nature, and the higher self does not develop in ease and comfort. Read the biographies of saints, initiates and the great Masters, and see how many ordeals they have had to undergo, how many battles they have fought before awakening their causal body, upon which evil and suffering have no hold.[4]

You want me to help you, and I too want to help you. I give you light and methods, but you must do the work, not me. The truth is that I help you in a way you do not realize. I may seem severe, I may even shake you up a little so you can decide to make some efforts, but then, without you knowing it, I help you from the invisible realms – with my thoughts I smooth your path and send you my support. You are unaware of this, and it is doubtless much better that this should be so. So, I help you in two ways, first by pushing you into making an effort and secondly by supporting you in those efforts. I behave like the Turkish grocer whom I knew in Varna. When a beggar came up to him to ask for a few coins, he would say, 'What kind of lazy chap are you? Why don't you work? I am not going to give you anything. Get out of here!' and so on, quite a speech. But the moment the embarrassed beggar turned away, he would slide a few pieces of change into his pocket. I loved to see that, and I decided to follow his example, to be both strict and generous.

When I have to make some comments to someone, I do not just reproach them; I give my time, my knowledge and my energy. I know how difficult it is to work on our character and behaviour. How can I not help those whom I am pushing to make more efforts? I would not help them much if I only opened my mouth to criticize. I must also support them, by giving them something they do not yet possess, and so I love them. When you do not love someone, you have no wish to give them anything. So, those who have no love should not begin to correct others but should, in fact, leave them alone. That is much the better for everyone.

When we meet together, I see you all sitting there before me, and sometimes I see such suffering on the faces of some brothers and sisters! I know how sincerely they seek the light, the efforts they make, but for all sorts of reasons they cannot find the remedies to their inner torment, and this is written all over their faces, engraved in deep furrows. You have no idea how my heart hurts to see this. I wish I had all powers to help them out of this state, but I do not have them. My powers are limited, but I do everything I can to support them. I see other brothers and sisters who are suffering too but who refuse to understand and make any efforts. Obviously, I feel quite differently about them, but do not think that I am happy and think they are getting what they deserve. They distress me even more, because I know that, whatever I do, I cannot help them; in one way or

another, they themselves will prevent me from doing so…
And especially when they have confided to me their difficulties, their grief and suffering, and then they will finally say, 'But you cannot understand me!…'

Now, I am used to it; I have heard these words so often, 'You cannot understand me.' And yet it always surprises me a little. If they are so sure that I cannot understand them, why do they come and talk to me? Not only is it a waste of their time but of mine, too. I listen to them, I am patient, and I end by saying, 'Don't fool yourself; I understand you very well because I, too, have been through these same difficulties and sorrows. It is you who do not understand what I say to you, because you have not yet begun on the path I am treading. So, it is you who must make efforts to understand me. Believe me, it would be so much better, as it is the only way out of your suffering.' But do they hear me? When I became Master Peter Deunov's disciple, I would never have allowed myself to tell him that he did not understand me. Firstly, what possible interest could he have in understanding me? I knew that I had to understand him in order to grow and become stronger.

I know your difficulties, because I have lived what you are living, and even much worse. I know what it is to be hungry, to be cold, to be ill, to have no money, to have nowhere to stay, to be unable to wash myself, to be badly dressed, to have to wait for hours in the corridors of power, to be continually under the threat of deportation, to have my name dragged through the mud, to be the target of plots against me and to be thrown into prison… After all the hardships, all the ordeals I had to bear but which I do not need to talk about, I can understand everyone's situation, even that of criminals. Yes, even that of criminals. I can very well understand that, in certain particularly dreadful conditions, if there has been nothing to prepare people for such trials they may be pushed into committing crimes. Obviously, I would never agree with their actions, but I understand them.

So, do not reproach me for being incapable of understanding your situation. It is exactly because I do know and understand it that I must be demanding, in order to help you triumph in all circumstances. It would be much nicer for me if I only had to give you my approval and to compliment you! If you think it is easy for me to have to underline your imperfections and deficiencies! Ah, you are surprised? You think it is easy; I just have to open my mouth to point out what is not right. Well, for me, it is very difficult, it takes a lot of effort, and I even recognize that it must seem unreasonable that I make myself so unpopular with people. But I do it for your good. For me, it is easy to be pleasant, to smile at you, to look at you with love, to speak to you gently, to forgive you, and I do it as much as I can. As a teacher, however, I have to be strict and raise my voice. Then, for the rest of the day, I am sad and unhappy, but too bad: I have to do my job properly.

How could you believe that it is easy for me to make remarks about you and to reproach you? When I speak of all the abundance God has placed in you, when I speak of the grandeur and beauty of the future awaiting you, then, yes, I am happy. But to show you that you are mistaken, that you have behaved badly, no, truly, that gives me no pleasure. If I do it, it is to free you and not to control you and take away your freedom. Have I ever asked you for any money for the right to come to my lectures? No, my teaching is free. So, if what I say does not please some, then they should not come and listen to me, that's all. In any case, they have no right to charge me with having misled them.

I told you that my own freedom is enough; I have no need of yours. Contrary to what many people may think, I have no desire, either, to preach to you. I am satisfied with presenting to you the realities of the psychic world, which, like nature, obeys laws. Yes, moral laws are, on the psychic plane, equivalent to nature's laws.[5] When you do not see you are walking on roads leading you to dead-ends and abysses, and when I can see them, how could I stand by unmoved? I am not here to preach at you; I explain, that's all. I explain what is healthy and what is harmful, what will save you and what you will lose. Before I risked speaking in public to explain anything at all, I had studied and had had years of experience. It was when I finally succeeded in living according to the rules of love, wisdom and truth that I began to speak. Speaking must always come afterwards, when we have learned how to accord our life with the laws we are asking others to respect. Otherwise, we are nothing but charlatans, hypocrites and imposters.

Above all, I would never allow myself to exact efforts from you that I have not undertaken myself. Everything I ask of you I have achieved myself. It is not theoretical. What I ask of you, I live myself, day and night. That is why, when I talk to you about my life, it is so that you may understand that we can overcome the greatest difficulties, thanks to the light given us by Initiatic Science.

Some years ago, in the street I met by chance a brother who I knew was going through some very difficult ordeals; he already had a depressive tendency and was really in a pathetic state. When I met him, I did not have time to stop, so I suggested that he come and see me the next day. So, the next day, I let him speak first and he told me, 'I have tried everything; the doctors can do nothing more for me, and I want to end it all. But before I do, I must tell you that during this difficult time the only moments of relief I have had I owe to you. In the truths you teach us, I have sometimes been able to draw a few moments of peace and even joy. That is why I want to tell you that I love you very much and I thank you, but now I can struggle no more.'

For a few moments I wondered what I should reply to someone who had come to calmly tell me that any moment he was going to end his days, for I felt he was capable of doing so. I looked at him for a long time, deeply, and I said, 'Do you think that my own life is easy? I, too, often feel overwhelmed and discouraged. You say that you love me and that you value my teaching, but you want to abandon me. If you truly love me, you would not contemplate death, you would live to help me. Like me, you would strive to do something for others. I beg you, please try, and I will help you with my thoughts and my prayers, because I believe you can heal.' I also shook him a little bit, because you cannot help people if you show them that you understand them all too well. He remained silent for a moment, and then he said, 'I hadn't looked at things from that point of view. It will be difficult, but I will try to do what you ask me.' Sometime later, he wrote to me that, even though he was still going through some really painful moments, he felt that he was on the road to healing and that he no longer contemplated suicide. He had understood that he could rise above his sufferings by trying to do something for other people, and that is what saved him.

What, for me, is still the most surprising is that people are always ready to suspect a spiritual Master of threatening the freedom of his disciples, but they never wonder what kind of freedom disciples give to their Masters. They think it is perfectly normal to create an image in their minds of him as they want him to be, they expect him to live up to all their expectations, and should he not do so, just watch the criticisms fly! Yes indeed, how many people expect me to support them in all their opinions and tastes, not to mention their weaknesses and their passions! I must tell them only what they want to hear, I should not upset their ways of doing things, and all they retain of my words are the ideas and advice which require no effort on their part. And, for my part, I must remain vigilant, like a pilot holding the helm firmly so that the vessel does not go adrift, swept away by conflicting currents.

Do you know what is most dangerous for a spiritual Master's freedom? The love of his disciples. Whether it be men or women, who amongst them does not long to attract his attention or be his favourites? This, of course, is quite normal, but what a lot of complications! Sometimes I notice in the hall a brother or sister who needs my support and encouragement. I could help with a look, because I can express so much from my heart and soul with a look. But I do not do it, because I know that others will think, 'Why doesn't he look at me too?' So, when I want to send my love and my light to those who, I sense, need my support in their efforts, I close my eyes. In the same way that we can speak in silence, so, too, we can look with our eyes closed.

Yes, for a spiritual Master the love of those who follow him can be the worst of chains.[6] Some years ago, a woman who had listened to some of my lectures came to tell me that I was the most extraordinary person she had ever met and that she had decided to marry me. She was married and she had children, one of whom was a little older than me, but that was no problem to her. When she understood that I was not going to give way to her advances, she became completely unhinged. I had been in France for ten years and I was due to get the authorization papers giving me permanent residence. She knew this, and, to get revenge, she went to the police and did everything she could to stop me getting the papers, by describing me as a very dangerous man.

All these declarations of love that I have received in my life! Pages and pages… But do not think that I am proud of it. Each time, I saw traps and burdens. You cannot imagine how much I have learned to mistrust the love of human beings. Sometimes, very young girls decide they are going to marry me. Some are barely twenty years old, I am an old man, and they want to marry me! They come to my lectures, and instead of listening carefully to the truths which are so useful for their future they sit there all tangled up in their feelings; they are just happy to look at me without listening or learning anything.

This puts me in a terrible situation with these young girls' parents, who want their girls to live a normal life with a husband and children. Nobody, not even I, can make these girls see reason, and then come more worries for me! Obviously, I am then judged to be responsible for inspiring such feelings in them. I assure you, you have no idea what goes on. Because I am sitting on a stage speaking about truths of the spirit and soul in front of people who look attentive, you think my life is simple. Don't you believe it!... How many times must I protect myself from the thoughts, feelings and wild ideas from one or other of you!

One day, at the Bonfin, I was warned that a young wo-man wanted to meet me. She was, it seems, talking about me in the most glowing of terms; according to her, I was the greatest living Master, and so on and so forth. I was shown her picture, she was very pretty, but there was something in her look that put me on my guard. As she was married, I asked that she come with her husband. They came together, we spoke of various matters, and she left even more enchanted by me.

But then, a few days later, I heard a knock at my door. I opened it, and there was this same young woman. Without me inviting her in, she walked into the house and told me that she had come to take care of me because, after her last visit, she had diagnosed that I had all sorts of illnesses. Yes, she listed all my diseased organs: lungs, heart, spleen, liver, intestines… Truly, I was gravely ill. In order to heal me, she had brought a bottle containing a blend of oils made especially for me. With the most incredible impudence, she told me to take my clothes off, so that she could give me a massage. I was completely dumbfounded! I told her, 'I have never allowed anybody to massage me. What makes you think that I would allow you to do so? First of all, tell me what you have mixed up in this bottle!' 'I cannot tell you that.' 'Fine, but, anyway, there is no possibility of you touching me.' This made her furious, and she gave me a terrible look claiming she was a great clairvoyant (if she could see just a little, she would have 'seen' how I was going to receive her!), that she had come through thousands of constellations, that she had received all initiations, that she was able to cure any illness… Then she turned towards the door to leave. Then, I said, 'No, since you have come here, you can stay for a few more minutes as there are certain truths you need to hear.' I do not need to tell you all that I said to her, but I was tremendously severe, because this kind

of woman is a public danger. At the end, she was so angry
that she jerked her arm and accidentally knocked over the
bottle which dropped and broke: liquid spilled everywhere
and I had to mop it all up after she had gone. Of course, she
went and complained about me to a lot of people and, all
of a sudden, I was no longer the greatest Master on earth.
Thank God for that!

I could tell you many other similar stories, and some are
much less funny, but I think this is enough. I do not complain, but when I am accused of taking away people's
freedom, perhaps those accusing me should ask themselves
what they do to *my* freedom. Do not think for a moment
that I gain great advantages from living amongst you! Some
days, I would feel so much better if I could go away for a
while and forget all the worries you create for me. In order
to be happy, I do not need to be surrounded by people.
Inwardly, I never feel alone, because I have learned to live in
communion with the most luminous and poetic presences
in heaven and on earth. All I need to do is to open my
window in the morning and fill my eyes with the light of
day to feel fulfilled.

Sometimes, when I am tired of hearing the same old
stories that people tell me, I call on the help of Nastradine
Hodja.* I call him, 'Nastradine Hodja, come here, please!'

---

* In 1396 Bulgaria was annexed by the Ottoman Empire and stayed under its
rule until 1878, and so its culture was much influenced by Islam.
  Mullah Nasrudin (known as Nastradine Hodja by the Bulgarians) was the
multi-faceted hero of many humorous tales illustrating certain aspects of the
Sufi religion. He is known from Afghanistan to the Balkans. See Idries Shah:
'The Exploits of the Incomparable Mulla Nasrudin', Octagon Press Ltd. See
also 'Sublimes paroles et idioties de Nasr Eddin Hodja' collected and edited by
Jean-Louis Maunoury in the Phébus Libretto edition.

Then, he turns up, wearing his big turban, and he talks to me about his wife Fatima, about his neighbours, his small donkey, and the minaret that he climbs to call the faithful to prayer. Oh, Nastradine Hodja is truly comical! He says all sorts of things, and you can never quite tell if they are very wise or complete nonsense, and his way of thinking is truly original! I listen to him, and I begin to laugh. Fortunately, there is no one to see me!

You will say, 'All the same, there are brothers and sisters who do not just cause you concern, and you must be happy sometimes to feel their respect and their love. And there must be some people whom you prefer to others.' Yes, of course, it would be impossible otherwise. Who can deny that, according to temperament, we feel naturally closer to some people than to others? But I never show my preferences because, from a pedagogic point of view, that never gives good results. If people feel that they are preferred, they slacken their efforts, they become both vain and demanding, and that does tremendous harm to their evolution. As for the others, who notice this preference, they feel it is unfair, because they, too, love their Master. They become jealous, and this kind of feeling does not help them. My position is identical to parents with their children; if parents prefer one of their children, there is nothing reprehensible in this, but they must never show it. I, too, must act like a father: if I have any preferences, I try not to show them.

A spiritual master makes a very great sacrifice when he incarnates on earth to teach people: he expends a great deal of time and energy which he could dedicate to his own development! You will say, 'But hasn't he already finished his work?' Perhaps he has finished a certain level of work, but there is always a higher degree to reach, a greater light and mightier powers to acquire. If he is always monopolized by his disciples, his time and activities are very restricted, but he accepts this, and even in the work he has begun with them he must be patient.[7] Sometimes he stops for a moment to wait for them, but he never goes back. When the disciples catch up, he is happy and then he takes off once again to take them even higher. I am often forced to stop and wait for you, because my heart tells me to do so. I sometimes blame this heart of mine, because it stops me from keeping to the decisions I have made. My heart keeps repeating, 'Try to be patient, and wait just a little.' I want to be strict, but within a minute this heart of mine (which my mother gave me and which behaves just like hers) nudges me into being lenient towards you.

All the same, I keep on at you so that you will make progress. It is true, I insist, for your future affects me; I want you to be healthier, wiser, happier and more beautiful. That is what I wish for wholeheartedly every day. You do not spend much time thinking about your future, and so I have to do it for you. How can I make myself understood? Day and night I seek arguments, methods, because I know that if you do not accept what I say, life will take it upon itself to make you understand, and life will do it uncaringly, with hard knocks.

But I must leave you your freedom; I have only been given the task of explaining, and I explain. If you pay no attention to what I say, well, that's too bad. Of course it is tiring, certainly discouraging, to use one's time and energy trying to convince those who are obstinate, who ask for my help but pay not the slightest attention to my advice. I, however, have no right to force you to do anything. Whatever you decide to do is up to you. I will carry on with my work, and even if you do not receive what I am giving you, it will not be lost but will come back to me: that is a law. But if I can help you, I will be the happiest man. Day and night, I think only of this one thing: to be useful to you. It is impossible for me to do otherwise, and I will continue whatever happens.

Humans always want to have nice friends who flatter their tastes and their instincts. If someone tells them how to evolve, how to surpass themselves, they flee in horror! Yet there is no better friend than a spiritual Master, because he represents the head, which knows the way. Certainly, this head does not always bring pleasant feelings. From time to time, when disciples are drowning or suffocating, when they no longer know where they are, they decide to make use of the head, which allows them to breathe a little and rediscover the path. Too often, that lasts only a short while, and they go back to wallowing in the swamps

Yet, one day, I know you will be forced to recognize that I have been your best friend, a friend you will find nowhere else, and then nothing and no one will be able to stop you in your journey towards light and freedom. For the moment, not only have you not yet understood that I am your friend, but you sometimes consider me your enemy, when all I want is that you avoid suffering. You will eventually understand this. Let's hope it's not too late! One day you will come looking for me on other planets in order to thank me.

Notes
1. See *Marchez tant que vous avez la lumière,* Izvor Coll. n° 244, chap. 12: 'Au service du Principe divin'.

2. See *Freedom, The Spirit Triumphant,* Izvor Coll. n° 211, chap. 6: 'True freedom: a consecration of self'.
3. See *The Wellsprings of Eternal Joy,* Izvor Coll. n° 242, chap. 5: 'In the school of life: the lessons of Cosmic Intelligence'.
4. See *Man's Psychic Life: Elements and Structures,* Izvor Coll. n° 222, chap. 10: 'The causal body'.
5. See *Man, Master of His Destiny,* Izvor Coll. n° 202, chap. 6: 'Natural and moral law'.
6. See *Truth: Fruit of Wisdom and Love,* Izvor Coll. n° 234, chap. 4: 'The love of a disciple, the wisdom of a Master'.
7. See *Le rire du sage,* Izvor Coll. n° 243, chap. 11: 'Le plus grand parmi vous sera votre serviteur'.

18

Others help you through me

Why did I want to be free? Why did I not have a family? Every intention to be free is justifiable only if one takes on other commitments. I have those commitments to another family, my spiritual family. I have children to feed, and each day I ask heavenly beings to enlighten me so that I can give them the best food. For that is my task: to feed you.

I have already told you that I am a cook, and, like all good cooks, before serving you a dish I taste it. If I find an ingredient is missing or that it is not sufficiently cooked, I wait a little. I have never yet offered you anything which has not been previously tasted and verified hundreds of times. Only when I have assured myself that the dish is both tasty and nourishing do I bring it to you; then, I move on to another recipe. In my restaurant, you are therefore invited to taste the best, most delicious and newest dishes.

You can transform the food I give you immediately into love and light, if you accept it with real attention, love and gratitude. If I doubted that this was the case, if I felt that it was indigestible or unhealthy, I would immediately close down the restaurant, because I do not want my name and my actions recorded somewhere, like those of evil people. I do not want the lords of destiny to summon me before them one day to say, 'Look how you led these poor humans astray. Go back to earth to remedy your faults!'

Like everyone else, I have travelled by train at night. It was at the time when railways were not as efficient as they are now, and the trains, which were powered by coal, gave off great clouds of black smoke. On these long journeys, I would think of the train driver, up there in front, eyes shining in the darkness, paying careful attention to each movement of his hands, so that he could bring all his passengers safely home. I thought to myself, 'While everyone else is sleeping or reading, talking or kissing, he stays watchful, not allowing his attention to wander or fatigue to creep in. Each time the train stops, passengers get off, happy to have arrived, but do they give a single thought or glance at this man thanks to whom they have arrived safe and sound? And as he watches them go, he is not even surprised that no one comes to greet and thank him.' Yes, those were my reflections. That is why, each time I got off a train, I would walk along to the engine to greet the driver and thank him. What joy and surprise I would see on his face! His eyes shone and he smiled at me, his teeth looking so white in his face blackened with smoke. And then I, too, would leave happy.

Why am I now recalling those memories? Because I feel like this train driver moving through the night with a crowd of passengers on board. This train is the Brotherhood, and I want you all to arrive safe and sound at journey's end. You do not yet realize how very strong my sense of responsibility is. I have practised the ideas and methods I present to you over many years before giving them to you. I quake at the thought of having to answer for any transgression before those who sent me. I am not upset by humans' judgment, as it is not they who made the decrees to which the universe and all its creatures are subject.

If I let my imagination run, I know I could tell you all sorts of incredible stories and lead you to realms which would look extremely attractive but where you would get lost. This is why I am vigilant and why I do not accept all the ideas which cross my mind. I look at them most carefully and sift them. I am conscious that I am responsible before God for the souls of all those who come to me, and that is the greatest of responsibilities; I know the risks I run should I deceive you or lead you astray. So, understand that I strive to lead you to the light not only for your benefit but to make sure that I, too, do not lose my way. The concern I have for my spiritual family forces me not only to be vigilant but also to keep looking for new treasures, new energies so as to help you. It is thanks to this concern that I receive more and more help and support from on high.

I always keep in mind that one day I will have to stand before heavenly beings, who will ask me what I have done to make you better, purer, stronger. First and foremost, I want to gain the love and respect of these beings; if I win your love and respect too, that is all well and good, but that is not what I seek. In order not to lead you astray, I must first look to the heavenly beings and put them in first place. Because my first thought is of them, you are protected. If my preoccupations started and ended with you, if it was you I tried to please, then, yes, you really would be in danger.

You have no idea of all the mistakes that can be made when our attention is focused only on people. With the best intentions in the world, involuntarily you can end up leading them astray. I know that sometimes you wonder if you matter to me. Of course you do, but not in the way that some would wish. What matters to me is your higher self; I work to make you aware of that self, by giving you the means to develop and nourish it. And it is precisely because I want to nourish your higher self that I look first to the divine world. The divine world matters to me as much as your higher self, your true self, matters to me. That is what you need to understand.

Just as it is desirable that you should understand the way you are important to me, it is also good for you to know the way in which I must be important to you, in order to avoid certain misunderstandings. What do you think I do when brothers and sisters write or tell me that they love me, and they are willing to put themselves at my service? I turn to the Lord and I say to him, 'Lord, this soul is giving its all not to me but to you. Take it under your protection and look after it. Send your angels to support this soul in all its efforts on the path of light. As for me, I have no need of this love, and I do not need to be served.'

I would never use your love and your devotion for my own ends. If you feel that thanks to this love you are blossoming, you are getting stronger and you feel inspired, carry on: you risk nothing. Why? Because I consider myself only as a letterbox, yes, a letterbox! Your love is in the letters I receive and then deliver on high. I say, 'Lord, through me, this love is really addressed to you. They seek you through me, they love you, they worship you, not me.' And so the letter is forwarded. Do you begin to understand me? I am only of value to you in the sense that I am this letterbox which forwards your love and devotion to God.

When I receive letters of thanks, paeans of praise and testimonies full of admiration, I transmit them on high where they are received by spiritual beings that will then use them for their work. I am most suspicious of compliments and praise that are bestowed on me, because I know what danger they represent. Even some of the greatest initiates lost their heads, because all the praise and admiration of their followers made them believe that they really were gods. That is why I take these precautions, and I hope they will be enough.

There is a certain inner work to be done to bear criticism, but there is another work to be done when you are showered with praise; never forget this! So, when I receive testimonies of love and admiration, I say to myself, 'Be careful, this is the time to be alert', and inwardly I link to the Lord. I say, 'If it is true that I have done a few good things, the merit is not mine but yours, Lord God.' Then I say to myself, 'You must not rebel when people slander and persecute you, and you must not become puffed up with pride when people praise you. Persecution or praise, you must place it all before the throne of God.'

I do not keep this love and gratitude that I receive from different people but, like gold, I put it in the banks of heaven. And when I need to be supported in my work with you, I know that I can look to heaven and I will be helped. In what form? It comes in all shapes and sizes. That is both the mystery and the richness of the spiritual life. When you tell me your worries, your sufferings, your hopes and dreams, you do not necessarily get an answer or a solution from me; that would be too heavy a burden for me to carry alone. You receive aid from my friends on high.

Each morning when we come down from the Rock of Prayer after the sunrise, have you noticed that the children all want to hold my hand? Have you thought about this meaningful gesture? If we want to be protected and supported, we must look for a wiser, stronger being and put our hand in his. Since I come down with these children, I think that I ought to behave just like them. Yes, I want to be like a child and put my hand in the hands of those higher beings, so that they will give me light and strength.[1] If I did not do so, I would be crushed by all the demands and worries with which I am assailed. But I put my hand in theirs, and they take care of sorting out all the problems.

Fortunately, I am surrounded by spirits that have agreed to look after you. You do not know them. You speak to me, but often others give the answers, and they are not always the same. Let us say, as an example, you dial my telephone number, but others hear you. I cannot see, feel or hear anything, but those who are around me do see, hear and feel. I am so privileged, because I have many friends in the invisible world who help me in my work, and sometimes these friends on high say to you, 'Don't worry if your Master is not as available as you would like to listen to you, to speak to you and to help you; we are here, and as long as you are looking for light we will help you.'

Our Teaching is spreading throughout the world through the books. How could I, alone, help all those souls who are far away and who will be calling to me? But I know that I can entrust them to my friends. Sometimes these friends humble themselves by taking on my face to appear before the inner eyes of someone, in order to help, to heal and to teach them while I am occupied elsewhere. For what alone matters to them is the work to achieve the kingdom of God. So, behind me are thousands of beings who are worth more than me, who are wiser, holier, who have placed themselves in service to the divine cause and who have agreed to help me in my task.

I am supported not only by friends around me, but also by those within me. To take another example, I could say that I represent a company; many entities live in me, and they take on my appearance without my knowing it. Many people have told me so! For example, they may have lost a very precious object, or they were ill or discouraged or grappling with a difficult problem. They asked for my help in their thoughts, and while they were asleep they saw me come to show them what they should do. Others, who have never met me, have recognized, on seeing my photograph, a face that they had already seen in a dream.

Of course, I am not aware when these things happen, but I know that they are possible. Some people have told me that by saying my name they avoided a bad car crash or their attacker was put to flight. That, too, is possible. Yet, I would ask you not to count too much on my miraculously coming to your aid, to heal you or to save you. Be vigilant; do not carelessly expose yourselves to danger, because even if I have some powers to intervene in the invisible world, the answer does not depend on me. I am unaware most of the time of what this part of me, which is a collective being, is doing. It acts without my knowledge, but it only acts in certain conditions, and it is never I who decide whether you should be helped at any particular moment.

How many times I have suddenly felt energies leaving me! It is a particular sensation which nearly always manifests in the same way: a feeling of tiredness comes down on me, but it is not mine. I know at that moment that someone needs me and has called out for help. I do not know who the person calling out to me is, and I do not need to know. I try to come to their aid as much as I can. I concentrate, and it is as if, for a brief moment, I leave my body to go to meet this person, and then I come back. Some time later I get a letter in which it says, for example, 'Oh Master, yesterday I had an unbearable pain in my right arm, so I concentrated my thoughts on you, and now that pain has gone.' Yes, I, too, had felt the same pain in the same spot.

That is just a small example. I get so many letters of this kind! Day and night, people call on me, and it is not always justifiable. Instead of trying to discover how to heal themselves and solve their problems by using the methods I have given, one way or another they always turn to me for help. If I were the only one to intervene, I would have died of exhaustion a long time ago. So I turn to this collective being that dwells in me and has been there since I know not when. It slips in everywhere, listening, watching… That explains the times when you have sometimes picked up my thoughts, or when I have followed a conversation you have had amongst yourselves when you were far away. Is it I who capture your thoughts, or the other way round?

I still do not know what this being that lives in me is capable of. From time to time I address it and I listen to it. Sometimes, though, I call on it, but it does not answer me, yet I do not become disheartened. I often say, 'I know that you know everything, that you can do everything. So, I beg you, turn your attention to so-and-so who is suffering. I am weak, but I know that you are powerful. Clearly, I cannot order this being to intervene, but it has often shown me what it is capable of doing. This being is the one that can help you at distance and that teaches you during the night. Do not, however, call on it for any trivial reason. In any case, nothing can force it to satisfy your requests. It comes when you demonstrate that you are children of God desirous of dedicating yourselves to noble work. It will never come if you want to make use of it for dishonest and selfish ends.

These realities of the spiritual life are difficult to grasp or even to believe, and I can only make myself understood by using analogies. When you address me, I am like an icon before which you pray, and then, through me, your prayers reach the highest beings.[2] Think of me as just an intermediary; if you trust me, if you are honest and sincere, you will always receive an answer. What matters is you, your goal and the manner in which you address me. It is helpful to have a wise and generous Master, but never forget that the determining factor is you! What you carry in you attracts from space elements and currents of the same nature.

The inner life conforms to the law of attraction. Even if I am not able to help you in the way you wish, others will do it through me. Since the starting point is you, if you adopt a suitable attitude, you will be heard. Begin by purifying and enlightening your feelings and thoughts, without wondering in what form the help you are asking for will come! And if it looks as if you are receiving the opposite of what you expected, do not rebel, and do not become discouraged either! Reflect rather on the reasons for what is happening to you and carry on working!

The responsibilities of a spiritual Master are overwhelming, and if he had not prepared for them over many years, he would be quickly crushed. Without realizing it, without wanting to do so, his disciples drain him, and they call this love! Yes, because they love their Master they clamour day and night for his attention, his time and his help. And when they find themselves in improbable situations, they turn to this Master whom they love so greatly, this Master in whom they trust. And what enables the Master to endure all this? I will answer once again with an analogy.

Imagine a great block of stone; as it is subject to the laws of gravity, it is very heavy and nobody can move it. However, if we discover a way to lift it away from the earth to the degree that it is no longer affected by gravity, it no longer weighs anything; it is light and even floats. The conclusion to be drawn is that those who have learned how to lift their burdens very high, beyond the limits of the earth's attraction, will find that their burdens not only no longer weigh anything but also will take them higher and higher like a balloon… Since a spiritual Master has dedicated his life to serving the Lord, to spreading the light, even the most crushing responsibilities do not crush him. The nature of his preoccupations lifts him, so to speak, above earthly gravity. By placing himself in service to the Lord and to the people he wants to enlighten, he is in fact serving his higher self. As his higher self lives in the sun, he finds that he is projected into the heart of the sun.[3] And there, in the sun, earthly burdens weigh nothing at all.

Notes
1. See *New Light on the Gospels*, Izvor Coll. n° 217, chap. 2: 'Unless you become like children', and *Love Greater Than Faith*, Izvor Coll. n° 239, chap. 8: 'Unless you become like children…'.
2. See *'In Spirit and In Truth'*, Izvor Coll. n° 235, chap. 12: 'An image can be a support for prayer'.
3. See *The Splendour of Tiphareth – The Yoga of the Sun*, Complete Works, vol. 10, chap. 3: 'Our higher self dwells in the sun'.

19

Only the unattainable is real

I was very young when I first came across initiatic philosophy, but I immediately felt that it was worth the hardship of sacrificing everything for it. That is why in my young, inexperienced head, I imagined that if I ever had the possibility to present the truths of Initiatic Science in all their beauty and clarity to humanity, they could only accept them. My God, how naïve I was! I have been amazed at how often these truths had absolutely no effect on people, and I might even say on most of them. Or else, the effect was so weak, that I was disappointed! I could not understand why it was that what had immediately and strongly convinced me could not convince others. This is what made me study the mystery of human nature: why is it that, in the face of evidence that is good, beautiful and true, people choose to deceive themselves and bury themselves deeper in disappointment, misery and ugliness?[1]

All human beings harbour desires and ambitions, which they try to achieve. Whether it is riches, beauty, knowledge, power, glory or pleasure, they spend all their time and energy in pursuit of them. But what happens once they have achieved their goal? After a moment of satisfaction, what they had longed for and dreamed about begins, little by little, to fade away... as if wiped from their consciousness. Nothing retains the aura it had when it was just a desire. Once fulfilled, the dream fades. Those who have the opportunity create new goals, but the same thing happens again, and after a short while they find themselves empty once more. Perhaps, one day, they will understand that life is not just limited to the satisfaction of a few ambitions or desires.

It is normal to be happy when you have achieved success, but unfortunately, or fortunately, it is also quite normal that, a short while later, this success is not enough; it now belongs to the past, and so you must find a new reason to carry on walking, with the same conviction, towards another goal. The only means we have of escaping the feeling of pointlessness and emptiness following the achievement of our goals is to give ourselves a distant goal, one that is so far off that we will never achieve it. This inaccessible, distant goal, which goes beyond everything, which contains everything we cannot even imagine, is what we call God, the Most High, the Eternal. If we make him the sole object of our search, we link to him, and on the path we have to travel if we are to draw nearer to him, we find everything that he himself has placed for our purposes: love, wisdom, beauty, strength, riches and glory.

You are thinking, 'Why should we aim for the impossible and unachievable? The meaning of life is found in reaching our goals.' No, absolutely not. The meaning of life is found in seeking that which is eternally unrealizable and inaccessible. If we long for something which, like the horizon, seems to move further away the more we advance, this longing penetrates our conscious, subconscious and superconscious selves, it galvanizes all our energies and opens the path to infinity, to eternity; nothing can stop us. Only the unattainable is real, and what is furthest from us is, in reality, the closest.

When Jesus said, *'Be perfect as your heavenly Father is perfect',*[2] did he really think that we, human beings, could reach the perfection of our heavenly Father? We do not even have any idea of who he is, so how can we think that one day we would be able to achieve his perfection? Yet, this ideal that Jesus gave us is the only one which can truly satisfy that fundamental need in us, fill our lives and give it meaning. A child may resemble his or her father, more or less, but is essentially made of the same essence as him, and since God is our Father we too carry the seeds of his perfection. I have made Jesus' text the cornerstone of my work, because all religions are in agreement with these words. Whatever their religion, and even if they do not have one, nothing is more essential to humanity's development than to try and reach the perfection of the Creator: all are his sons and his daughters, and this unattainable ideal impels them to keep on walking towards him without stopping.

'Be perfect as your heavenly Father is perfect' says it all. But just to get closer to this ideal of heavenly perfection requires that we acquire such vast knowledge and learn such self-discipline! And that is what is so marvellous – always to be moving forward, advancing, climbing towards an inaccessible summit. On this upward path, benevolent beings come to our aid, draw us up behind them, and as long as we make the effort to keep up with their rhythm we are supported, protected and enlightened. If I keep returning

to these words of Jesus, it is because I have understood that what is written there is the meaning of life, and not just the meaning of our present life, but of all our future lives, and for eternity.

Those, who work towards the unattainable, the perfection of God, remembering that they have been created in his image, are living in reality. Since they have put God at the heart of their existence, he participates in all their activities; in all they do, think and feel, God is there, even if they do not know it. That is why each day their faith, hope and love grow, and each day their light and peace increase.

Cosmic Intelligence has foreseen everything. When humans are tempted to stray down cul-de-sacs, it places obstacles to make them turn back and meditate on their lesson. Whereas, on the right road, even though it is difficult, they are never hindered. The right road is clear. Yes, it is true, the end is unattainable, but what does that matter? What seems far away is in reality quite close, whereas those things within reach are only mirages. Our ideal is present, inside us… ideally! All our strength, joy and peace come from that, whereas when we try to grasp the things that are nearby, we lose them.

How can I make you understand this truth, which is such a great part of my life? The secret of our blossoming lies in this apparent contradiction: from the moment we start seeking God, who is inaccessible, unimaginable, inconceivable, he is there close by. He is in us. The true riches we long for are not here on earth; they are on high. Here on earth we only see reflections, and they will leave us hungry, as long as we do not seek to discover them in our soul and spirit.

The higher we go, the more we are able to capture subtle realities, and yet we will never be able to probe completely the mystery of God. Let's say that we may catch a glimpse of... his feet! But we can know his names, and that is a great deal. This science of God's names is given in detail in the Cabbalah.[3] God does not allow his creatures, whoever they are, to know him totally, and that is all to the good! We will always have something to make us happy, because we will always have something to discover. In the universe forms are infinite; they change all the time and are always producing new combinations of elements. It would be terrible to have nothing left to learn and to understand; the only thing left would be to die. But God is eternal life.

Since experience shows us that, once attained, the goal that seemed so important no longer holds much interest for us, we must look for what cannot be found, pursue the ungraspable and aim for the impossible; in this way we will always be kept in suspense and alive. As we follow this path, we will experience all the riches we long for. That is why Jesus also said, *'Strive first for the kingdom of God and his righteousness, and all these things will be given to you as well.'*[4] Once again, who can believe that we will see the coming of the kingdom of God soon? But since Jesus told us to seek the kingdom of God, I have decided to take his request seriously, without worrying if I will ever see it come true.

In order to immerse myself in the idea of the kingdom of God, in order to go more deeply into it, to feed it and to protect it within myself, I have had to make every sacrifice. But this idea has brought me such fulfilment that I feel I have sacrificed nothing at all, and life has shown me that I am not mistaken. This idea of the kingdom of God does not live here on earth; it is an entity that has its roots, its home, in the divine world. So, by nourishing this idea within me, I felt that I penetrated the realm in which this entity lives, breathes and blossoms, and the awareness that I was working for something immense and sublime filled me with inspiration, courage and joy.

The idea of the kingdom of heaven is echoed, has ramifications, in all regions of the universe, from the top to the bottom of creation, because everything is connected. Nothing truly great can be realized on earth unless an idea has been put in motion on high, as we know that an idea is not an abstraction but a living, active being. So, may all those who have been touched by the divine Word, by the sun's rays, make the decision to work for the idea of the kingdom of God and his righteousness! Even if the realization of this idea has to wait, even if it never happens, they will at least have brought it alive within themselves.

When I started, a long time ago, to read the Gospels seriously, I felt there was such richness in them that it would take me years to interpret Jesus' words correctly. So I said to myself, 'I have this great field inside me, my brain, and in this field, I will sow seeds, all these truths, these words of Jesus that have not yet been properly understood.' So, I sow them, I water them, I give them heat and light, and then, from time to time, I harvest the fruits that I distribute to you. I understand that you do not yet have the patience, yourselves, to sow these truths within you and make them grow; I understand the difficulties, but when I give them to you, at least be willing to appreciate them and study them.

Some people who learn about our Teaching are surprised that it does not draw its inspiration from Hinduism and

Buddhism, or that our Brotherhood does not resemble an ashram. If that is what they need, they can go to an ashram in India or elsewhere. But they should first ask themselves a few questions. They were born in the West, in a country with a Christian tradition, and it may not have been by chance; perhaps there was a reason for it. People do not pause to reflect, and think now they must go to India, Tibet, Japan or China to find spirituality. So, off they go, without having studied or practised their own religion at home, to look for different food, which was not made for them. I am not saying that it is a bad thing to want to know about other forms of religion and spirituality. On the contrary, for those who are intelligent and thoughtful, these religions and spiritualities shed light on their own and help them understand it better, providing they begin at least by studying it seriously. If the immeasurable wisdom found in the Gospels does not mean much to some people, it is quite simply because they do not have much in their head.

How many truths expressed in the Gospels escape Christians, because, quite simply, they do not know how to interpret them! Why do they not know how to interpret them? Because they have not tried to study them with the light of Initiatic Science.[5] For myself, I can acknowledge the greatness of all religions, yet I will never abandon Christianity, and in the Brotherhood it is the teaching of Christ we try to study and to apply.

Many of those who leave Christianity for oriental spirituality say it is because they find there both disciplines and philosophy: meditation techniques, breathing techniques and the knowledge of the laws of karma, which give meaning to our destinies. But what is there to stop a Christian from practising meditation, breathing exercises and even different yogas? And what is there to prevent a Christian from accepting reincarnation? I have shown you that some of Jesus' words in the Gospels can be explained only by reincarnation.[6]

For years, I have had all sorts of opportunities to talk with priests and clergymen, and I have found that some of them were really so stupid! As soon as I wanted to touch on certain topics with them, they were terrified, as if right there before their eyes was the devil in person. Others, on the contrary, were very open, and I know that some read and appreciated my books. I have had some good conversations with some, but they admitted to me that, on many topics, such as reincarnation, in fact, they had to keep quiet about their convictions and beliefs in order to avoid clashes with their superiors.

One day, a bishop asked to see me. When he came into my house, imagine my complete surprise to see him fall to his knees before me and kiss my hand! I was most uncomfortable, and I immediately got him to stand up again. We spoke together, and he asked me questions about some of the ideas in my books, and he was very happy with my answers. But he had to admit to me that he could never say that he had been to see me. Imagine the reaction if he had said he had been to see a dangerous heretic like me who was the leader of a sect! He showed me a photograph of himself, at the Vatican, with Pope John Paul II. I have a lot of empathy, respect and love for this Polish pope. He was a man of great intelligence, great spirituality, with a magnificent soul. Fortunately, he survived the assassination attempt made on him. All sorts of accusations have been made against him, but I am sure that he will be seen by history as one of the best popes. Certainly, he lacked certain initiatic knowledge. But let us leave that topic...

One day I received a letter from a sister, who wrote saying that she had been intrigued to notice how often I said the word 'work'. 'This is the first time', she said, 'that I have become aware of it. I wonder about this work that you are always talking about and attributing such importance to? I understand that you are doing something we cannot grasp, but I am beginning to discover it is grandiose. I cannot go very far as yet, and I know there is a limit that I cannot break through, but I want to go on searching.' I was happy to receive this letter.

I have never revealed what my true work is. It is my secret, the one thing that I have always protected most jealously. I never even spoke of it to my Master, but I am sure he guessed it. In the inner life, in the spiritual life, there are things we should always keep secret. If we talk about it, it is like losing some vital fluid, a precious quintessence. But I have never forbidden anyone from trying to guess what my work is. What work is Jesus speaking about when he says, *'My Father is still working, and I also am working'?*[7] Everyone talks about the love of God, of his wisdom, but who speaks about his work? This saying from Jesus gave me much to think about. I made it the foundation of my own work, and it is constantly present in my spirit. As Jesus worked with his heavenly Father, I too want to work with my heavenly Father. And I ask, who are you working for, who are your companions, what are your methods and what realms are you working in?

It is up to each one to discover how he or she can participate in the work of the heavenly Father. This work is never over, and that is precisely the reason that it is worth undertaking. Some people have said to me, 'But what exactly are you seeking? Where do you want to get to? We do not understand, and you will surely fail in this undertaking of yours.' Someone else told me that I am running after the wind. The intent was to irritate me, because to run after the wind is to do the most useless and stupid thing possible. Apparently so, perhaps, but from the symbolic point of view there is an analogy between the wind and the spirit, and in Hebrew it is the same word, *rouah*. Do you remember the words of Jesus in the *Gospel of St. John: 'The wind blows where it chooses, and you hear the sound of it, but you do not know where it comes from or where it goes. So it is with everyone who is born of the Spirit.'* The truth is that I never ask myself if I am going to be successful or if I am going to fail; I work, that's all.

The history of humankind teaches us that we can never pass judgment on the worth of human beings if the only criterion is their success or failure. Those who succeed are not necessarily the greatest, and those who fail are not necessarily less elevated. Each creature comes to earth with a particular mission, and, often, those who are given the most important missions are destined to fail, at least that is how it seems. They have laid the groundwork, which is what is most difficult, so that others may succeed. Then, those who do triumph should never forget that they owe their success to the efforts and sacrifices of those who preceded them.

You are here in an initiatic school and my Teaching is based on Christ's philosophy: *'Be perfect as your heavenly Father is perfect'... 'Strive first for the kingdom of God and his righteousness, and all these things will be given to you as well.'*

I want to help Christ by saying these words to you that you are not hearing; so do not expect me to give you the same points of view and the same advice as anybody else. You have plenty of people around you on your level, who can speak your language, who give you the food you like and clothes that are your size. Do you not think that you need someone who is an exception? Yes, that is why I offer you clothes that are a little too big, saying, 'Look, these are for you, but you must work to grow into them.'

I can only speak to you of what I myself live. So do not ask me to give you some easily achievable ideal, because an ideal that is easily achievable is not really an ideal. I will always give you the most distant and unattainable goals, because that is where truth reigns, that is where beauty reigns. Try not to be like those travellers who, when they find themselves at the foot of a mountain, keep from climbing it. They are happy to see that the mountain is there, they admire it, they praise its beauty, but the mountain is what it is, and those down below remain what they are. From time to time, they glance towards the summit, and they would like the summit to descend a little towards them, but the summit keeps on thrusting up towards the sky. If they do not want to climb, too bad, but the summit – and I mean by that a spiritual teaching or a spiritual Master – will never come down to them.

You will say that what I am saying is cruel. No, because even if the summit does not come down, it will continue to project to the valley below something of its thoughts and its love. Like the sun… The sun sends its rays to earth, and these rays are like long ropes it hands us to hang on to. In this way it tries to hoist us up to its level, without coming down itself. I am here to demand efforts from you, so that you can undertake the long climb to the summit, to the sun, for that is your predestination.

Even if you sometimes have the impression that I am dragging you towards inaccessible and even unreal realms, I never give you abstract theories. I speak to you only of events happening (or that will happen) inside you, in your psychic and spiritual life. I know where you have been and where you will go, what ordeals you will be forced to undergo and what work you will have to do in order to accomplish your mission as sons and daughters of God here on earth. I know that you will make progress and also that sometimes you will fall, but that is not serious. The important thing is that you should not go backwards, that you pick yourself up and carry on walking forward without ever worrying about the time it will take to accomplish each stage.

Do I worry about time? No, because I know that those who want to approach divine perfection work with elements that belong to a different dimension. So, I tell myself, 'Even if I have to do this for eternity, I am not going to stop. Even if I do not succeed, I will still carry on. As long as I keep walking, I am alive.' Those who are committed to the path of true initiation sense that the greatest joys lie in the expectation and not in the realization of what they desire

Their professional life, their social life, their personal life oblige people to pay attention to time, and for some it even becomes an obsession: meetings they must arrive on time for, work timetables, times for trains and planes, the opening and closing hours of shops or offices, and so on. Not to mention saving time, which they have to try to do, because, as they say, 'time is money.' Time dominates people. In the spiritual life, time does not count. What is essential is the goal. And even if this goal is impossible to reach, it matters little; we must keep moving without being preoccupied with time. So, now, set to work; show your heavenly Father that you are conscious of being of the same quintessence as him, and he will recognize himself in you!

I am speaking to you so that you will decide to open your doors and windows onto this new world, the divine world, which is our true homeland. And the sun speaks to you too, nature speaks to you, life speaks to you… what more can I say? Nothing. I can only invite you to remember all that I have told you for all these years. Go back over it. Whatever changes have happened and will happen in the world, the truths that I have given you are valid throughout eternity: how to acquire self-mastery, how to receive the light, how to enter into harmony with all the beneficial and life-giving forces of the universe, this will always remain. Whether there is war or peace, whether you are rich or poor, whether you have a family and friends or are alone, abandoned by everybody, your deepest needs will always remain the same. You will always have a physical body, a heart, a mind, a soul and a spirit, which you must nourish so that you can draw ever closer to your heavenly Father, who has made you in his image.

So, in the hope that my insisting does not make you rebel, ask yourselves, rather, what you have done with all these truths you have been given. I am a jeweller, and when I give you a diamond I say to you, 'This stone is of incalculable value.' Think, if you wish, that this is vanity, I do not mind. What would you think of a jeweller who, wishing to appear modest, lays out rubies, emeralds and sapphires before his clients saying, 'Well, you know, these are nothing but a few pebbles, a few bits of glass…' I am a good jeweller, I know the value of what I give you, and that is why I tell you: these truths are priceless, and they will shine one day like precious stones in the firmament of your existence.

Of course, I also know that many of you, aware of the importance of the light you have received and the unique moments you have lived here in the Brotherhood, would like to retain the memory of them in a future incarnation. Some of you have asked me if that is possible. Yes, it is possible, and I gave them a method I will give to you, too.

Take as your starting point a mountain, for example, something which will resist the attrition of time. It could also be a well-known building, because even if it is destroyed one day there will still be pictures of it in books. Look frequently at this mountain or at this building, and think to yourself, 'When I see this again in another life, I want such and such events in my present life to return to my memory.' In this way you create a link between you and this mountain or building; you are stamping an indelible mark, which will continue to work on the matter of your subconscious, so that when you reincarnate you will come back with this link intact. The moment you set eyes on the mountain or the building you concentrated on, this indelible mark will reawaken the memory of those life events you recorded as you went along. I have often spoken to you of the law of recording.[8] It is this law you must call upon if you are to remember the precious moments you have lived in this lifetime.

I pray the celestial beings will allow you to glimpse, if only for a few moments, the distant destination of the work we are doing here. You will never forget that splendour, and nothing will stop you or make you draw back ever again.

Little by little, you will surmount all obstacles, because this vision will fill your soul with the longing to reach this goal which is ever more distant. Of course, you will suffer at never being able to reach it, but this suffering will sustain your enthusiasm and your need to keep progressing. This blessed suffering ennobles your being, and it is the only suffering which I hope you experience as I do.

All the worries, questions and longings of the child and the adolescent we were we can understand and interpret much, much later. I did not know what I was looking for when I read so many books and did so many experiments and exercises that I nearly died. Now that I know, I know too that I will never succeed in achieving it. But it is that which gives meaning to my life: the pursuit of the unattainable, the impossible, for, in the spiritual life, only the unattainable is real.

Notes

1. See *Man's Two Natures, Human and Divine*, Izvor Coll. n° 213, chap. 1: 'Human nature or animal nature?' and chap. 2: 'The lower self is a reflection'.
2. See *The True Meaning of Christ's Teaching*, Izvor Coll. n° 215, chap. 3: 'Be perfect as your heavenly Father is perfect'.
3. See *Angels and Other Mysteries of the Tree of Life*, Izvor Coll. n° 236, chap. 4: 'The names of God' and *The Fruits of the Tree of Life – The Cabbalistic Tradition*, Complete Works, vol. 32, chap. 4: 'The tetragrammaton and the seventy-two planetary spirits'.
4. See *The True Meaning of Christ's Teaching*, Izvor Coll. n° 215, chap. 4: 'Strive first for the kingdom of God and his righteousness'.
5. See *The Philosopher's Stone – in the Gospels and in Alchemy*, Izvor Coll. n° 241, chap. 1: 'On the interpretation of the scriptures'.
6. See *Man, Master of His Destiny*, Izvor Coll. n° 202, chap. 8: 'Reincarnation'.

7. See *Vie et Travail à l'École Divine*, Œuvres Complètes, vol. 31, chap. 3: 'Le véritable sens du mot "travail"', partie 4.

8. See *The Book of Divine Magic,* Izvor Coll. n° 236, chap. 11: 'The three great laws of magic'.

Addenda

Appendix 1

Meeting of 28 September, 1947 at Izgrev (Sèvres)

Notes taken during the weekly meeting

Today I have come to say goodbye to you...

Since I have been with you, I have given you everything I could, and I can give you still more. You have no idea what this love I hold in my heart is capable of doing. But it appears that those who have come especially from Bulgaria to prevent me from fulfilling the mission the Master entrusted to me are succeeding.

Look at my situation: some of you treat me with great respect and call me 'Master', a title I have never asked for – for me the only Master of the Brotherhood remains Peter Deunov.* Others, however, describe me as a public danger, treat me as a swindler obsessed with sex and threaten to gun me down. Are these the conditions in which to pursue a spiritual life together? My resistance has its limits. If I am still standing, it is because I struggle inwardly without respite against all these forces trying to throw me to the ground. I have been censured for the pettiest acts, and intentions I have never had are attributed to me. I know, I sense, that the plots against me could lead to imprisonment, and this could happen so much more easily since I am a foreigner in your country. All it needs is just a few lies, and there are so many being invented right now!

* He died December 27, 1944.

Of course, knowing human nature as I do, I could have been more careful and kept certain people at a distance. Why did I not do this? I was like a lake into which these people threw their rubbish. They have burdened me with their ambitions, their desires, their physical and psychological illnesses, and now they accuse me, because the way that I helped them did not suit them. But whom did they think they were addressing? Did they believe I was going to perform miracles just to satisfy them? From now on, I seek only to burn all the filth that is being thrown at me in the fire of divine love. If I do not succeed, this is the last time that I will be with you; we will not see each other again.

A great responsibility weighs on me. I am, and I remain, the Master's disciple. When he sent me to you, it was not because he thought I was perfect, but because he thought that I would improve in this shared work we would be undertaking together. Without my knowing it, he had been preparing me for a long time, and then one day he said to me, 'Your strength is not for here, but for somewhere else.' Since my arrival in France, he has never stopped encouraging me in my work and my methods, through his thoughts, his letters and also his messengers from Bulgaria. Now that he has left the earth, some are beginning to claim that I have betrayed his teaching, and they are stirring up trouble everywhere by spreading lies, saying not only that I came without his agreement but that he even banished me from his school. Why did they wait until his death to circulate these rumours? If those who knew me in Bulgaria think that I have taken the position I occupy unlawfully, let them come forward and say it clearly; I am waiting for them...

(There was silence, and those to whom he was speaking left the room never to return.)

Do not be so focused on me personally. If the philosophy I bring you can help you, it is because it comes from the Master. He worked for years on me, I am his spiritual son; one day you will understand this. Until then, pray that all that is overwhelming me with the hope of making me fall may be deflected, because I have much more to give you. If some of you want to leave me, do so, but I ask only that you never leave the Master's teaching, for he has left us a treasure. The decision you take should not depend on my person; you should not follow this Teaching because you like me, nor reject it because you do not like me…

I thank those who continue to put their trust in me.

My dear brothers and sisters,

The events of this past year have been foreseeable for a long time. I had warned you of them and told you of the precautions to take. When night falls, we can no longer keep on the move; we must stop and light a fire in order to protect ourselves against wild animals, by which I mean that we must link to the Lord with all our strength and wait for the moment when the sun rises and lights the road.

It is not difficult for a spiritual guide to guess the nature and intentions of those around him. But his mission is to give everyone the chance to learn, to improve, and he must use only the forces of love, so they will preserve forever in their memory the imprint of the sacrifices that he has made to save them from themselves. I saw Master Peter Deunov act in this way in our Brotherhood in Bulgaria: some of his disciples did him a great deal of harm. They did not come with the intention of harming him, but they did not know themselves; they were not conscious of the motives driving them, and they became his worst enemies. Sometimes I wondered whether he realized what was being plotted against him, but one day he said to me, 'True love wants to hold out its hand to everyone. They have the right to reject divine grace, but it is not up to me to exclude them.' Since the Master behaved like this, would the disciple with the responsibility of continuing his work have the right to conduct himself differently? Misunderstanding, lack of gratitude and malice are poisons which must be digested and neutralized, and so I strive to act like the Master.

Many different signs made me quickly aware that some were wicked beings, who were waiting for the right moment to destroy me. In spite of these warnings, I continued to treat them in the same way as I do each one of you, trying to help and enlighten them. It may seem as if that did no good at all, but the truth is that, without their realizing it, I imprinted something on their souls which will never be erased. Those who think that it would have been better to sever all connections with these people show a great lack of understanding. My work, like that of my Master, is a very particular one; I must not consider my own wellbeing and peace of mind.

For ten years, I have given you a teaching whose true value you will one day appreciate, and then I have found myself in the position of an observer watching the inevitable unfolding of events. This has been a school for you, but even more so for me. But nothing could make me change my behaviour toward those who had been busy plotting my downfall. I can say before the Eternal and for his glory that I saw clearly into each one of them; not one of them deceived me. Yet I was obliged to continue to be patient, kind and humble; they will never be able to erase that from their memory. One day, the rotten seeds they have been nurturing for incarnations, and which were waiting for the perfect moment to surface, will be neutralized by the growth of the good seeds the Master's Teaching has planted in them. You are unaware of the power of good in the long term...

1948 will be the most extraordinary year.

Blessed are those who understand me!

Your brother Michaël

Appendix II

Prison de la Santé
February 1948

My dear brothers and sisters,

... I do not want to distress you by speaking of my ordeals. Never forget that the designs of God are unfathomable. My path takes me via prison, but it will not stop there, and my real work is beginning now. Believe me if I tell you that even in the depths of this abyss in which I am plunged, there are moments when I feel not only happy but privileged. I had to go through this. From now on, everything is possible.

Jesus said, 'Love your enemies and pray for those who persecute you.' Now, more than at any time in my life, I must prove myself capable of doing so. I pray and I send light-filled thoughts to all those who are the cause of my suffering but who, in fact, have given me a great blessing. The Master predicted this suffering for me, without telling me exactly what form it would take.* Disciples must be prepared for the best and for the worst, but nothing must stop them in their ascent to the summits, and if they hold to their faith and their love, all that comes to them will be for their own good. With such an understanding of things, we can be happy everywhere, even in prison, whereas many others, who are free and have the best conditions, are unhappy and outraged.

I am a prisoner, but my spirit is free, and it often comes to visit you to say, 'You, too, can strengthen your faith, your love and the light inside you. Sing and pray with all your heart. Set

---

* See chapter 8: 'Meeting Master Peter Deunov: The revelations of Psalm 116'.

an example of courage, patience and perseverance.' The new life demands strong souls.

Prison de la Santé
March 1948

… I am ready to make every sacrifice as long as I am allowed to do the will of God and bring souls to him. It would be hard for you to imagine the love I have for all beings. I would like them to weep with happiness every day before beauty and light, as I myself have often wept when my inner eyes gazed upon the splendours of creation. If this is the price of reaching it, I accept being locked up in a small cell with seven others, as well as rats roaming around at night; I accept being deprived of light, heating and decent food, except for what you send me. Heaven has given me a very difficult problem to solve. It tells me, 'Mikhaël, you are so sensitive to cold that you cannot drink cold water, you cannot stand cigarette smoke, and what you long for is silence, harmony and beauty, and you also claim to love people and want to transform them. Very well, let us see what you are capable of now that you are forced to accept dirt, noise, ugliness and violence…'

The first day I arrived in this cell, I was absolutely stunned by the hostility which greeted me. I was in a jungle surrounded by wild beasts which all banded together against me. Whatever I did they were ready to blame and insult me. When I was called outside the cell, they took from me all they could, ate the provisions you had sent me, even though I had shared everything with them. Without my knowing it, they ordered cigarettes, sausages and all sorts of other things, which I then had to pay for. Everything I told them in an attempt to help them just stirred up their hatred and mockery. Those first days were truly a living hell; they were totally against me, and no matter how patient and forbearing I was it all had no effect.

And then, I saw the power of good thoughts and words. One day, one of them spoke up in my defence and began to stand up against the others. Little by little, some of the others began to change their behaviour to the point of making my bed, or cleaning the cell when it was my turn, guarding my food when I was not there, washing my billy can, or stopping the others from stealing from me, heating water for me when I was thirsty, and many other things hereto numerous to mention. They are ashamed now of having been so brutal towards me. Of course, they will not change from one day to the next, but they want to learn, they ask me questions, and what makes me happiest is that their behaviour towards each other has changed; they talk to each other quite differently. Reason is returning to these hardened beings, who have a rage against society. I point out their abilities and qualities they have not known how to use. My soul is filled with compassion for them, for even if they are guilty they have also been the victims of harsh conditions.

So, my beloved brothers and sisters, use my experience to progress further into love and light. Everything fades away in life, except for good thoughts, good feelings, good words and good actions. Do not be troubled by what is happening to me, but let my ordeals be an opportunity for you to make progress.

Often, I receive ten or twelve letters a day. This has an extraordinary effect on those who sort and distribute the mail, but the most amazed are my cellmates. Sometimes, I give them these letters to read, and I observe the impression that their content has on them. It helps them by opening doors into a world that is virtually unknown to them, a world of love, goodness and gratitude. God alone knows what the future consequences of this reading will be for them!

466

The guards themselves are impressed, and now, more and more, they have long, friendly talks with me. Each morning, they say, 'Good morning!' to us all, and in the evening, 'Goodnight!', which they do not do to prisoners in other cells. For the first time, perhaps, the Prison de la Santé is filled with so many luminous rays and currents. When I sing the Master's songs or the Paneurhythmy, I can feel that there are unusual changes in the atmosphere of the prison.

God descends into the depths of hell to extend a helping hand to all these unfortunate beings who do not know where they come from or where they are going, nor why they are here on earth. Yes, God comes here through the letters you send me. However difficult the conditions are here, they are as nothing if he can use them to awaken the consciousness of the inmates.

Continue working with love and wisdom; do not worry about public opinion, as it changes so easily. Only those who are not afraid of demonstrating their faith in the power of the new life are worthy of receiving the gifts of the Spirit, which will be eternally distributed to the children of the light.

Your brother Michaël

On this first day of the year 1949, I send you all, dear brothers and sisters, my very best wishes for your health, peace, joy and courage. I have never felt closer to you since I had to leave you for prison. You are my preoccupation, my constant concern.

I have already told you, but I will tell you again, it is here in prison that I verify the greatness of the teaching of love and wisdom, its power to enlighten, guide and strengthen people. Since time immemorial, initiates and great Masters have investigated the human being, the universe and the Creator, by constantly communicating with the Creator via an entire hierarchy of spiritual beings. I have always known that this Teaching is the quintessence of all their research. But now, thanks to the exceptional conditions in which I am placed, I have still greater opportunities to verify this science they have bequeathed to us; we can use it, even in a human hell, for the good of all. I have tested the powers of thought over and over again. I must drink poison, I must drink hemlock, and not only must I not die, but I must turn it into ambrosia.

Do you remember the example I gave you some time ago of the opposite reactions of two people deprived of food for a few days? Whereas one of them will become irritable, rebellious and aggressive, the other will say, 'Since I have never had the opportunity to fast, I will make use of this situation', and this person will become purer, more enlightened and more sensitive to spiritual realities. I have had plenty of experiences of hardship over the years, but I did not know what being in prison was like. So now I accept it as a continuation of my learning. Those who are always spared should not necessarily congratulate themselves; having nothing to fight for, what can you gain? When you know how to view ordeals, they are a privilege. That is why, even here, I can continue to love, to sing and to communicate by thought with all the beings living in the world of beauty, light and love.

One day, once again, I will have my freedom, pure air and peace. The Lords of Destiny foresee everything with absolute precision. When the time comes, events will occur for the glory of the Universal White Brotherhood on high. May it be blessed forever! I am participating in a work which is based on unshakeable laws. Even if the whole world took up arms against it, they could not destroy it, but rather they themselves would be destroyed.

And now I tell you that a great future is opening up before us; a new culture is coming into the world, a culture of brotherhood. Humanity has already passed from the subconscious life to a conscious one, but now it must give way to superconsciousness by steadily opening to a higher life, marked by the seal of sacrifice, which is the manifestation of the Godhead. Through sacrifice, the man and woman of this new culture will acquire a new consciousness and be like the sun coming up over the horizon.

Your brother Michaël

Appendix III

Izgrev (Sèvres)
12 February 1950

My dear brothers and sisters,

The river which flowed in broad sight of everyone has had to plunge deeply underground in order to fertilize other regions and explore the deepest mysteries of human nature, where hell dances and sings over everything. But now the river has risen once again to the surface, and it flows once more along its course, watering plants and quenching the thirst of animals and people.

During this long absence, I have never left you. I have become enriched: in the depths of this ocean of darkness into which I have been thrown, I have not only discovered gold and precious stones, but I have learned how to transform wickedness and hate into the elixir of life.

Now, do not be upset if I tell you that we cannot see each other again immediately. The magistrates, recognizing that I had been unjustly imprisoned, freed me, but, in view of the forthcoming trial, they have given me to understand that it would be better if I did not resume my old activities of meetings and lectures right now, as it could be said that I am trying to influence public opinion. Furthermore, I have little time to study all the documents which I must understand before the trial begins. I would have been so happy to be with you all again, as I have so many things to tell you, but I will continue to do so in my soul and in my thoughts as I do each day.

I know and I can sense that great changes have taken place in you. You see far more clearly the need to participate in the creation of this new life that is forming in the subtle realms of the planet to improve humanity's destiny. Good and evil have been engaged throughout time in a pitiless battle. So many times evil has been victorious, and in all realms! Now, however, conditions are forming for the triumph of good.

Nothing is more important for disciples of the Universal White Brotherhood than their conscious participation, every day, for the victory of the divine cause. The more people who vote for this ideal, the sooner the kingdom of God will be installed here on earth, and life will take on new colours. From the moment our will is committed to working for this divine cause, all the powers of light and beauty will shine through us, and peace will become an almost tangible reality. Patience is one of the greatest virtues. The future belongs to those who continue to work, no matter what happens, with unshakeable faith.

Once again I thank the brothers and sisters for both the material and moral support they have given me, their expressions of loyalty, the efforts they have made and the time they have taken to defend me.

'The sun of love is already rising on the world. It shines its light everywhere; it spreads its warmth everywhere. We are sunbeams, and we are bringing the new life', says the Master's song.

Your brother Michaël

BIBLICAL REFERENCES

'Be perfect as your heavenly Father is perfect' – *Matt. 5:48, p. 264.*

Demonic Gadarene, the – *Mark 5:1-16, p. 73.*

'For everything there is a season' – *Ecclesiastes 3:1, p. 179.*

'For God so loved the world' – *John 3:16, p. 97.*

'God, come from the four winds' – *Ezekiel 37:9, p. 364.*

'Hear, my child, your father's instruction' – *Proverbs 1:8, p. 71.*

'Here is the lamb of God' – *John 1:29, p. 405.*

'I am going to create a new heaven and a new earth'
   Isaiah 65:17, p. 278.

'I am the light of the world' – *John 8:12, p. 264.*

'I baptize you with water' – *Matt. 3:11, p. 283.*

'I walk before the Lord in the land of the living' – *Psalms 116:9, p. 157.*

'I will put a sign on everyone's hand' – *Job 37:9, p. 235.*

'In the beginning when God created the heavens and the earth'
   Gen. 1:1, p. 40.

'In the beginning was the Word' – *John 1:1, p. 140.*

Jesus casts the demons into swine – *Matt. 8:28, p. 38.*

'Love your enemies and pray for those who persecute you'
   Matt. 5:44, p. 464.

'My father is still working, and I also am working' – *John 5:17, p. 449.*

'No one can enter the kingdom of God…' – *John 3:5, p. 47.*

Noah takes refuge in the ark – *Gen. 7:1-9, p. 41.*

Parable of the five wise virgins and the five foolish virgins
   Matt. 25:1-13, p. 90.

'Strive first for the kingdom of God and his righteousness'
   Matt. 6:33, p. 445.

'The snares of death encompassed me' – *Psalms 116:3-4 , p. 155.*

'The wind blows where it chooses' – *John 3:8, p. 450.*

'Those who are well have no need of a physician…'
  Matt. 9:12, p. 378.

'Those who love me, I will deliver' – *Psalms 91:14-16, p. 210.*

'What is your name? – Legion' – *Mark 5:9, p. 73.*

'You are the light of the world' – *Matt. 5:14, p. 265.*

Books by Omraam Mikhaël Aïvanhov
(translated from the French)

Complete Works

Brochures

Daily Meditations:
A thought for each day of the year

By the same author:
(Translated from the French)

Izvor Collection

World Wide - Editor-Distributor
Editions Prosveta S.A. - Z.A. Le Capitou - B.P. 12
F - 83601 Fréjus CEDEX (France)
Tel. (33) 04 94 19 33 33 – Fax (33) 04 94 19 33 34
Web: www.prosveta.com – e-mail: international@prosveta.com

Worldwide copyright for the works of Master Omraam Mikhaël Aïvanhov belong to Éditions Prosveta S.A. This publishing house publishes mainly in French and in English, granting translation and editorial or joint-editorial rights to others languages. The different companies or organizations throughout the world which use the brand Prosveta® are independent and not affiliated to each other.

*** Editor in his own language - ** Distributor - *** POS**

Distributors

ARGENTINA
** ASOCIACIÓN SOPHIA – Chile 1736 – Ciudad Mendoza
Tel (54) 261 420 10 47 – e-mail: info@sophia.org.ar
AUSTRALIA
** PROSVETA AUSTRALIA
16 Galway Gardens – Warnbro WA 6169 – Tel. (61) 8 9594 1145
e-mail: prosveta.au@aapt.net.au
AUSTRIA
** HARMONIEQUELL VERSAND – Hof 37 – A- 5302 Henndorf am Wallersee
Tel. / fax (43) 6214 7413 – e-mail: info@prosveta.at
BELGIUM & LUXEMBOURG
** PROSVETA BENELUX – Chaussée de Merchtem 123 – 1780 Wemmel
Tel./Fax (32) 2 460 1362 – e-mail : prosveta@skynet.be
** N.V. MAKLU Somersstraat 13-15 – B-2000 Antwerpen
Tel. (32) 3/231 29 00 – Fax (32) 3/233 26 59
** S.D.L. CARAVELLE S.A. – rue du Pré aux Oies, 303 – 1130 Bruxelles
Tel. (32) 2 240 93 00 – Fax (32) 2 216 35 98
e-mail : info@sdlcaravelle.com
BRAZIL
* EDITORA NOVA ERA um selo da EDITORA BEST SELLER LTDA (Grupo Editorial Record)
Rua Argentina 171 – Rio de Janeiro, RJ – 20921-380
Atendimento e venda direta ao leitor:
mdireto@record.com.br ou tel. (21) 2585-2002
BOLIVIA
** BELTRÁN – Calle Muñoz Cornejo, Sopocachi – La Paz
e-mail: mariabelre@yahoo.es
BULGARIA
*** NOVA EPOHA – Rue Chesti Semptembri n°28 – Sofia 1000
Celular: 0359 (0)88 981 98 98 – Tel. 0359 (0)2/981 98 98
Fax. 0359 (0)2/981 32 79 – e-mail: novaepoha@novaepoha.com
CANADA
** PROSVETA Inc. – 3950, Albert Mines – Canton-de-Hatley (Qc), J0B 2C0
Tel. (819) 564-8212 – Fax. (819) 564-1823 – *in Canada,* call toll free: 1-800-854-8212
e-mail: prosveta@prosveta-canada.com / www.prosveta-canada.com
CONGO
** PROSVETA CONGO
29, Avenue de la Révolution – B.P. 768 – Pointe-Noire
Tel. : (242) 948156 / (242) 055531254 – Fax : (242) 948156
e-mail: prosvetacongo@yahoo.fr
COLOMBIA
* PROSVETA COLOMBIA
Calle 174 Número 54B – 50 Interior 6 – Villa del Prado – Bogotá
Tel. (57 1) 6 14 53 85 / 6 72 16 89 – Fax. (57 1) 6 33 58 03
Celular: (57) 311 8 10 25 42 – e-mail: prosveta.colombia@hotmail.com

CZECH REPUBLIC
PROSVETA – Ant. Sovy 18 – České Budejovice 370 05
Tel / Fax: (420) 38-53 10 227 – e-mail: prosveta@iol.cz
FRANCE – DOM TOM
* Editions Prosveta S.A. - B.P. 12 – F - 83601 Fréjus CEDEX (France)
Tel. (33) 04 94 19 33 33 – Fax (33) 04 94 19 33 34
e-mail: international@prosveta.com – www.prosveta.com
GERMANY
* PROSVETA Verlag GmbH – Heerstrasse 55 – 78628 Rottweil
Tel. (49) 741-46551 – Fax. (49) 741-46552 – e-mail: prosveta7@aol.com
GREAT BRITAIN – IRELAND
** PROSVETA – The Doves Nest, Duddleswell Uckfield – East Sussex TN 22 3JJ
Tel. (44) (01825) 712988 – Fax (44) (01825) 713386 –   www.prosveta.co.uk   Jk
orders@prosveta.co.uk
GREECE
* PYRINOS KOSMOS – BOOK - PUBLISHERS
16 Hippocratous Str., 106 80 ATHENS
Tel. 30/1/3602883, 30/1/3615233 – Fax : 30/1/3611234
e-mail : info@pyrinoskosmos.gr – www.pyrinoskosmos.gr
HAITI
** PROSVETA DÉPÔT HAITI – Angle rue Faustin 1er et rue Bois Patate #25 bis
6110 Port-au-Prince
Tel. (509) 22 45 18 65 – Mobile : (509) 34 64 80 88 – e-mail: rbaaudant@yahoo.com
HOLLAND
* STICHTING PROSVETA NEDERLAND
Zeestraat 50 – 2042 LC Zandvoort
Tel. (31) 33 25 345 75 – Fax. (31) 33 25 803 20
e-mail: prosveta@worldonline.nl
INDIA
* VIJ BOOKS INDIA PVT. LTD. *(Anglais et Hindi)*
2/19, (Second Floor) Ansari Road, Darya Ganj, New Dehli - 110 002
Ph: + 91-11-43596460, 011-65449971 – Fax +91-11-30126465
e-mail: vijbooks@rediffmail.com – www.vijbooks.com
ISRAEL
** Zohar, P.B. 1046, Netanya 42110 – e-mail: prosveta.il@hotmail.com
ITALY
* PROSVETA Coop. a r.l.
Casella Postale 55 – 06068 Tavernelle (PG)
Tel. (39) 075-835 84 98 – Fax (39) 075-6306 20 18 – e-mail: prosveta@tin.it
IVORY COAST
** Librairie Prosveta
25 rue Paul Langevin Zone 4C – 01 B.P. 2 – Abidjan 01
e-mail: prosvetafrique@yahoo.fr – Tel/Fax: (225) 21 25 42 11
LEBANON
** PROSVETA LIBAN – P.O. Box 90-995
Jdeidet-el-Metn, Beirut – Tel. (03) 448560 – e-mail: prosveta_lb@terra.net.lb
LITHUANIA
* LEIDYKLA MIJALBA
Gedimino G 26 B – 44319 Kaunas – Tel. 370.687 8760 – Fax 370.37 353088
e-mail: info@mijalba.com – www. mijalba.com
NEW ZEALAND
* PROSVETA NEW ZEALAND LTD
90 Potae Avenue – Gisborne
Tel. (64) (0)9 889 0805 – port. 027 3560107 – e-mail: info@prosveta.co.nz
NORWAY
* PROSVETA NORDEN – Postboks 318, N-1502 Moss
Tel. (47) 69 26 51 40 – Fax (47) 69 26 51 08 – e-mail: info@prosveta.no

POLAND
*** WENA Studio Tworczej Ekspresji s.c. – ul. Nowina 36, PL 60-589 Poznan
Tel. 0048 61 843 65 25 – e-mail: biuro@wenastudio.pl

PORTUGAL
* PUBLICAÇÕES MAITREYA – Rua do Almada, 372, 4° esq – 4050-033 Porto
e-mail: flora@publicacoesmaitreya.pt – www.publicacoesmaitreya.pt

ROMANIA
* EDITURA PROSVETA SRL
Str. N. Constantinescu 10 – Bloc 16A - sc A - Apt. 9 – Sector 1 – 71253 Bucarest
Tel. 004021-231 28 78 – Tel./ Fax 004021-231 37 19 – e-mail : prosveta_ro@yahoo.com

RUSSIA
* EDITIONS PROSVETA
143 964 Moskovskaya oblast, g. Reutov – 4, post/box 4
Tel./ Fax (495) 525 18 17 – Tél. (495) 795 70 74 – e-mail: prosveta@prosveta.ru

SERBIA
* ÉDITIONS GLOSARIJUM (for the Serbia Language)
Rige od Fere 12 – Beograd
Tél./Fax 011/2182-163 – e-mail: glosarijum@glosarijum.com

SPAIN
* ASOCIACIÓN PROSVETA ESPAÑOLA – C/ Ausias March n° 23 Ático
SP-08010 Barcelona – Tel (34) (93) 412 31 85 – Fax (34) (93) 318 89 01
e-mail: aprosveta@prosveta.es

UNITED STATES
** PROSVETA US Dist.
29781 Shenandoah LN – Canyon Country CA 91387 – Tel. (661) 252-9090
e-mail: prosveta-usa@earthlink.net. / www.prosveta-usa.com
** FBU - USA – P.O. Box 932 – Locust Valley, 11560 New-York
e-mail: fbu_usa@hotmail.com

SWITZERLAND
** PROSVETA Société Coopérative
Ch. de la Céramone 13 – CH - 1808 Les Monts-de-Corsier
Tel. (41) 21 921 92 18 – Fax. (41) 21 922 92 04 – e-mail: prosveta@prosveta.ch

VENEZUELA
** PROSVETA VENEZUELA C. A. – Calle Madrid
Edificio La Trinidad – Las Mercedes – Caracas D.F.
Tel. (58) 414 134 75 34 – e-mail: prosvetavenezuela@gmail.com

Updated list 25.05.2011

The aim of the Universal White Brotherhood association
is the study and practice of the Teaching
of Master Omraam Mikhaël Aïvanhov,
published and distributed
by Prosveta.
All enquiries about the association should be addressed to:
Universal White Brotherhood
The Doves Nest, Duddleswell, Uckfield
East Sussex TN22 3JJ, GREAT BRITAIN
Tel: (44) (0)1825 712150 – Fax: (44) (0)1825 713386
E-mail: uwb@pavilion.co.uk

Achevé d'imprimer en Juin 2011
par XL PRINT - V004595
42010 Saint-Étienne – France

Dépôt légal : June 2011